To my family

Contents

Preface

THE NIGHT DRAFT OFF THE GLACIER brought a penetrating chill as I sat on a piece of driftwood in skimpy clothes and hip boots, marooned at a remote lake in the mountains of Southeastern Alaska. During intervals between the groaning of the glacier ice and the splashing of spawning salmon in a nearby creek, the natural silence was absolute. I glanced away from the small fire of willow that I gingerly tended and saw only blackness, except for stars above and, on a nearby mountain, startlingly bright snow patches illuminated by a hidden full moon.

The time was late August 1997. I knew that my wife, Christa, and others would be worried about me, but at the same time I felt a deep sense of freedom and joy. The wild beauty here was intense, stirring me to reflect on the events of my life that had finally brought me to such a place. As the hours passed and the Big Dipper rotated overhead, I recalled the early security of a loving home where values were rooted and from which I could venture at first tentatively, then with more daring. A fascination with what lay beyond the horizon led to perilous trips on freight trains, airplanes, and dogsleds. An affection for nature and a love for hunting and fishing helped bring me to Alaska and to a career journey from laboring in a Civilian Conservation Corps camp to shaping the management of some of the North Country's major fish and wildlife resources.

I made up my mind right there to set down on paper the story of my life, with its risks and setbacks, its rewards and successes. I hoped that readers could identify with the story of a boy and his adventures; that people who want to learn more about Alaska would enjoy reading of the

7

trappers and bush pilots and Natives that I encountered daily; and that those who care about the future of this land would gain from firsthand stories about Alaska's wildlife.

But first, of course, I had to get out of my current predicament, stranded at this lake.

Just that afternoon I had landed my Cessna 185 amphibian on the glassy waters of Antler Lake, a long, curved body of water that penetrates the Coast Range from the west. I beached the airplane and secured it firmly to some tough little willows, then took a look around. I was hoping to find cutthroat trout. Dimples appeared on the water close to shore, some distance to my right. I quickly rigged my fly rod, grabbed a small canvas bag containing flies and lures, and headed down the beach. My happy anticipation slumped when I saw that the disturbances were caused by finning red salmon, not feeding trout. Still, there was a chance of trout lurking here so I cast my best proven patterns, but no luck. While the fish ignored my offerings, I was attacked by a swarm of the fierce biting insects known as white sox. I had to go back for my hat and insect repellent.

Walking leisurely toward the airplane, I was momentarily puzzled by its position. The heels of the floats that had been on the cobbled beach were now several yards out in the water. The airplane was in the grip of a steady breeze and moving away fast—faster than I could hope to swim in the frigid water. I discovered that the anchoring willows were shallowly rooted on a thin layer of soil; they had simply peeled off, freeing my beautiful white Cessna to sail unguided across the lake.

Like it or not, I was here to stay. To protect against the voracious white sox, I put my stockings on over my hands and arms and pulled my sweater over my head. I could even see pretty well: the beloved twenty-five-year-old cashmere from Orvis now had the character of cheesecloth.

With darkness, the attackers returned to the hangar. But without matches, I faced the serious threat of hypothermia. I built a windbreak using willows. My plan was to walk around until I got warm, then to rest in the windbreak, then walk again—and so on through a miserable night. My mood instantly changed to exultation when I found a book of matches in a long-unopened pocket in my tackle bag. Thanks to a fire, the night proved to be a marvelous and rewarding experience.

Christa knew where I had planned to go, and when I didn't return, she called for help. At daybreak a Civil Air Patrol Beaver on floats found my empty airplane sitting quietly in the middle of the lake. Pilot Tom Meisner and copilot Alex Hazelton then taxied up the lake, saw my fire, and approached to ask whether I might be looking for an airplane. "Yes," I assured them. "Come aboard," Meisner said, "and we'll take you to it."

I was soon back with Christa, apologizing for the sleepless night I had caused her. I also told her of the surprising result of my bivouac: a decision to write an account of my life. Close friends had long urged me in this direction, and the time seemed right to flesh out the memories that had swept over me during that long night beside the lake. This book is the result of my efforts, a personal story of adventures that intersect with an astonishing period in Alaska history.

Acknowledgments

I AM GRATEFUL TO MY WIFE, Christa, for encouraging me to work on this memoir even when the blue grouse were hooting or the trout rising less than an hour away from my desk. Her critiques helped greatly in discarding extraneous detail and focusing on the story line. My son, Lewis, with extravagant patience taught me, a computer illiterate, the perplexities of a word processor program.

My first Alaskan friend, Harold Hansen, contributed wisdom, humor, and support to my life over many decades. Professors Druska Carr Schaible and Brina Kessel motivated me to strive for scholarship. For rewarding personal and professional associations, I am indebted to Loren Croxton, Robert Hinman, Franklin Jones, Robert McVey, Robert Rausch, and Ronald Skoog. Alaska governors Jay Hammond and Willian Egan remained constantly supportive of me during times when doing so surely caused them political stress.

I am indebted to Jim Rearden, who first inspired me to write outdoor magazine articles while he was a professor and I was a student at the University of Alaska; without his later urging I likely would not have begun this book. I am thankful to two dear friends, Lynn Wallen and her husband, R. T. Wallen, for their continuous and inspiring assistance in both grammar and substantive content.

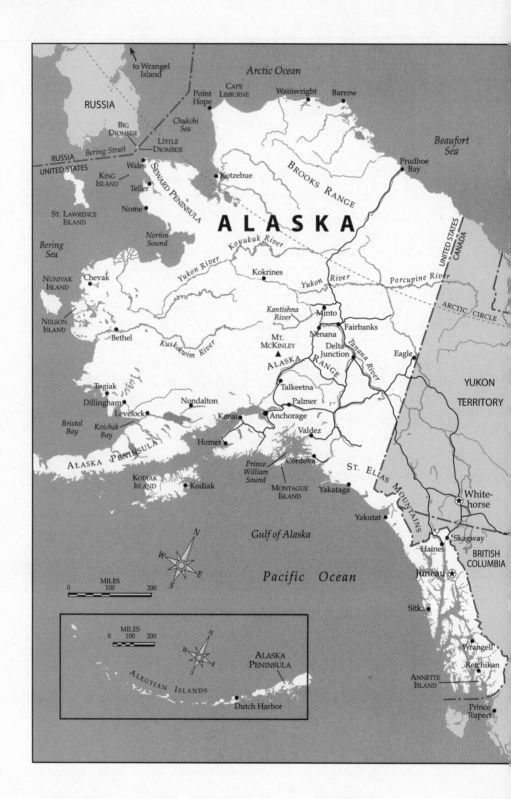

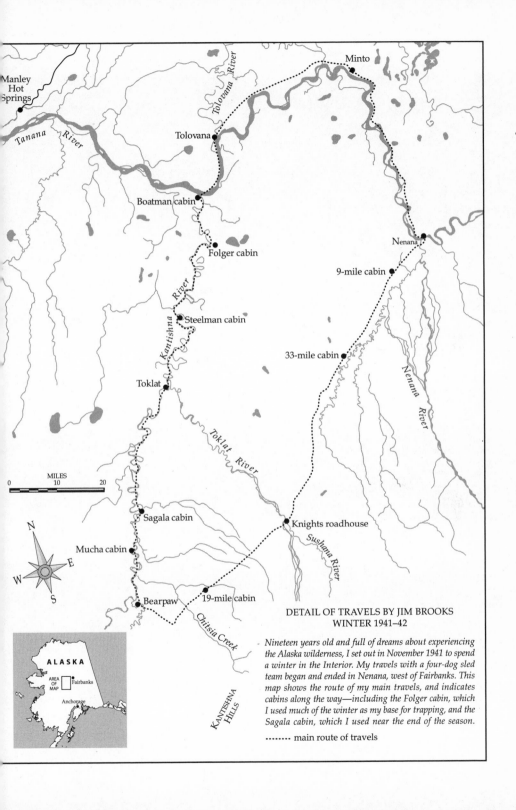

Manley Hot Springs

Tanana River

Tolovana River

Minto

Tolovana

Boatman cabin

Folger cabin

Kantishna River

Steelman cabin

33-mile cabin

Nenana

9-mile cabin

Toklat

Toklat River

Nenana River

MILES
0   10   20

N
W   E
S

Sagala cabin

Mucha cabin

Knights roadhouse

Sushana River

Bearpaw

19-mile cabin

Chitsia Creek

ALASKA

AREA OF MAP   Fairbanks

Anchorage

KANTISHNA HILLS

DETAIL OF TRAVELS BY JIM BROOKS
WINTER 1941–42

Nineteen years old and full of dreams about experiencing the Alaska wilderness, I set out in November 1941 to spend a winter in the Interior. My travels with a four-dog sled team began and ended in Nenana, west of Fairbanks. This map shows the route of my main travels, and indicates cabins along the way—including the Folger cabin, which I used much of the winter as my base for trapping, and the Sagala cabin, which I used near the end of the season.

.... main route of travels

CHAPTER ONE

Hobo Days

IN THE SPRING OF 1939, at age sixteen, I felt driven to see more of the world. For thirty-five dollars I bought a 1927 Buick sedan; my parents weren't at all pleased. With my dog, Pal, a friendly and gentle mutt, and my good buddy and fishing partner Dock Darrow, I set out westward from Detroit, destination indefinite.

Plagued by tire and engine problems, we rolled through Wisconsin, Minnesota, and North Dakota, leaving a trail of blue smoke. It was uncommon to go a hundred miles without changing a flat tire. For each tank of gasoline, the engine burned at least a gallon of oil—usually used crankcase oil that we got free at gas stations. We paid a quarter apiece at junkyards for old tires, and extended their useful lives with repair patches that cost less than fifty cents at Western Auto stores. We lived mainly on bread, apples, canned pork and beans, and corned beef, and we slept in the car.

I felt enormous pleasure in viewing this beautiful, wild country. I got excited every time we spotted a pheasant, a rabbit, or a skunk from the car. Traversing the Badlands near the North Dakota-Montana border was especially thrilling. I had read about the Badlands in Zane Grey stories and felt we were now truly in the Wild West. Dock was less taken by the wonders unfolding, but he was nonetheless a perfect companion, always pleasant and quick to do at least his part of whatever needed doing.

We were disheartened by the increasingly loud complaints from the engine's connecting rods. The used crankcase oil had been the wrong medicine for the rod bearings. We limped into a used car lot in Miles City, Montana, and I sold the car for ten dollars. We were now stranded, but we still had our hearts set on further travel into the West. Dock said he had heard fellows at the pool hall talk about riding freight trains; we decided to give it a try.

In the Northern Pacific Railroad yards a kindly switchman gave us a timetable that listed when trains were leaving in either direction. Friendly hobos offered information and advice. We climbed into an empty boxcar on a train we were told was heading west. On schedule, there were two blasts of the powerful steam whistle—the signal known as the highball—and a great racket and clattering from the slack in the car hitches, and we were on our way. But we soon found this mode of travel would not be easy.

At Billings, Montana, railroad bulls—the security police—carrying night sticks caught us and several other hobos and ordered us to stay off the train, or else. The other hobos just planned to go to the other end of the yards and catch the next train on the fly as it departed. We couldn't do this with my dog, so the highway was our only recourse. A rancher picked us up in his truck and took us to Laurel, a railroad water station where we caught another train. This time we climbed aboard a loaded coal gondola.

Looking to the west as we rode across the prairies, I was startled to see snowcapped mountains rising on the horizon. The view made me ecstatic. Here was a world I had dreamed about. I was seeing the Rocky Mountains in real life, even grander than the stereoscopic pictures that had awed me back home. As we passed the towns of Three Forks, Butte, Deer Lodge, and others with familiar names, I thought of my father's stories about these places. As a General Electric Company representative, he had supervised the electrification of parts of the Great Northern and Northern Pacific Railroads. Electric motors that pulled the trains up the mountains would turn into generators on the down side, putting electricity back into the line. But for whatever reason, the Northern Pacific trains we were riding all used huge sixteen-drive-wheel, coal-fired, Malley steam engines, sometimes with a pusher behind on the steeper grades.

The exhilaration of moving through this mountainous country was dampened somewhat by our grimy condition aboard the coal gondola. Coal soot covered us, and on my scalp it felt like coarse sand. I longed for a bath and clean clothes almost as much as I hungered for a big piece of apple pie and a thick malted milk.

By the time we crossed northern Idaho, we were traveling in one of the empty ice compartments of a refrigerator car. The two hobos who were sharing the other ice compartment were friendly and invited Dock and me back to their end of the car to play cards. One of the men, from Eau Claire, Wisconsin, had been on the road for five years, two years longer than his buddy, who was from Lincoln, Nebraska. They bragged that they had been in every state. After a bit, Dock and I returned to our own compartment.

Some time later, the men shouted to us from their compartment, inviting us to return. Dock was busy reading a pulp magazine so I went alone to join the two men. I was immediately aware of a changed atmosphere. Their nervous, tense expressions communicated something about to happen. I instantly felt peril and the need to act first. As I leaped for the compartment's handholds to climb out, one of the men, a hunting knife suddenly visible in his hand, began to stand up. I scrambled out before he could reach me.

I was now on top of the refrigerator car, kneeling on the narrow wooden catwalk that ran down the center of its roof. Suddenly it was dark. Everything was black and noisy, and it took a moment to realize the train had entered a tunnel. Fearing the men were pursuing me in the dark, I crawled ahead. When the train cleared the tunnel, the men were not in sight. I called Dock to come up with Pal, and we sat on top of the car until the next stop, where we joined some other hobos in a coal gondola. We felt safer traveling in a larger group.

At Wishram, Washington, we stopped at a "hobo jungle," a collection of ramshackle shelters constructed of odd pieces of lumber, cardboard, and flattened five-gallon cans. Dock and I thought some of these shelters looked almost luxurious after the boxcars we had slept in since leaving Miles City. A few of the hobos said they were traveling to visit relatives or friends. Others were going somewhere down the line in hope of finding employment, though many seemed to be just hanging out or drifting. These included veterans of the road who took pride in their lifestyle. They knew which parts of the country were favorable at various seasons, were accomplished at minimizing discomforts, and usually carried a small bundle (called a balloon) that contained a blanket, maybe a rain slicker, and some food. Theirs was a domain of men, for we had seen only a couple of escorted women and no children on the trains. Dock and I were acquainted with the distress of people in Detroit suffering through the Great Depression, and it was easy for us to understand how these hobos could feel satisfaction, even superiority, in their unstructured, roving life.

We left the train again at the Northern California mountain town of Alturas. Adjacent marshes held many ducks and shorebirds. Avocets caught my attention; I had not seen them before except in pictures. Even more surprising were the familiar largemouth bass in a stream at the edge of town. They seemed out of place here compared with their habitat back in Michigan, and I correctly guessed they had been introduced artificially. It was puzzling that people weren't trying to catch the bass for food. Fishermen at home would make short work of them. It was July 5, 1939, and we got a day of employment cleaning a large ballpark that was littered with trash from the Fourth of July celebration. The wet snow of a summer storm blew horizontally as we worked, and we shivered through the day.

At the post office, as I wrote a card home, I noticed a sack of bright yellow grain on the floor. I picked up a handful and was about to taste it out of curiosity when the postmaster told me it was prairie dog poison. I remember feeling saddened at the thought of the animals and birds that would die from eating this substance.

At this stage in our journey, after many days of feeling cold, hungry, and tired, Dock was turning somber despite his pleasant nature. His enthusiasm was waning, partly because he didn't share my excitement and uplift at seeing wildlife and the countryside. We caught a train heading south, and after reaching Reno, Nevada, in fine warm weather, we discussed for the first time the question of heading home. But we turned westward instead, back into California.

The train stopped at Truckee, just inside the California border, where we sat on a flatcar gawking at the cascading Truckee River. Suddenly, uniformed men appeared from behind the screen of boxcars ahead. We were promptly taken into custody by the California State Police. Calling us "damned Okies," they rudely herded us to a small guard station where papers were filled out charging us with vagrancy. The big, well-fed officers, with their pressed uniforms and polished leather belts and gun holsters, had obviously cultivated their technique for intimidating hopeful souls seeking to share their great state of California. They referred to us as trash and talked about taking us to jail— then volunteered we might escape deep trouble if we would leave the way we came. When the next eastbound train arrived, they made sure we were aboard.

Our train moved slowly through the edge of Reno as we sat on a catwalk on the side of a tank car. A large dog saw Pal and began to chase alongside, barking viciously. Pal tried to jump, and I very nearly fell off in restraining him. It was a close call and had a very bad effect on Dock, whose already sagging spirit had been further dampened by our run-in with the police at Truckee. He decided to continue on alone, by hitchhiking on the highway, and off he went.

The next surprise: at Winnemucca, Nevada, a couple of days later, Dock came walking up to the flatcar where I was sitting. He had managed to hitchhike only to Sparks, a short distance from Reno, where he stalled for lack of highway traffic. Then by chance he had boarded the train I was riding. We were happy to be together again.

We viewed Utah's Great Salt Lake while passing over a long trestle. Just outside Ogden, where the train stopped, we built a small fire about thirty feet down a slope from the tracks to heat a can of pork and beans. Without warning, two shouting policemen came running down the slope toward us. Pal was frightened, and he bristled up and barked. One of the officers yelled, "I'll kill that son of a bitch." I grabbed my dear Pal and shoved him behind me. The other officer kicked our can of beans, soiling his trousers and making him more furious. To my relief, they didn't attack us, but settled for a violent, scurrilous scolding. We were told to get far away and fast; if caught again, it meant jail.

The furor seriously upset Dock, who was already worried by a warning that the meanest railroad bull on the Union Pacific, a man known as Green River Jim, was still ahead on our route. Dock now lost his last bit of enthusiasm for this kind of adventure. He said he was going to try to join the Army right there in Ogden. I waited while he went into the city. He returned several hours later to report he had enlisted, and we parted a second time.

I was expecting the worst at Green River, Wyoming, so it was a pleasant surprise to see a large hobo jungle by the river and no sign of the notorious bull. A few hobos were fishing, including one fellow who became the butt of a practical joke. While a couple of hobos distracted the fisherman, another cut his line nearly through. The next fish he hooked was barely out of the water when the line parted, allowing the fish to fall back in as the pranksters roared with laughter.

While I was in a restaurant the next morning, a young gentleman came in with a trout he had caught earlier and asked the cook to fry it up for his breakfast. This fisherman was neatly attired in a checkered shirt, a Stetson hat festooned with fishing flies, a vest with many pockets for holding fly fishing paraphernalia, and folded-down hip boots. That ensemble looked real classy and stirred a feeling of envy: my clothing was on the shabby side, and I was washing dishes for my breakfast.

Near the railroad yards at Kansas City, I found a Volunteers of America hostel that offered a meal and a cot but didn't allow dogs. I accepted a bowl of stew and hid several slices of well-buttered bread inside my shirt for Pal. We then wandered back to the rail yards and found a train composed of loaded and sealed boxcars. These cars have catwalks on top, with a metal roof that slopes down on either side. Pal and I rode on top of one of the cars through the night to Des Moines. I lay down on the narrow walkway and fell into a hard sleep while the train sped along. The next thing I sensed was that one of my arms was being jerked and that I was sliding off the boxcar roof. Pal's leash, attached to my wrist, was tight and threatened to pull him off the walkway. By desperately pulling back, he had awakened me just an instant before tragedy, because my lower legs were already over the edge. Pal had saved both our lives.

Dock beat me home to Detroit. He had traveled there in a passenger train after his father refused to approve his army enlistment. School now seemed useless to me. Instead I worked through the fall and winter for a small business that repaired and sold used radios, washing machines, and refrigerators. During this time, I was overwhelmed with grief: Pal had disappeared from the yard while I was at work one day. I never found my loyal protector and companion, superb pheasant hunter, and puller of burrs from my trouser legs. My situation became less satisfying with every passing day, and I tried to figure some way of venturing out again. When I told my boss I was thinking of moving on, he offered a small salary increase and sage advice about a rolling stone gathering no moss.

CHAPTER TWO

Growing Up in Detroit

I'M TOLD THAT MY BIRTH on August 6, 1922, in an Erie, Pennsylvania, hospital caused my parents to debate whether my given names would be James Knox Polk or James Washington. Since my father's given names were Lewis Knox Polk, my mother, Mattie, felt Knox Polk had been sufficiently honored. James Washington was agreed to, and I recall early guidance about the virtue of confessing should I ever chop down a cherry tree. I suppose my parents wanted me to identify with respected men, for at a young age my father arranged for me to meet and shake hands with composer and marching-band leader John Philip Sousa, a man he somehow knew from his service in the Navy.

My father traveled extensively during his time as an engineer for General Electric. To remain closer to the family, he found work as an engineer for the City of Detroit and moved the family there in 1923, when I was just an infant. The world of my juvenile and adolescent years was the Detroit of the Great Depression. Detroit anguished in poverty during the 1930s, while reveling in naughtiness and flashes of progress. By street talk, if not in fact, Frank Barbara controlled the bookies, prostitution, and the illicit liquor trade. Walter Reuther rallied union members to bloody stalemates and eventual successes. The Ambassador Bridge, the world's largest international suspension span, was built to link Detroit with Windsor, Ontario. Detroit's Gar Wood and his Miss America powerboats repeatedly won the Harmsworth Trophy Race, and the boxing of Joe Louis brought pride to all of Detroit and to blacks everywhere. The Detroit Tigers terrorized baseball's American League and contended often in the World Series while the Lions in football and Redwings in ice hockey offered additional inspiration and vicarious success to the multitudes struggling under dire economic conditions.

Among my first vivid memories are, at age six, peeping into a giant Ford Trimotor airplane and watching thundering warplanes racing low around pylons at Selfridge Field, an army air base near Detroit. At about the same age, I became excited at seeing my father catch sunfish and perch from a rowboat during a family picnic. His stories about hunting quail and ducks in his youth with

26

his Irish setter and water spaniel validated in my young mind the high place of hunting dogs and game-bird shooting.

I was raised with two older sisters, Blanche and Virginia, and a younger sister, Hazel, and this surely influenced my behavior and attitudes. If my sisters liked to dance, that was a girlish thing to be avoided. The same applied to dishwashing, fragrant shampoo soaps, and whatever else I associated with their preferences or activities. But like it or not, Blanche and Virginia's uninvited counseling probably had some noble effect on me, imparting proper table etiquette, courteous manners toward women and the elderly, personal cleanliness, and above all, honesty.

Our annual family vacation to Ohio and Indiana always fulfilled my yearlong anticipation of venturesome travel through towns with Indian names and reunion with gracious relatives. A few of these folks lived on farms with birds, animals, orchards, and even woods to explore; it was all so exciting I could hardly wait to tear out each morning on new adventures.

Until I was eight years old, we lived on the west side of Detroit within walking distance of Navan Field, a stadium then home to the Tigers. Occasionally, usually when the Yankees came to town on a weekend, my father took me to the ball game. We would sit in the left-field bleachers in order to be close to Babe Ruth, who played left field for the Yankees. The Babe was so famous that all baseball fans, no matter their favorite team, wanted to see him perform. After one game, we encountered a boy who had recovered a home run ball the Babe hit over the left-field fence into Cherry Street. My father's offer to buy the ball was rejected, though the boy proudly gave us a look at his prize, which showed the mark of the Babe's mighty bat as a gray smudge.

The year I entered third grade, our family moved to the far east side of Detroit near the city limits and just a block from the Detroit River. My new elementary school was blessed with wonderful teachers and I truly enjoyed my years there. Penmanship was stressed, and we students felt special pride as the teacher awarded fancy certificates and complimented us on having a "nice hand." Spelling was taught and practiced by sounding out letters and syllables. Frequent spelling bees kept interest lively, and it seemed to me the teacher chose easy words for the less apt pupils so everyone seemed competitive and maintained good spirits. Reading and arithmetic were also taught in ways that encouraged confidence. The basics were leavened with athletics, plays, music, and lively discussions. We learned the national anthem, "Home on the Range," English madrigals, and even the stories of some operas. It was puzzling and saddening to me that the heroine always had to die in the last act of these operas.

In the spring we made and flew kites, the electric wires around the schoolyard becoming decorated with kite skeletons and tails. Playing marbles was important too, each boy bragging about his special shooter. My favorite was a red marble called a "bloody" — and what unhappiness when I lost that beauty through a hole in my pocket. Mother didn't understand the importance of shooting marbles and complained because my trouser knees got dirty.

There were enough boys in our neighborhood to field a couple of scrub baseball teams, and we occasionally played teams from distant neighborhoods. Lacking a coach, we weren't very good. We rarely won, being baffled by opposing pitchers who could actually put stuff on the ball. Practically all of the neighborhood boys and many of the girls learned to swim in some pool or in the Detroit River. The river soon became the main focus of my interest. Early attempts, with the help of my sister Hazel, to build a small boat from scrap lumber didn't work out well. We put the boat on a wagon and pulled it to a nearby canal, where it filled with water as I put one foot aboard. Its tendency to sink was puzzling because the boat was made of wood and we knew wood floated. The mystery was solved when my father explained the principle of water displacement and the need for tight seams.

Later I acquired two things that brought enormous joy. First, my father agreed we could keep a stray dog that seemed from his color to have either black-and-tan hound or Gordon setter in his ancestry. I named him Pal, and we became inseparable adventurers. Then, my father gave me a small rowboat. That boat opened new horizons. Baseball, roller-skating, and kid's games lost much of their attraction. At rowing speed, Pal and I explored the upper Detroit River and Lake St. Clair from Belle Isle to the Clinton River on the American side and to Belle River on the Canadian side. I learned to handle the boat in water sometimes so rough I didn't know whether we would make it. My confidence and self-reliance grew.

My father finally gave in to my pleas and bought a one-and-a-half-horsepower Evinrude outboard motor for the rowboat. Being a restive fourteen-year-old, I once set out—over my mother's strong objection—to motor the entire perimeter of Lake St. Clair. There was no doubt my father would be disturbed that I disobeyed my mother, but the venture seemed worth the consequences. My logistics were simple: a fishing rod, a blanket, some sandwiches, and much less gasoline than required for the trip. With a little money in my pocket, I expected to be able to buy gasoline along the way. By evening, I made it to Belle River on the Canadian side of the lake, where I ate my sandwiches and went ashore to sleep. Mosquitoes soon found me. To escape, I rowed out into the lake, but they followed. Then the rain started. There was nothing to do but curl up on the boat seat under my blanket and soak up the rain; it was the most miserable night of my young life.

Already needing more gasoline, I took the boat up the Belle River and found a road, then hitchhiked to a gas station. Back at the boat, the rain continued and I was thoroughly soaked, tired, chilled, bug-bitten, and hungry, with 80 percent of my planned travel still ahead. At that point, the comforts of home were far more enticing than pioneering uncharted waters and I headed back.

As I approached our home mooring stake, I saw my father standing on the bank. There was no doubt a stern reprimand in store for me, but I was not prepared for what actually happened.

"Mother told me you were taking the boat around the lake," he said. I answered yes. "Did you make it?" he asked. I replied no. He turned and walked away.

That response signaled my failure in a devastating way. I took it to mean that he might have been pleased, even proud, if I had not quit short of my goal. Had I anticipated his reaction, I would have pushed on with the trip no matter the difficulties; instead I felt only embarrassment and disgust with myself.

During my early teen years, an obsession with fishing kept me out in the boat most days during the summer, and I usually managed to catch something. Peach Island, in Canada at the entrance to the Detroit River, was a favorite destination, though an unauthorized port of entry. Canals had been dug on the island in earlier times for winter storage of small ferryboats, and these channels provided excellent spring fishing for largemouth bass, sunfish, bluegills, crappie, and an occasional northern pike. Bullheads bit best in the evening and were a great excuse for staying out late. They were tough to clean but good to eat. Walleyed pike, which we erroneously called pickerel, was our favorite fish on the platter. My mother always seemed pleased to cook my catch for the family, but on two occasions the fish gave off such unpleasant odors that they went from the frying pan to the garbage can.

On one of the rare times when I ventured to take my single-shot .22 rifle to Peach Island, I was stricken with excitement on seeing a flock of black ducks settle on a small bay. Could I get one of them? Stripping down to my underwear, I slithered into the marsh and very slowly moved in the direction of the birds. With water around my chin and the gun barrel parting the reeds, I moved very slowly to avoid making sound or waves. In half an hour, I progressed about fifty yards. Occasionally the low chuckle of feeding ducks gave me direction and encouragement. Then, through the reeds, I saw movement and the shiny dark eye of a duck within ten feet. It hesitated, probably not sensing danger from my quarter. Despite a pounding heart, I aimed and shot at the duck's head. There was a swirl of air from the noisy flapping of wings as the flock jumped, but they left one member behind. I rushed forward through the waist-deep water and grabbed the bird, which had died instantly.

The thrill of possessing and caressing the warm, soft duck was like nothing I had ever experienced. I examined it from beak to tail, almost feather by feather, marveling especially at the iridescent purple patch of wing color known as the speculum. How good I felt, going home with this prize. The bird was so beautiful I could not consider disturbing its plumage by picking it until every member of the family had an opportunity to admire it. That my three sisters were less than interested was disappointing. Bagging this duck surely provided the purest joy and fulfillment of my youthful hunting fantasies, yet unmarred by any pangs of conscience about killing.

During the fall, my father and brothers-in-law sometimes took me on hunting trips for pheasants, rabbits, and even deer. These outings always ended too soon. By my early teens, the streets and playgrounds where my friends hung out came to appeal less and less to me. Yearning to be in the woods or on the lake, I gradually came to dread school. Only the biology courses interested me, and they were not a priority in a system designed to support the vocational character of a great industrial city. Nevertheless, I persevered and graduated from Foch Intermediate School In 1937.

In my bedroom at home as a child, I sometimes stared in wonderment at a framed color print depicting a lone wolf in a snow-covered, moonlit landscape. The animal gazed from a hill across fields at a small cluster of buildings below. While free, it still seemed to be a lonely fugitive. I sadly reflected that the wilderness had been conquered by pioneers before I had a chance to see it. Confirmation came in a memorial service for my grandfather Brooks, which made reference to wolves howling in Dark County, Ohio, when he was growing up in the 1850s. The Indians lost wars and were gone; the trees were turned into buildings, rail fences, or firewood; and the wolves, except for the pictured survivor, were purged from the land. How insecure and lonely that animal must be, and how long could it hold out? I hoped it would survive for a long time. From reading the books of Ernest Thompson Seton, I even felt I had become an expert on wolves. If there were still places in the far north where wolves roamed, I longed to go there.

CHAPTER THREE

Alaska Boy

IN THE SPRING OF 1940 I told my boss at the repair shop that I was quitting. I had already responded to an advertisement seeking drivers to move cars from Detroit to dealers throughout the country. My application resulted in an unbelievable opportunity to travel in class. I drove a shiny new Pontiac from Detroit to San Francisco. From there I rode a Dollar Line bus to Seattle (eleven dollars), where I purchased a steamship ticket to Ketchikan, at the lower end of the Alaska panhandle (twenty-one dollars).

The Alaska Steamship Company's SS *Yukon*, a seven-thousand-ton freighter, had a few cabins for those who could afford them and many steel bunks stacked four high in the fo'c'sle for steerage passengers like me. The place was nearly full and I ended up in a top bunk, which was fine because I was nimble enough to climb up and down easily and could better hear the talk of the other travelers.

Most of these men had been to Alaska before. They were miners, fishermen, construction workers, even a radio announcer. I envied those who were going back to jobs, because I had little money and great uneasiness about what faced me. For three days I listened to stories about gold nuggets, bears, red light districts, poker games, fish pirates, and other exciting subjects. I felt I was headed toward adventure.

With curiosity and optimism tempered by a good deal of apprehension, I got off the ship in Ketchikan, where a sign over the main street read "The Salmon Capitol of the World." But the salmon canneries were not yet open for the season. I visited the sawmill, marine ways, and other businesses to ask for work and met disappointment at every turn. That evening, much discouraged, I checked into the Knickerbocker Hotel, something between a hotel and a boardinghouse. In the morning the owner, Dorothy Sorensen, offered me a job as a pearl diver—that is, as a dishwasher—and a cleaning person. I was tickled pink, as my mother would say; the pay was low, but board and room were included.

I invested in a copy of *Alaska Sportsman* magazine and was rewarded with an article about the exciting work of the field agents for the Alaska Game Commission. Some of them even flew airplanes. I would later encounter several of these agents, including Clarence Rhode, who gave me my first job as a biologist. In the article, the commission's executive director said he hoped to hire more agents—"Alaska boys" who had been here at least two years and knew the country. This seemed to disqualify me—at least for now.

A few weeks after arriving in Ketchikan, I learned that applications were being accepted for the Civilian Conservation Corps, a Depression-era employment program started under President Franklin D. Roosevelt. I hustled to the U.S. Forest Service office and met a man in uniform named Chester Archbold, who was businesslike but kind in helping me fill out the forms and explaining the program. He seemed genuinely interested, not in what I could do, but in what I aspired to do. I have always felt grateful to this gentleman.

The CCC in Alaska accepted men of all ages, usually assigning them work near their homes. The ranks expanded and contracted with seasonal employment opportunities, mainly in fishing. Construction of trails and cabins were the major CCC projects, though some Natives carved and restored totem poles.

I was put up at the Ward Cove CCC camp for a few days to get outfitted with field clothes and await transportation to my assigned camp. With free time on my hands, I explored the waterfront and particularly the bridge over Ketchikan Creek, with its access to Creek Street, the famous red light district. Men on the ship and at the hotel had talked about this place, so I knew the girls charged three dollars for a visit and fifteen dollars to stay all night. I felt conspicuous and self-conscious after several passes by the entrance as I tried to work up nerve to turn in there in broad daylight. With heart pounding and driven by a force common to young men, I walked up Creek Street trying to project innocence but entertaining another idea. I had never seen a naked woman, much less touched one, so this was a daring venture.

The house fronts lined the street, which was really a boardwalk; you could see through the windows directly into the living rooms. In some, women smiled out at me as I walked by. At one house, a thin curtain drew back as I approached, and a pretty young woman smiled and waved toward the door. She opened the door and led me into another room, where an older woman was seated. This was the madam. She told me to have a seat and asked if I wanted a drink. When I said no in a quivering voice, she turned to the younger woman and said, "Maybe he wants to go upstairs." I agreed to that, and followed the younger woman upstairs to a bedroom, where she turned, smiling, and said, "Three dollars please." She then proceeded to remove all of her clothes, which weren't a lot, and lay face up on the bed, telling me to get undressed.

My hands were shaking so badly I had trouble unbuttoning my shirt. As I was trying to undress, she asked me how I wanted it. I had no idea what my options were. I said, "Oh, the regular way." I guess that's what I got and it didn't take long. Thereafter, I was not so much in awe when men talked about the creek. I had been there.

A mail and supply boat took me to Loring, about thirty miles north of Ketchikan, where a dozen CCC men plus a cook and foreman lived in a dormitory on a houseboat designated *Wanigan 12*. My new companions had been together only a couple of weeks. They were a varied group, all older than I and more familiar with ax, crosscut saw, and the tools of the woods. Our foreman, Louis Richmond, was a civil engineer and a fine leader. After he clearly set out the rules of behavior, a mere frown was all it took to alert folks that they might be close to the line. I never heard him raise his voice.

In the several months this group lived and worked together, there was never a serious dispute among us. Part of the reason may have been our diversity of backgrounds and interests. There was Clarence Ruffcorn, who had traveled widely with a carnival as a prizefighter, challenging all comers in the small towns they visited. Anyone staying three rounds with Clarence would win a little money and much local prestige. He and his manager, whom he called Pops, got their payoff from betting on the outcome.

Cal Johnston was from a wealthy family in Bellingham, Washington; his presence here was related somehow to an automobile wreck while he was drunk. With the only shortwave radio in camp, Cal controlled the audio environment. Until the required shutdown at night, he would bring in an endless stream of pulsating static, foreign languages, and exotic music from all over the world, trying mostly in vain to find western music.

Al Swatch, a quiet, serious-minded Lithuanian immigrant, had hoboed and worked his way across the United States and western Canada. For a time he handhewed railroad ties in British Columbia, where he became an artist with an ax. Al loved nature and the outdoor life, and he had a fly rod that he would sometimes lend to me.

Wanigan 12 was moored near the mouth of the Naha River in a beautiful country of rounded mountains covered with forests of giant Sitka spruce, hemlock, and lesser amounts of yellow and red cedar. Around the edges or wherever light could filter through, there was a dense, almost impenetrable, understory of alder, huckleberry and salmonberry bushes, skunk cabbage, devil's club, and other shrubs. The Naha River, connecting a chain of lakes, entered the brackish water of Roosevelt Lagoon, which in turn emptied into saltwater through a shallow, narrow channel known as a salt chuck, where the direction of flow reverses on every change of tide.

The only permanent inhabitants of the area were an old man and his Airedale, at the nearby abandoned cannery, and the Orton family who lived beside the river. Mr. Orton, with his wife and their two young children, cultivated a large vegetable garden. In summers he worked as a stream guard for the Bureau of Fisheries, protecting salmon from poachers, or creek robbers as they were called.

Some of our crew built a portage around the salt chuck so skiffs could be taken into Roosevelt Lagoon at any stage of the tide. The rest of us reconstructed old trails that led from Loring to the salt chuck, then along the edge of the lagoon and up the river to Heckman Lake. With no maintenance for many years, the trails were grown over with brush and obstructed by wind-thrown trees. Here is where I learned to pull a two-man crosscut saw, and not push it, as the faint scars on the back of my left hand still remind me.

At a low falls on the river just above Orton's place, black bears congregated to catch salmon. Here we built a bear observatory. While others prepared the ground and erected the frame, I packed cedar shakes for roofing and siding from Heckman Lake, where a large quantity of shakes were stored at the old Fortmann salmon hatchery.

As I ferried the shakes from the hatchery across the lake in a skiff, I was thrilled to see feeding trout breaking the surface and black-tailed deer standing along the lakeshore. With Al Swatch's fly rod, a sleeping bag, and a little food, I enjoyed spending an occasional Saturday night at this old hatchery. After catching enough rainbow and cutthroat trout to make a nice meal for the crew, I spent hours reading the documents and reports that had remained undisturbed for years in the hatchery office.

After more than twenty years of operation, the hatchery closure in 1926 apparently was intended to be temporary, because everything was left in such good order. Dishes, silverware, pots, spices, and even towels were neatly arranged in cabinets and on shelves. I discovered the hatchery was named after a man named Fortmann who was head of the Alaska Packers Association, which owned both the hatchery and the cannery at Loring. Heckman Lake was named for J. R. Heckman, superintendent of the cannery, and the next lake upstream in the system, Patching Lake, was named for hatchery manager Fred Patching.

A federal law exempted cannery owners from taxation if they built and operated hatcheries, an arrangement that failed the salmon. Newly hatched salmon fry with yolk sacs attached, which in nature remain in the gravel for protection until the yolks are absorbed, were prematurely dumped into the lake. This expedient procedure, while inflating the production credited to the hatchery, caused the quick death of the fish.

Coho salmon were considered predators on red salmon, so the natural coho runs were deliberately wiped out, as were fish-eating birds and mammals that chanced into the area. Having reduced the salmon stocks below commercial viability, the packers association walked away from its Loring cannery and Fortmann hatchery to open new facilities where the salmon had not yet been overly exploited. I began to develop a skepticism about federal/industry management of Alaska's salmon fisheries that continued to intensify until statehood. And it seems ironic that men who destroyed the once great Naha salmon runs for profit and out of ignorance should have their names forever associated with the beautiful lakes of the Naha system.

At dinner following the arrival of the mail boat in early July, Louis Richmond told us we would be moving. *Ranger 10*, a Forest Service vessel, would arrive in a few days to tow *Wanigan 12* to Tamgas Harbor on the south side of Annette Island. *Ranger 10* turned out to be not a tug, but a sleek fifty-five-foot cruiser built to transport light cargo and people. The *Wanigan* was a heavy tow, and our progress depended on the *Ranger* skipper's skill in using a favorable stage of the tides. The trip went slowly but smoothly for the first half day, but late in the day we were surprised by a tremendous southeast storm while entering Tongass Narrows from the north.

Even before the wind got strong and the seas began to break, the dimly visible shoreline told us we were not moving ahead. As wind and seas continued to build, the ride aboard the *Wanigan 12* became more violent and noisy. We sat on our bunks, wearing life preservers, holding on and bracing against the plunging and jolting as each wave crashed over the blunt bow and struck the cabin. Some of the fellows became nauseous, and all were uneasy if not frightened. I rather enjoyed the force of the elements. Crossing the Detroit River in a small rowboat with a strong wind against the current had seemed to me more exciting and dangerous than our present situation.

We were being blown backward into the more open water of Behm Canal, and the seas became ever larger. But after several hours, the whistling and roaring of the wind seemed to lessen, raising hopes the worst was past. Then someone looking aft called out that he could see a shoreline. That was alarming; we might be blown into shore. But the wind was clearly moderating, and the danger passed. When things calmed down, we discovered that our skiff, oars, antenna, lines, and everything on deck — except the anchor and winch, which were bolted down — had been carried away. The only further excitement during the trip was at the poker table, where my small losses were somewhat offset by gains in my poker playing skills.

To my eyes, Tamgas Harbor was pure wilderness. We saw several deer on the beach as we entered, and we flushed blue grouse and found wolf tracks on the beach when we first went ashore. Land to the south of our anchorage was dominated by sparse stands of trees, mostly jack pine, and open muskegs. Standing high to the northeast was lovely Purple Mountain and, to the west, a most unusual prominence named Yellow Hill. I felt a sense of adventure just being here.

Richmond told us we would be building a plank road from the beach across a muskeg for about three hundred yards, and then boardwalks and platforms upon which we would erect tent frames. He said about a thousand men would be coming in to construct an Army airfield.

For the next few days we cut brush and helped Richmond shoot the initial survey lines for access to the planned airfield site. In the evenings we beach-combed for Japanese glass balls, which were said to be floats for fishing nets. These were something of a mystery to us: why would so many net floats be here? Al Swatch said they were carried clear across the Pacific Ocean by the Japanese current—but years later it was discovered they came from nets deployed much closer to our shores. They were, in fact, just a hint of the enormous high-seas gill-net fisheries the Japanese operated both before and after World War II, extending into the 1990s, with monstrous destruction of sea life.

A tug and barge soon arrived in the harbor, loaded with timbers, planks, and lumber of all sorts. We had no power equipment or tools; everything was carried by hand and on shoulders, except heavy timbers that required four or six men with timber carriers. There was a feeling people were depending on us to have things ready, and eight hard weeks later we were finished. With the last of the lumber we even built some outhouses, and in the nick of time.

That night a ship arrived bearing scores of Corps of Engineers troops, suntanned and fresh from Puerto Rico. We were pleased to see their vehicles on our plank road and their tents nicely fitted over the tent frames we had built. This was the vanguard of the construction force, Navy Seabees, that converted the substance of beautiful Yellow Hill into a 7,500-foot runway in record time. (After World War II it became an international airport, serving Ketchikan and surrounding areas until the new Ketchikan Airport was built in the 1960s.)

I was homesick and longed to see my parents and sisters, so rather than going to the Ward Cove CCC camp with the other fellows in early October, I returned to Detroit via steamship and bus. Although the homecoming was joyful, it quickly became apparent that job opportunities for a person like me were still dismal. A neighbor who had taken me grouse hunting several times near West Branch in the central part of Michigan knew of a cabin there that I could use. I jumped at the chance and stayed at the cabin through November, sensing it would be a real north-woods experience. I even earned some money by trying my hand at trapping muskrats, skunks, and raccoons while I pondered my return to Alaska.

CHAPTER FOUR

A Desperate Move

IN EARLY DECEMBER 1940, I once again drove a dealer's car west, this time as part of a caravan to Phoenix. From there, with barely enough money to buy food for a couple of weeks, I resorted to a mode of travel that was within my budget: riding freight trains north to Seattle. As my train crossed a Sacramento River bridge, I saw two men each carrying a huge king salmon. It could never have occurred to me that the survival of this great salmon stock would one day become threatened.

In Seattle, I didn't have the money for a boat ticket, but I went down to the wharf and gazed at the ship. It seemed to me that such an enormous vessel would not feel an extra burden if one more small person were aboard. The stub from the ticket I purchased in May was still in my wallet. The idea came to mind that I might mix with the boarding passengers and flash that ticket stub as we went up the gangway. Well, it didn't work, and I don't know whether it was the shabby ticket or the nervous look of guilt that betrayed me.

I decided my chances would be better at Prince Rupert, British Columbia. I had heard that fishing boats bound for Alaska usually stopped there. Prince Rupert was only ninety miles from Ketchikan, which had no road or train access. But first I had to get to Prince Rupert.

Trains entering Canada from the United States along the West Coast were stopped and searched at White Rock, B.C., so I hitchhiked to Blaine, Washington, on the highway and looked for a way to avoid Canadian immigration officials. In Blaine, U.S. Border Patrol officers nabbed me, thinking I might be a Canadian. When I told them I was an American from Detroit, one asked: "Who lives at the foot of Piper Street?" This was within a mile of home, so I instantly replied: "Gar Wood, the racing boat champion." The other asked me to spell Arizona, which I did with a Z rather than the Canadian term Zed. That convinced them.

That night, chill and fatigue persuaded me to seek shelter at an office of the Blaine Police Department. Pointing to a small jail cell, the officer there said "Sure, no one has slept there but my dog for quite a while, but I will have to lock you in for the night." So I planned my next day's activities from the luxury of a jail cot and a blanket covered with dog hair.

Next morning I walked east from Blaine a few miles until I could go north along fencerows and through woodlots while staying mostly out of sight of buildings. I felt like a fugitive. The sun was my only reference for direction, and it was impossible to know just when I crossed the border into Canada. Making a wide arc north of White Rock, I intercepted the railroad tracks and walked back to a place where I hoped to see an incoming train stop to be searched. I intended to climb aboard as it began moving again.

It was getting dark when the train arrived and stopped for inspection. When the train got under way again, I miscalculated its acceleration; it was clattering along awfully fast when it reached me. To make matters worse, the light was so poor I could barely see the ladder rungs on the boxcars. In desperation I ran as hard as I could beside the train and grabbed the forward ladder of a car as it moved past. I was immediately slammed back almost horizontally against the side. When I swung back down, my feet dragged the roadbed, keeping me from stepping onto the bottom ladder rung. It was a life-or-death moment, and panic may have provided the shot of strength that allowed me to hang on and find the foothold.

With the noise of the train and rushing of air, it took a few moments to realize I was OK. Youth, luck, and a determination not to miss the train had barely overcome my terrible miscalculation. After this test, I had a feeling I would be able to handle whatever awaited me down the road.

In the railroad yards at New Westminster, where Christmas passed me by, a switchman gave me a timetable and told me I needed to go northeast to Red Pass Junction and then back northwest to Prince Rupert. When my train stopped at Boston Bar, hunger forced me to leave it and walk into town. On the main street I encountered a uniformed Provincial Police officer wearing a black great coat and a fur hat; there was no way to avoid him. Anxiety and fear surged within when he signaled for me to approach. Now I had to create a monstrous lie in response to his questioning. I told him that my name was James LaBelle, and that I was from Hamilton, Ontario. When he asked to see my military draft registration card, my heart sank. All I could think of saying was that I had been on the road for some time and didn't know that I was supposed to register. His response was hopeful. He said "You had better get right over to the post office and register now before it closes. It's in the back of that store."

The store was a kind of trading post, with an elderly man discussing some Cowichin woolen sweaters with the two Native women who had made them. They were very slow in completing their business, and more than once I saw the police officer walk by and look in at me. Finally it was my turn. I filled out a packet of variously colored forms and was handed a small white card. I was now registered, under the name of James LaBelle, for the Canadian military draft.

After I left Boston Bar in an empty boxcar, the weather got very cold, far below zero Fahrenheit. In addition to the clothes I had worn in Phoenix, I had a sweater, long underwear, and woolen socks and gloves, but it wasn't enough. I jogged around the boxcar trying to generate heat while my chill deepened. In despair, my wits came alive. The car had been used for hauling grain, and the sides were covered with heavy brown paper, evidently to keep the grain from leaking out. I tore long strips from the walls, laid them on the floor for insulation, and rolled up like a giant cocoon to await my fate. To my relief, I began to get warm.

Red Pass Junction consisted of a depot, a station house for railroad workers, and a Provincial Police post. The next train to Prince Rupert wouldn't come through for three days, but the depot attendant said I could stay there. I asked the cook at the station house for work in exchange for a meal, and she sent me to a shed to split wood for her range. As a result, I enjoyed a fantastic Christmas dinner, albeit a few days late. Two more hearty meals before my train arrived carried me through in fine shape.

I had noticed the Provincial Police officer in the depot a couple of times, and though he said nothing, his presence gave me an uneasy feeling. The morning the train was to arrive, he approached me and asked where I was heading and why. Again I had to fabricate a story. I said I was going to Prince George to work for a cousin who had a contract with the railroad to furnish ties. This line came from listening to Al Swatch on *Wanigan 12*, but it was the truth when Al said it.

The officer examined my draft card and seemed satisfied. He was, however, truly concerned about my well-being, saying that the temperature was nearly forty below zero and that I would never survive to reach Prince George. When the train arrived, he talked to the engineer and got permission for me to ride in the engine cab. My deceit of such generous and caring people caused me shame, a feeling I didn't like.

The fireman directed me to a low metal seat on the left side of the cab, out of his way as he shoveled coal into the roaring furnace. When he wasn't shoveling, I was permitted to stand and watch the scenery move by. At one point we passed a snow-covered lake that was crossed by a track laid down by a person on snowshoes. The remarkable thing about the track, that stuck indelibly in my mind, was that it seemed as straight as an arrow clear across the lake. I would later try to emulate that straight track when walking across expansive open areas by focusing on a distant object.

With darkness and the heat from the open furnace door, I felt an uncontrollable urge to doze off. The engineer and fireman were afraid I might fall between the engine and coal car. They spoke harshly to me, threatening to put me off at the next water stop if I didn't stay awake. It was a struggle; I had never before felt such a compelling need to close my eyes. I was permitted to ride in the train cab all the way to Hazleton, and from there again hopped inside a cold boxcar.

I arrived in Prince Rupert at night, greatly fatigued, after more than two days without sleep, with little food, and only a few opportunities to drink water. I sought out the warm shelter of the railroad roundhouse and lay down in a secluded niche. Later I became vaguely aware of climbing a steep bank and moving toward distant lights. Coming awake, I was startled to realize I didn't know where I was or how I got there. I had been sleepwalking. This incident made me wonder if I were near the limits of my endurance.

Canada was now involved in the war against Germany, and security measures around the waterfront were formidable. Still, I had to somehow find a boat heading to Ketchikan. Early in the morning I ventured toward the boat harbor and found it protected by a metal fence. While I pondered how to deal with the fence, two police officers stopped their car to question me. I suddenly felt a sinking sensation caused by weariness and a realistic sense of futility in carrying my ruse further. I told them I was an American, trying to hitch a boat ride to Alaska. They took me to jail, where they gave me the number of the American consul, Mr. Anderson, and access to a telephone.

Anderson promised to come see me on Monday; it was now Saturday.

Despite the bars and confinement, the jail was a clean, warm, even fascinating place. I joined four Canadian sailors who had been embroiled in an alcohol-fueled disturbance. They tried to top one another with stories about storms and German submarine encounters in the North Atlantic while escorting convoys. For emphasis they relied on risqué language. I had never heard such an unbroken stream of off-color words, many of them new to me.

Sunday morning brought a miraculous transformation in their behavior. Four Salvation Army folks—a middle-aged couple and two attractive young women—came into the jail to hold a service. The sailors attended, projecting devotion, a knowledge of the hymns, and great enthusiasm for singing. I was impressed by their versatility.

Consul Anderson appeared Monday morning. He and his wife had been assigned to Eagle, Alaska, before being transferred to Prince Rupert, and he was sympathetic with my attempt to return to Alaska. He came back later with a steamship ticket, had me released, and took me home to meet his wife. That evening they drove me to the dock and saw me aboard the *Princess Patricia*. So I disembarked at Ketchikan a second time. But now I felt like I belonged.

The CCC camp seemed my best immediate refuge. Chester Archbold obligingly signed me up again, after hearing an account of my trip Outside—the Alaskan term for anyplace outside the Territory. It was a happy reunion with some of the *Wanigan 12* gang who were now at the Ward Cove camp. A couple of them warned that I had committed a criminal act by registering for the Canadian draft and recommended that I destroy the draft card, so I hastily burned it.

CHAPTER FIVE

High-liner

A HANDSOME FELLOW several years older than I, Harold Hansen, occupied the bunk below mine on *Wanigan 12*. He was of Danish descent, or claimed to be, a distinction that he delighted in calling to the attention of his Norwegian associates. Of course, he added his version of history, alleging a preponderance of Danish blood in the veins of Norwegian royalty. Most enjoyed his humor; some chafed under it.

Harold, who owned a commercial salmon fishing boat, and I became good friends. Our common work project was building a spur road and large timber culvert between the main road and a cove several miles north of Ward Cove. This is where I learned to drive trucks and operate a Caterpillar bulldozer.

By mid-March, with the first hint of spring in the air, Harold was ready to return to fishing.

"Why don't you come along?" he asked. "I could use a hand on the boat and it will get you away from these lousy people."

He meant it literally; crab lice were indeed a problem there. It didn't take long to stuff my few belongings into a seabag and check out of the CCC camp for the last time.

Harold had run his trolling boat up from the Oregon coast the previous summer to fish for king and coho salmon. Talk around the harbor was that he was a high-liner—an extraordinarily successful fisherman—from Outside. He was generous to himself and others; money slipped through his hands easily. Harold enjoyed drinking and the company of women. He admitted that time spent on Creek Street had used up much of his last season's earnings. Not one word of regret, however.

We spent several days getting the boat, engine, and gear cleaned up, work I thoroughly enjoyed in anticipation of an exciting venture into commercial fishing. While Harold was in town one day, I spent many hours polishing metal fishing spoons that had tarnished. When Harold saw what I had done, he picked up the whole lot and he threw them overboard. I was stunned and confused.

56

"Jim, if we can't afford new spoons every year, we had better give up fishing," he told me. "Besides, once the spoons tarnish badly, you can't keep them bright. They don't fish."

Finally, with ship's stores aboard that we charged at the Tongass Trading Company, everything looked right to Harold. It was now the first week of April. We freed the mooring lines, stopped for fuel, ice, and frozen herring, and headed for Dixon Entrance.

We commenced fishing the next afternoon off Cape Chacon and caught a single small king salmon, which to my dismay Harold shook off without landing. From the glimpse I got of the fish, it looked like a beautiful thing.

Harold had shown me how the fishing gear worked, how to read the chart, and a myriad of other things. The gear was complicated, and my apprenticeship dragged out because Harold so much enjoyed operating it himself.

A trolling pole made from a seasoned spruce sapling was hinged to each gunwale, port and starboard, so that by means of a hauling line they could be raised straight upward, parallel to the mast, or lowered outward at any angle. When they were in the lowered position to fish, two fishing lines were attached to each pole by a system of tag lines and clips. A heavy lead ball was fastened to the end of each fishing line and above that, at intervals of ten to fifteen feet, leaders were clipped to the line for the lures or bait. The fishing lines were lowered and raised by reels known as gurdies that, in Harold's boat, were powered by the propeller drive shaft through sprockets and chains. With the gear rigged and fishing, we had many baits working at various depths.

The next morning we caught a couple of larger kings. Now at last, he counseled me on dressing the fish. Harold commented that the fish were slow in biting, and he wished that other boats were around.

"Are you worried that if we have trouble, there would be no one out here to help us?" I asked. He was incensed.

"Hell no!" he shouted. "The fish are where the boats are."

We raised the gear and set a course for Cape Muzon, where sure enough, we found a half dozen trollers following each other around. Harold steered in behind another boat, and we began to catch fish right away. The fishing was good for a week, with only one day being too rough to leave the nearby harbor where we anchored each night. Harold was a wonderful companion and teacher, and it made me feel good when he said how much he appreciated my help.

With not much ice left for preserving any additional fish, and the weather looking good, we returned to the Ketchikan dock. Before my fishing days with Harold, I had stood on the dock and watched as fishermen loaded their catch into baskets to be hoisted up to cold storage. I thought they were some of the luckiest people in the world. Now I was doing it.

Harold explained the way receipts from commercial fish landings are shared, with the crew being low in priority. But my share still amounted to more than two months' pay in the CCC. I was tickled with the arrangement and the outlook was even more promising. I went shopping for groceries for our next trip, while Harold went to another part of town. When he failed to return to the boat by evening, I had a strong hunch he was on

Creek Street. He showed up bleary-eyed the next morning and rolled into his berth. With the groceries, fuel,
ice, and bait herring taken aboard the previous day, we
were ready to go as soon as Harold felt up to it. In late
afternoon, he got up, had a shot of whiskey, and said,
"OK, let's go." It was back to Cape Muzon.

Our fishing was good again, and I learned a lot more
as Harold let me work the gear and gaff some fish. But it
was disheartening to see wonderful game fish, like giant
trout, towed to the gaff by the powerful gear without a
chance to fight.

Harold really enjoyed catching fish, showing an especially happy face when we got a large, prime salmon,
the kind that were processed into lox, a salt-cured, cold-
smoked product esteemed by gourmets. It didn't seem to
be the value of the fish that gratified Harold so much as
the achievement of getting them. Maybe it had something to do with his reputation, too, because he quietly
glowed with satisfaction at mention that others had referred to him as a high-liner. On the way back to
Ketchikan, Harold said we should have really hot fishing later when the coho salmon came in. I could sense
he also considered the current trip a very good one. My
share this time more than doubled. My optimism
soared.

All cleaned up and wearing clothes fresh from the
laundry and cleaners, Harold was anxious to get uptown.
I asked him when he would be back, and he said, "Hell,
I don't know exactly. But I'll see you later, Jim. You can
get the boat ready."

Remembering our last visit to town, I found that reply both encouraging and ominous. Thirty-six hours later

he had not returned. I looked in all of the town's bar-
rooms and then realized he might still be on Creek Street.
Checking the houses on the creek seemed impossible, and
even if he were there, he would be upset that I sought
him out. An officer at the police station advised me to
check at the hospital.

That's where I found him. A nun escorted me to
Harold's room. He was unrecognizable. His eyes were
mere slits on the side of a pink, green, and purple ball;
his rib cage was encased in wide strips of adhesive tape.
His voice was guttural and weak, though his mind was
clear. Two "asshole Norwegians" from the Ward Cove
CCC camp had beaten him up in the Arctic Bar. I knew
these fellows. They were the big, powerful, authorita-
tive kind of people that Harold loved to taunt. Later, as
the face swelling subsided, it became evident that
Harold's nose had been broken because the middle part
was no longer straight. Eventually he went back to the
boat to recuperate and soon began walks around the harbor.

Harold returned to the boat for lunch one day in a
most somber mood. He said we had to talk. A friend of
his from Oregon had just arrived in the harbor with a
seine boat and was heading to Kodiak for the salmon
season. He wanted Harold to come along on the seiner,
and Harold said yes. But leaving me behind was clearly
upsetting to him. He knew the depth of my disappointment, after the promises of a great season that grew out
of our two successful trips. He said I could live aboard
his boat as long as I wished, and he insisted on giving
me some of his best clothes. Except for a fine leather and
canvas vest, which was too tight for him, I refused his

charity. We fought back tears as I left the boat. Despite the setback, my passion for Alaska was undiminished. I boarded the SS *Alaska* with a cabin-class ticket that night, bound for Seward, the gateway to a larger Alaska.

CHAPTER SIX

Gandy Dancer and Grease Monkey

SEWARD, AT THE SOUTHERN END of the Alaska Railroad, was bustling. Stevedores unloaded freighters laden with cement and other construction material for military airfields being built at Anchorage and Fairbanks. The main street, only a couple of blocks long, was dominated by the Brown and Hawkins general store. There was a mission school for Native children from all over Alaska, and a sizable red light district.

I asked at the railroad building about work, and I was promptly hired as a section hand at the Divide station house, nine miles north of town. I was now a gandy dancer—the odd term used to describe a worker in a railroad section gang. The work involved leveling the track by jacking up places where vibration at rail joints caused it to settle, and then tamping gravel under the ties with a straight-edged shovel.

The scenery was spectacular, and the sight of white Dall sheep on a mountain above the Snow River seemed almost unreal. We saw moose every day. There was no doubt I was approaching the heart of Alaska. Although the foreman and a few of the workers at the station had been there for years, I didn't see much future in being tied to the railroad track. The hard work was all right, but the simple repetition became unbearably boring. After barely a month, I continued north to Anchorage.

Trudging up the slope from the depot to town with my seabag over my shoulder, I encountered the Anchorage Hotel. It looked a little too highbrow for my pocketbook. I spotted a likely looking place on the north side of Fifth Avenue. I knocked, and a black woman opened the door. I asked, "Do you have a room?" She smiled, looking me up and down, and asked, "With or without a girl?" In surprise and embarrassment, I blurted, "Oh, without a girl!" She said, "I'm sorry, I have no vacancies." The woman, I later learned, was Zulu Swanson, perhaps the city's most famous madam.

Folks in the government employment office told me that gold mines in the Willow Creek district north of Palmer hired quite a few people. I bought a bus ticket, went up to the mining district, and was hired at the Lucky Shot Mine to work in the mill. A condition of employment was that I own a hard hat, a carbide lamp, and rubber boots—even though I wouldn't be working in the mine itself and thus wouldn't be using them. I walked to Kelly's store, about two miles down the road, to buy the items. The walk was an adventure in itself as I experienced the fresh breeze and the beauty of this alpine setting. With ravens calling, ground squirrels scurrying and chattering beside the road, some money in my pocket, and an interesting job, the world seemed wonderful.

The job was satisfying and paid more than I expected. The mill building contained two independent systems, one processing thirty tons of ore a day and the other eighteen tons. Within a few days the superintendent left me in full operating charge of the smaller mill. I was proud of having that responsibility and enjoyed the respect that most of the older men showed toward me.

During off-duty hours, many of the miners played poker. The three tables in the bunkhouse lounge were almost continuously in use, and the stakes were high. These were no-limit games, only stud and draw poker with no confusing variations. After watching for a few evenings, with fast-beating heart I joined a game. My experience in the penny-ante games on *Wanigan 12* at least taught me the rules. Playing cautiously for a few sessions, I won and lost little. One evening during a draw game, the pot got large as no one had openers after several deals. Then someone opened with a big bet. I held two small pairs. I stayed and drew one card, which gave me no help. One player then tried to buy the pot with another big bet. All folded except me. I decided it was my time to gamble: I saw the bet and raised. My opponent studied that for a minute or two and folded. The pot was several hundred dollars.

My immaturity then surfaced, unfortunately, for I showed my hand. While some people laughed, I knew I had violated the etiquette of good poker playing and badly irritated at least one person. But I wished the *Wanigan 12* gang could have seen me play that hand.

In late summer of 1941, a problem developed in the operation of my mill. A key component of the equipment is the ball mill, a rotating drum filled with iron balls that tumble about, breaking and grinding the ore. The balls wear down and new ones are periodically needed. The superintendent called me to his office and explained that my mill would be shut down because no more iron balls could be obtained. This notice was not a serious disappointment. The money I had already earned gave me freedom to go anywhere.

IN ANCHORAGE I BOUGHT a train ticket to Seward and a steamship ticket to Seattle, intending to go to Detroit and visit my parents and sisters. The train wouldn't be leaving Anchorage for a couple of days. In beautiful weather I wandered to the end of Fourth Avenue and stared for a long time across Cook Inlet toward the snow-covered mountains beyond. The scene fired up such a strong yearning to see more of Alaska that I couldn't leave. I cashed in my tickets and caught the next train for Fairbanks.

Again I found joy and excitement in moving beyond my known world. At Curry, about midway between Anchorage and Fairbanks, the Alaska Railroad operated a hotel where travelers were fed and housed overnight. At dinner I met a fellow passenger named Fred Hill who was on his way to Nenana to work on construction of a new airfield. He knew the superintendent and was sure I would be hired if I stopped there. He was right. At Nenana, Sam Kelly told me to see his timekeeper; I was to report for work in the morning. This time I'd be a grease monkey. My job was to grease and fuel the tractors. Before the day was over, I also signed up for occasional hourly work with the Alaska Railroad, using hand trucks or carts to load government riverboats when they were in town.

Fred and I both checked into the Southern Hotel, a two-story frame building on the main street. The owner and operator was a gracious elderly lady named Dolly Laferrie, credited in local lore with being a once-beautiful and successful prostitute and madam in Dawson during the heyday of gold mining. Thin walls that didn't reach the ceiling separated the rooms, a feature to enhance the circulation of warm air, but it also enhanced the transmission of sound. It was my misfortune to get a room adjacent to one occupied by a tractor driver and his girlfriend, a demure schoolteacher up from Talkeetna for a visit. Seeing her in the lobby, it was hard to believe she could be so uninhibited when making love. I soon found a small house to rent, which Fred was happy to share. We could do our own cooking and finally get some undisturbed rest.

Nenana captivated me. The railroad, riverboats, whistling little wind generators, fish wheels, sled dogs, Natives, old-timers, and village culture created an almost bewildering mix. The main street on the west end of town boasted one block of wooden sidewalks and several businesses. The Northern Commercial Company (popularly known as the N.C. store) was the main trading center. The post office, Sid Sheldon's bar, and Alex Fowler's drugstore shared the west side of the street. On the opposite side, Don Clark's tiny barbershop and Mr. Kaiser's power plant adjoined the small theater, with its benches for seats. This diesel-powered generator, which was fired up between 6 and 11 P.M., blew smoke rings in the air and all but drowned out the scratchy loudspeaker during the Saturday night movie.

On the east side of town the Coghill family operated a general store and seemed quite prosperous, for they had sent a son to Fairbanks for flying lessons. He caused much excitement one day by returning with an airplane and landing on a tiny airstrip near their store. (The son was Jack Coghill, later to become Alaska's lieutenant governor.)

When time allowed I frequented Sheldon's bar, rank with tobacco smoke and sour spittoons, where the old-timers drank, talked, dispensed wisdom and information, and played poker. Here I picked up more feel for the country and even began to dip snuff, which I had first tried in the CCC camp.

In Sid's bar just after dark one rainy evening, we heard an airplane over town. George Hupprich excitedly said, "We have to go light the pots." I jumped on the back of his flatbed truck with one of his sons and we went to the airstrip, where others were already lighting fires in cans containing kerosene-soaked rags.

Somehow the pilot managed to land his large trimotor Stinson on that patch of blackness guided only by these few small, flickering fires. He was alone, and we drove him to the Southern Hotel, where I learned he was Bill Lavery, of Lavery Airways. He said he had flown from Anchorage, following the railroad tracks as the sky's ceiling lowered. He wore the clothes of a businessman and carried a briefcase—not the appearance I had expected of a famous aviator.

One of the regulars at Sid's bar was a man named Al Wiggan, who had a glass eye, the result of a brawl. Al occasionally asked Sid for a glass of water for rinsing the glass eye clean. When he was sober, Al was discreet about taking the eye out and cleaning it. At other times, he would do it while sitting with the other patrons at the bar. I was presented with a bizarre scene one evening when I entered the place. In poor light, Al was crawling on his hands and knees and others were bent over, looking for something. Al had spilled the glass containing his eye, and it rolled away into some shadowy place. The eye was soon found. The finder claimed it was peeking at him from behind a cuspidor.

In late September, Sam Kelly told us that frost and snow would stop our work on the airfield in a few weeks. The riverboats had already taken their last cargo from Nenana for the year, so my job loading the boats was finished too. Fred Hill left for the Lower 48 states, but as a gesture of friendship he sold me an ancient Colt Frontiersman .44-40 revolver at a giveaway price. It was time to think about my next move.

CHAPTER SEVEN

An Idea Comes to Life

ON A QUIET SEPTEMBER EVENING I walked east through Nenana, past St. Marks Mission and the Native village of small cabins and tents, and climbed to the railroad bridge that spanned the Tanana River. The sun was low but still brilliantly illuminated the yellow leaves of birch, aspen, and willow trees along the river and on the hillside to the north. A strange stillness seemed to have settled over the country, softly broken by swirling water below, rhythmic squeaking of a fish wheel downstream, and distant howling of sled dogs. This gentle atmosphere carried an ominous message. Soon a long, frigid winter would grip the land.

It was decision time. I longed to visit my parents and sisters, but I also wanted to experience the sort of things I had read about in Robert Service's poems of the far north, copies of which I had bought for a quarter from a crippled street vendor in Detroit and still carried in my wallet. I could not leave. I wanted to spend the winter on a trapline. Having decided that, I remained sitting on the bridge until deep twilight descended, exulting in the promise of new adventure.

It was now urgent that I prepare for winter. The old-timers in town were generous with advice about areas for trapping. They mentioned two abandoned cabins and traplines in the Kantishna River country that sounded attractive. With a wonderful map of Alaska produced by the Knoll Publishing Company in Seattle that depicted dog-team mail trails and shelter cabins, I studied the lay of the land and tried to estimate distances to the places suggested to me. It became increasingly clear that I would first have to make a reconnaissance trip to decide the best place before the trapping season opened in mid-November. This notion was reinforced by the realization that I had never driven sled dogs, never worn snowshoes, and never camped in Alaska during the winter. But no matter; I had read and thought endlessly about these things and happily looked forward to dealing with them.

John Burchard was an especially valuable source of woodcraft and trail wisdom. Widely known as Whiskey Jack, Burchard was a Nenana resident and, he claimed, graduate of Brown University who came north during the gold rush and drifted to Kokrines on the Yukon. He married a Native woman, began a large family, and moved to

Nenana in the 1930s. I soon became aware that the strength of his helpfulness was related to his hope of pairing me with one of his daughters. He had four daughters of marriageable age, three were still single, and prospective husbands were scarce. I felt totally unprepared to get seriously involved with any of the daughters, even though the youngest, Alice, was surely a beautiful girl. But for whatever reason, I did spend a lot of time eating dried salmon strips and listening to John talk in his kitchen.

Much of the trail knowledge that John conveyed proved to be useful in the coming months. When taking snow for melting, dig down close to the ground where the snow will have changed to a granular form, almost like rock salt, and the volume of water and rate of melting will be much greater. The dead twigs next to the trunk of black or white spruce offer the best and maybe the only dry tinder and kindling for starting a fire along the trail. Carry a long-handled ax—not a hatchet, which is useless for any serious chopping. Get single-tree harnesses with leather collars that fit your dogs; the *siwash* or racing harnesses are no good for dogs that have to pull a heavy load. Wear a long cloth parka that reaches your knees to help you keep from freezing vital parts when it's cold and there is some air moving. Have a bottle of Everclear (pure grain alcohol) in camp, but don't touch it unless you need it. (I thought about asking how I would know if it were needed but decided the question would sound too naive.) John also showed me the Native method of tying a simple and practical snowshoe binding from a strip of moose hide, webbing, or canvas. Learning these and dozens of other bits of lore gave me confidence that I was ready to undertake a long winter of trapping in the very heart of the Alaska wilderness.

Most of the white men in Nenana had come to Alaska during the gold rush of 1898, and they were more interested in talking about prospecting than about trapping. Aging and the rigors of past work had taken a toll on them physically, though they still talked and probably dreamed about finding and working rich placer ground. More than one of these fellows recognized that I might be a strong worker and offered to take me to places where the bedrock was shallow and coarse gold was within easy reach. I would, of course, have to buy the outfit and pay the transportation. Others cautioned me to be wary of such proposals.

I cultivated the friendship of John Sagala, who trapped in the lower Kantishna country, and Slim Carlson, whose trapping grounds were near Lake Minchumina. My chats with Slim usually started in the lobby of the Southern Hotel and then moved to Sid Sheldon's bar, where talking was easier and time didn't matter. Slim was a veteran dog musher and, to my comfort and delight, clearly loved dogs. In response to my questions, mostly about dogs, he responded with stories that were carefully seeded with illustrative answers. What I heard was captivating and undoubtedly influential beyond what he could have known.

John Sagala had been a rural schoolteacher in Wisconsin, where he also developed the strong interest in trapping that eventually brought him to Nenana. In the summer of 1940, John bought a trapline and cabins on the lower Kantishna River from two trappers who had moved upriver to the Lake Minchumina country. John paid Carl Hult and Fabian Carey four hundred dollars. Some weeks before freezeup on the river, he hired Joe Justin and his big flat-bottomed boat to transport him, Ethel Kokrines (Whiskey Jack's oldest daughter), two large sled dogs, and their winter outfit to his trapline cabin.

74

Nearly every family in Nenana had sled dogs, and I was able to buy four animals. John Burchard sold me Patty, a cream-colored male husky. Charley Shade offered me Tony, a trained leader that had become too slow to lead the huge team that he used for hauling the mail. French John was eager to part with a dog that appeared to be half German shepherd and half malamute or husky. When I asked about his name, French John said, "Oh, he has two names, Mutt and SOB." I called him Mutt. My fourth dog was a rather small, black male with one blue eye that I bought from a Native. He came with the name Seagram. With my little team of four dogs, new collars and harnesses from the N.C. store, and a beautiful basket sled made by the fellow who sold Seagram to me, I was pleased and felt well prepared.

Buying the old .44-40 Colt Frontiersman revolver proved to be a mistake of lasting consequence. After buying a box of cartridges for the gun, I set up a shooting target. When I pulled the trigger, the gun recoiled sharply with a very loud blast that blew bits of hot powder back in my face. The intensity of the shot surprised me, but I thought it was just in the nature of such a powerful gun. The second shot proved otherwise. I said something like "wow," but I couldn't hear myself. I was either deaf or had lost my voice. It soon became apparent that I could no longer hear. Terribly distressed, I went home to bed. Sometime during the night, I awoke with a loud ringing in my ears. Despite this noise, it was a wonderful relief to discover that I could indeed hear myself speak again.

In the following days, the tinnitus—the ringing in my ears—diminished somewhat, but it has never left me. The ear damage robbed me of certain high frequencies of sound, and I could never again have the pleasure of hearing certain songbirds. The cartridges were evidently loaded with modern smokeless powder, much too powerful for an ancient firearm probably intended for black powder cartridges.

In late October we had ten inches of snowfall, but the Nenana River was still running slush ice and sleds couldn't travel on it yet. I spent several days learning how to manage the dogs on local trails. I felt excitement and also a good bit of uneasiness the first time I hitched them up to the sled. I knew how much depended on my dogs being able to pull a loaded sled through a wilderness I had not yet seen, but I had never before harnessed or driven dogs.

I tied the sled to a small tree, laid out the tow line, tug lines, and harnesses in the order that I had decided to place the dogs, and started to harness them one at a time. They barked eagerly, jumping over and around each other, creating a tangled mess. They sounded like a dog team, but they didn't look like one. Frustrated and overheated, I tried desperately to get the animals and lines untangled.

When I finally straightened it all out, we flew off down the road with the air whistling by my face. It thrilled me, and the dogs obviously felt whatever joy dogs feel. In the following days, I could judge the performance of each dog, and moved their position in the team accordingly. Tony, the old lead dog from Charley Shade's mail team, was the only one that would respond to the command of *gee* or *haw* (right or left), but his tug line was always slack when he was in the lead. I moved him back next to the sled opposite Mutt, with Patty and Seagram in front. We stayed with this arrangement.

Outfitting with gear and food at the N.C. store was by far the largest shopping spree of my life. I spent many hours choosing the variety of items that seemed essential while trying to balance need against weight. I knew that warm bedding was vital. A Woods Three Star eider down robe was recognized as the ultimate sleeping bag, but it was far too expensive and bulky for me. A compromise that worked out fine was a Hudson Bay blanket and a large flannel sheet that I sewed into sacks to be used as liners in my old kapok sleeping bag.

I bought a four-foot-long crosscut saw, an ax, a seven-by-seven-foot canvas wall tent, a small sheet-metal stove with pipe, a case of candles, steel traps and snares, corn-meal, flour, sugar, cocoa, bacon, tallow, dried fruit, dried salmon for dog food, and sundry other things including cloves, which I had learned would quell a toothache. When I finally looked at the size of my outfit in relation to my sled, I could see that my dogs and I faced a formidable challenge in moving it to some as yet unknown destination.

CHAPTER EIGHT

Into the Wilderness

ONE MORNING IN EARLY NOVEMBER, the ice in the Nenana River stopped moving and froze solid. I saw that a dog team had crossed, heading out the Diamond mail trail, which leads to the upper Kantishna country and to Lake Minchumina. I started out at dawn the next day with about half of my outfit on the sled, although I went very light on food. I intended to return to town in about two weeks for the rest of the supplies. After an initial happy burst of running, which carried us a few hundred yards, the dogs settled

79

down and I realized that our load was heavy, maybe too heavy.

Where the trail was level and straight, we moved at two or three miles an hour with me walking behind. But with a slight uphill grade or bend in the trail, I had to push to keep the sled moving. The dogs were panting heavily and I had to peel off my outer clothes to cool off, so we stopped frequently to rest. During the rest stops I felt especially sensitive to the continued ringing in my ears from the tinnitus, to my heartbeat, to the heavy breathing of the dogs, and to the colorless surroundings. Under the cloudy sky I saw only white, black, and shades of gray unless I was focusing on very close objects. Although we were not having an easy time of it, I was so stimulated by actually living what I had so often thought about since being a small boy that the long miles of unknown trail ahead seemed more inviting than intimidating.

That day we made it to the first shelter cabin, nine miles from Nenana. It was a fine little log cabin with a stove, and firewood already cut and split. The Alaska Road Commission contracted to have such cabins built and maintained along dog-team trails throughout the Territory. The daylight was going fast when we arrived. I quickly tied the dogs to small trees, cut spruce boughs for the bare bunk, and gave each dog a dried salmon and piece of tallow before making my own dinner. By candlelight I recounted the day in my small diary and was just dozing off when I heard a terrific commotion outside. My dogs alone could not possibly make such a racket.

With heart pounding, I got up and opened the cabin door. I was relieved to see a man with his dog team. He tied up his dogs and came in, and I recognized him as a Native I had met in Nenana. He was on his way home to

Bearpaw, a small village on the Kantishna River, and said he had left Nenana just before dark. Traveling with five dogs on a fast trail, he had covered in little more than an hour a distance that had taken me and my dogs eight hard hours.

In the morning the man and his dogs continued down the trail, moving at what seemed fantastic speed. My second day on the trail was a repeat of the first, ending at the eighteen-mile shelter cabin. I imagined that the other dog team was already forty or fifty miles ahead of me.

My goal the third day was to reach the thirty-three-mile shelter cabin, and the dogs and I were soon to learn what real work meant. A foot of new snow now covered the trail, and the dogs were unable to keep the sled moving. I had to put on my snowshoes and try to walk ahead of them, breaking trail. But the dogs kept crowding up behind me, stepping on the tails of the snowshoes and causing me to fall. The poor animals couldn't understand the problem despite my explanations. They tired as the day wore on; the hazard lessened, as did my tendency to fall. But we did have an accident.

My rifle, a beautiful lever-action Winchester .25-20, was on top of the load, under the lashings. I noticed that it had slipped down to the side and when I went back to rearrange it, I was appalled to see that the barrel had dropped down so that it caught the trail surface. Pulling it free, my heart sank as I saw that the barrel was badly bent and the tubular magazine was kinked. In disgust, I threw the rifle as far as I could into the woods. I had no real need for it because I had not intended to shoot anything on this trip, though it was comforting to have that little rifle along. Having no firearm at all gave me an uneasy feeling a little farther down the trail.

After resting a day at the thirty-three-mile cabin, we continued on toward Knights roadhouse on the Toklat River, mile forty-two on the trail. Whenever we crossed animal tracks, it was an occasion to rest the dogs and examine the tracks carefully. I saw lynx tracks that seemed large enough to have been made by mountain lions. The real shock was to see the size of wolf tracks; compared with the tracks of my dogs, they appeared to have been made by huge animals.

About a mile before reaching the roadhouse, I came to a large stream, Sushana River on my map, that more than got my attention. Spruce trees grew tall along the banks, and with the fading afternoon light the atmosphere was quiet, almost eerie. Then I noticed that the fresh snow in the streambed was packed down with large bear tracks, and there were scattered blotches of blood on the snow. The loss of my gun flashed into my mind. I could see only fifty yards or so upstream and about the same distance downstream, but no bears were visible. The dogs were absolutely quiet, with quick apprehensive glances back at me.

Then my attention was riveted by the sound of water splashing around the bend to my left. There was something familiar about it. Could it be salmon spawning in shallow water?

I tied the sled to a tree and nervously sneaked up the streambed to peek around the corner. No bears, but indeed the backs of salmon were visible in small puddles of open water. I saw that in addition to blood on the snow there were salmon heads left after the bears had eaten the preferred parts. It had not occurred to me that salmon would be alive and spawning in November, but this stream seemed to be fed by warm springs, and some fish apparently adapted their spawning time to it. I was relieved to get across and away from this stream and on to Knights roadhouse.

No one was at the roadhouse, but the door was unlocked and a note on the stove welcomed travelers. George Knight and his partner spent summers placer mining and operated the roadhouse in the winter. Sharply reduced travel over many of the traditional trails had already spelled the end of most roadhouses. There were fewer miners than in the past, and bush planes were transporting people and mail that formerly moved by dogsled. The presence of several grizzly bear hides on the floor and draped over chairs in the roadhouse indicated that the bears of Sushana River were not always left unmolested.

From the roadhouse it was necessary to cross the Toklat River before picking up the trail on the west side. The water must have been quite high when the river first froze, and then dropped several feet, for there was a precipitous break in the ice near the shore. I ran the dogs parallel to and within a few feet of the abrupt drop-off, looking for a safe place to get down to the lower ice. Unfortunately the dogs sensed that the trail was to the left, out on the river ice, and seemed ready to jump off into space. When I said, "gee," hoping to swing them to the right, away from the edge, they turned left and jumped off the ice ledge. Four dogs, the loaded sled, and I crashed down to the ice below. The sled landed on its bow in the midst of the dogs and I fell on top of the mess. I was afraid the dogs would be injured, but when I took inventory none were hurt, the sled was sound, and so was I.

Just west of the Toklat, we entered the most beautiful stand of white spruce I had yet seen. The trees were uniformly almost four feet in diameter near the base, closely spaced, tall, and straight. Only unusually good fortune could account for their escaping the wildfires that are common throughout Alaska's Interior. To not suffer a killing fire or damaging pestilence for two centuries or more allowed these trees to become an extraordinary forest, almost like the spruce-hemlock rain forests I knew in Southeastern Alaska. This stand had no doubt provided a perfect environment for uncountable generations of red squirrels and species of birds adapted to a closed-canopy forest, but at ground level there appeared to be little to support life. I wanted to spend more time examining this place, but we had to push on to a shelter cabin that was nineteen miles beyond Knights roadhouse. Heinie, an old-timer I met in Nenana, had given me directions from that shelter to another cabin, one that might be suitable as my base camp for trapping in the area.

The daylight hours were noticeably shrinking by several minutes each day and now amounted to less than six. Still, in that time the dogs and I were pretty well spent and happy enough to call it a good day on the trail when we reached that nineteen-mile shelter cabin. Next morning, leaving the dogs tied at the cabin, I left on snowshoes to find the cabin said to be in the Chitsia Creek valley on the north side of the Kantishna Hills. It would be about a twenty-four-mile round trip, according to my map and best guess. Again I felt uneasy without a gun, a feeling I did not experience when the dogs were with me. The long-unused trail I hoped to follow was supposed to leave the mail trail a couple of miles west of the cabin and head south toward the mountains. Sure enough, I not only found the trail but also discovered that a dog team had been up and down it. This was the first recent sign of other people that I had seen since leaving the cabin nine miles from Nenana, and it certainly raised my curiosity.

Soon a few caribou tracks appeared, then scores of tracks, then hundreds of tracks, but not a single live animal. I came across places where caribou had been butchered, so it seemed probable that Natives from Bearpaw had been there just the day before. I extricated a couple of frozen hearts that had been left behind with other viscera and stuck them up on sharpened sticks in the middle of the trail so I could pick them up on my way back—tasty morsels for me and the dogs.

The country became more open, with scattered black spruce merging into alpine tundra. About noon, approaching the entrance to the valley, I heard wolves howl for the first time since I left *Wanigan 12*. As I continued into the valley, which began to look more like a canyon, the animals moved from my right side to my left, but I couldn't see the wolves' tracks because of the maze of caribou tracks. I looked carefully for the cabin as I walked upstream and eventually found its sad remains. Snow had collapsed the roof some years earlier, and I could barely make out rusty utensils and a pile of moose hair that seemed to be part of a mattress. It took only moments to decide this was not a place to spend the winter. Then wolves began howling again, so close that I expected to see them on the sides of the canyon within a few hundred yards of where I stood. But they stayed out of sight.

About 2:30 P.M. I started my retreat back down the trail, with the light already fading. The wolves followed, periodically howling; they seemed ever closer as the light waned. Although I had read that wolves never harm humans, their howls sent chills to my neck and scalp. The last four hours of my tramp were in darkness that made it difficult to follow the trail. I was at peak alertness and, with a little help from my imagination, could almost sense the nearness of the wolves when they were quiet. I found the sticks that held the caribou hearts by blindly stumbling into them. When I was within a couple miles of the shelter cabin, I heard my dogs barking. What a welcome sound. The dogs received an especially good feed that night, and I enjoyed their company even more than usual.

WE HEADED FOR BEARPAW the next day and encountered the most vexing trail conditions I had yet experienced as we crossed large tussock-grass meadows. This grass grows in a compact mass some ten or twelve inches in diameter and fifteen or more inches high, with deep fissures between adjacent masses or heads. The dogs had great difficulty with these monsters, the sled high-centered, and I feared spraining an ankle.

At Bearpaw I stayed overnight with an old Finn named Gus Harju, who treated me to a marvelous dinner of home-made bread, boiled salmon, and potatoes from his garden. I learned that the Native who showed up at the cabin on my first night out of Nenana was the person who had killed and butchered the caribou two days earlier. Gus had helped the two Native families at Bearpaw, each headed by a widow, establish gardens and he was obviously proud of how well they all lived.

My intention now was to go down the Kantishna River to look at a cabin located on the east bank between the mouth of the Toklat River and the Tanana River. This cabin was well known to the old-timers in Nenana because one or two of them had accompanied a government official there by boat a few years earlier to investigate the death of a man named John Folger, who had ended his life there.

Their conclusion, as I recall, was that illness and pain probably led him to commit suicide.

Gus gave me valuable advice about traveling by dogsled on the frozen river, the treacherous character of the ice, how to spot the portages (shortcuts across loops or meanders of the river), and the locations of cabins owned by the few trappers who worked the region. In moving down the river, I kept the sled and dogs toward the middle, away from the cutbanks where the current ran swiftly and eroded the ice from below. There were some small areas of open water with steam rising from them; these were easily avoided. But avoiding risky places sometimes made me miss the portages and travel needless extra miles around a large loop or meander in the river's course.

The sled was becoming lighter as I and the dogs ate our way through the food, and our condition was improving every day, so we had relatively easy going on the hard-packed snow. While I still walked behind the sled most of the time, there were places where I could keep one foot on a runner and push with the other, in the manner of riding a scooter. One chronic problem was the formation of ice balls between Mutt's toes because of his rather splayed feet. After stopping scores of times to help him clear this ice, I finally cut pieces from the sled tarp and tied them over his feet for protection. He did some pretty fancy stepping while getting used to the booties, but they were a success.

We arrived at Fred Mucha's home cabin in deep twilight and received a most sincere greeting. I was touched by the realization that Fred, a lifelong bachelor, was truly thrilled to have a visitor. That evening he plied me with the story of his life, the mines he had worked, his summer job with the Alaska Road Commission at Fairbanks, and much advice about staying healthy by eating properly.

It struck me that if Fred had at least one dog for company he would have seemed less lonely, although he must surely have enjoyed the solitude to return to it annually for so many years. He hired a power launch to bring him and his outfit from Nenana to this cabin, so he felt no need for a dog team. Trapping was not particularly important to him; it was more a way of explaining why he spent winters in the bush than a means of making money. But gardening was important, and I was told in great detail how to start seeds germinating in the cabin and to plant them outside before leaving for the summer. He brought out new potatoes from town each fall, which he used for planting half of his potato garden while using those from his last crop in the other half. He was clearly fascinated by the different results he got from year to year, and I'm sure that harvesting the garden was the main attraction bringing him back each fall. I have rarely met a more enthusiastic and generous person. (I was delighted some decades later to notice on an aeronautical chart a little lake near Fred's home cabin named Mucha Lake.)

Sledding downriver, we reached John Sagala's cabin in a couple of hours. John and his companion, Ethel, were out on the trail so I left a note on the door and continued toward Toklat, where a few Native families lived. Our arrival there in good light set off pandemonium among many sled dogs and brought people out of tents and cabins to see what had appeared in their neighborhood. A man approached me, smiling, and introduced himself as Joe Justin. He invited me to stay in his cabin, showed me where to tie my dogs, and directed two of his sons to bring four frozen dog salmon from his cache. Even after the salmon sides were slashed with an ax, my dogs didn't know quite how to tackle these whole frozen fish, which were plump with eggs or milt, but they obviously enjoyed this rare feast.

Joe and his family treated me royally. Joe's wife, Margaret, had graduated from the government boarding school at Eklutna, near Anchorage, and was an excellent cook, seamstress, and housekeeper. All of their several older children could speak English and even read and write pretty well, as they delighted in demonstrating to me. During the evening, other residents of Toklat came to visit. I was of some interest to them. There was Frank Justin, Joe's brother, with his wife and two infants. Next came Amos James and his sister, a girl of about seventeen, but Amos's mother was too feeble to walk over. The James family lived in a large wall tent and did not speak English.

I learned there was a late run of dog (chum) salmon up the Kantishna during October. Joe would take the fish directly from his fish wheel in the river and hang them on high poles, where they froze before spoiling. It appeared he had an ample supply to keep all dogs and people well fed until spring. He also had parts of two moose hanging nearby, but commented that there were not many moose in the country. I had already concluded this, since I could count on my fingers the number of moose tracks I had crossed since leaving Nenana. It was a surprise and of serious concern to these folks that I didn't have a gun. Suppose you see a moose or a bear or some caribou, they asked. Of course their first concern is always food, while my immediate interest was moving quickly through the country. Until I settled someplace, a lot of meat would be more burdensome than useful. A gun would have been comforting on my trek along Chitsia Creek with the wolves, but otherwise it would just be extra weight.

The next person living downriver was a white trapper named Jim Steelman. Joe suggested that I might want to go past Steelman's place without stopping. "Steelman doesn't like people," he explained, and that was about all I could learn. But coming from such a friendly person as Joe, I took this admonition seriously and pondered what I should do. As it turned out, I had plenty of time to think about it because we missed some portages and were following big loops in the river when it began to get quite dark. I realized we would have to bivouac that night in the open.

The temperature was probably near zero as I got a fire started, tied up and fed the dogs, and cut a good amount of firewood and spruce boughs for my bed. After a meal of pilot bread, dried salmon, and hot cocoa, I prepared a pile of kindling for morning and crawled into the sleeping bag with most of my clothes on. The positive thing about cold weather is that it usually doesn't snow. I was thankful for that during the night, which went well. The bivouac was a great confidence builder.

Next morning I reached Jim Steelman's cabin and decided to risk a meeting. A tall, rangy man of about fifty greeted me in a soft-spoken way, saying, "Why don't you tie your dogs and come in for a cup of jamoch?" He asked a number of questions about what I was up to and didn't volunteer much about himself. With a little reticence, I asked how he got along with the Natives. He said, "Oh, some of them are all right, but if you're at all friendly with them, they become nuisances, always stopping to borrow things."

I could tell he had reservations about the Justin family when he related a story about Chief Justin, father of Frank and Joe. Steelman said that Chief Justin had been briefly jailed by the U.S. marshal for breaking a front window in the N.C. store in Tanana during a drinking bout. Not long afterward, a large government riverboat heading up the Yukon near Rampart struck boulders and sank. Chief Justin claimed credit, through his medicine, for the sinking as retaliation for his jailing—a claim that obviously rankled Steelman. It bothered me more when he warned me to be careful of Frank Justin, saying it was Frank who had pulled out a knife during a scuffle with Al Wiggan, putting out Al's eye.

Steelman came from Oregon and had been a cowboy. Though a recluse, he was capable of being friendly with certain people. He spoke kindly of Mrs. Callahan, a Native woman who had made his marten skin hat, mittens, and moose hide moccasins and put new webbing in his snowshoes. It appeared to me that he wanted to control his social contacts and not have them happen by chance. He bade me good-bye with word that the cabin I was interested in didn't amount to much, and I sensed he wasn't keen about having a new neighbor who was interesting in trapping.

Later that day I found the John Folger cabin and, perhaps because my expectations were so low, I brightened considerably at its possibilities. Although one of its two windows was gone and the chinking had fallen from between the logs in several places, the roof was good and it was reasonably clean inside with a table, a chair, a bunk, and even several books. I installed the Yukon stove and stovepipe that had occupied the sled for so long, fastened my wall tent over the missing window space, and enjoyed a first-class camp that night. Although I had little idea what kind of fur country I might be in, this was a good enough place. We had even crossed some moose tracks within a mile of the cabin. The next day I chinked the cracks, cut wood, and generally cleaned up the place.

My planned route back to Nenana was much shorter than the trip out. We would go down to the Tanana River, then up to Tolovana and intercept the mail trail to Nenana.

This trip would be only about seventy miles, compared with more than two hundred that we had already covered.

THE DOGS WERE RESTED, we had only a light sled, and snow conditions were good: for the first time we could really move well and cover a lot of distance in a hurry. But after leaving the cabin to head toward Nenana, I was unable to locate the portages, so we had to travel around the great meanders of the river. Early in the afternoon I sighted a blazed tree marking a portage. The light was fading as we left the river and entered the timber, and we were in near darkness as we approached the river again. I couldn't see the riverbank until it was too late. The dogs suddenly dropped from view and the sled nosed over and fell about twenty feet down a near-vertical bank.

The dogs were able to keep their feet and scoot ahead to avoid being hit by the sled, which nosed into a snowdrift and stopped. The tow line connecting the dogs to the sled parted. I tumbled over the sled and saw that the dogs were running on ahead. They ignored my calls and quickly disappeared into the night.

The crash was followed by a deathly quiet. Never before had the sensation of being alone gripped me so strongly as it did while standing there in the dark. Almost like being outside looking in, I wondered how I would work out of this fix.

I rigged a shoulder harness and began walking down the river pulling the sled, hoping intensely I would come upon my dogs. For about two hours nothing appeared, and then I saw a dim orange light ahead. I realized it must be the cabin of Clarence Boatman, an elderly man who lived near the mouth of the Kantishna. The cabin was back from the river just far enough to be out of sight, but a kerosene lantern set on the bank guided me in.

My dogs were there. What a wonderful feeling of relief to see them again. As I went toward them, greeting them by name, a tall, gray-haired, round-faced man came out of the cabin carrying a Coleman lantern. Clarence Boatman said the dogs showed up more than an hour earlier, and he first thought they belonged to Natives from upriver until he saw their leather collars and the style of their harnesses. He was concerned that someone might be in trouble and set out the kerosene lantern as a beacon.

Joe Justin had told me that Clarence Boatman was a friendly and generous man who talked a lot; it was a good description. Clarence insisted my dogs needed a hot meal and set about cooking rice and cornmeal mixed with dried salmon. Before, during, and long after our own dinner, he plied me with stories, mostly dealing with his many Native friends. Clarence said he didn't bother to trap because he had a pension from his service in the Spanish-American War. He seemed very proud of having married (common-law relationship) a young Native woman when he was in his seventies. The idea came suddenly in Nenana when she teasingly raised her dress and flashed a view of her nicely formed body from the waist down. This presentation stirred sufficient vigor in Clarence to persuade the woman to accompany him home to the Kantishna. He was stoical about her leaving him after a few months because she was homesick.

In the morning I was treated to sourdough hotcakes, lowbush cranberry syrup, and bacon before hitching the dogs and heading up the Tanana River. How good I felt now, especially when reflecting on my sad state just sixteen hours earlier.

CHAPTER NINE

Bush Winter

EARLY ON NOVEMBER 13, 1941, we hit the Tanana mail trail again, well rested but with a very heavy sled. Although the trail was good and we reached Minto before dark, it was a tough day for I had to help the dogs by pushing the sled almost continuously. Johnny Campbell seemed pleased that I stopped. Except for Charley Shade on his mail runs, he rarely had guests at the roadhouse.

Johnny was getting along in years and seemed content to be the only resident trader in the area. The Native community depended on him, and he was generous in extending credit. In return, he got most of the fur produced by the village trappers. But it really upset him that Johnny Sweggler, known to most residents as Muskrat Johnny, and sometimes other fur buyers would arrive by bush plane to buy furs from people who owed him money. At that time he carried thirty thousand dollars in bad debts, a fortune in those days. It was late before Johnny Campbell let me retire to the luxury of a feather bed with a snowshoe-hare fur robe over it.

We arrived home at our Kantishna cabin without incident. In a couple of days, the place was shipshape. I began going afield on snowshoes to scout the area, carrying my rifle and a pack containing traps, snares, and an ax. It quickly became evident that trapline trails close to the cabin were being used by my reclusive neighbor, Jim Steelman, who had evidently extended his trapping effort in this direction after Folger's death. There was still plenty of open country for me, but without established trails, travel would be slower and more strenuous.

I focused with fascination on animal tracks in the snow, for they portrayed much about the animals that shared this wilderness with me. Fox, mink, marten, land otter, and lynx, all valuable furbearers, left their distinctive marks, but except for fox, none seemed plentiful. Even snowshoe hares were scarce. Each day I broke more trail, traveling on snowshoes without the dogs, to find promising places to set traps and hang snares. My first success was grand indeed. Near an unfrozen slough, two otters had left tracks. I set traps in shallow water beneath where the animals had been sliding down the bank, and the next day one very lively otter was in a trap. Its pelt would bring twenty dollars or more at the N.C. store.

I discovered that otters are not easy animals to skin. Getting that job done and the pelt on a stretching board took all of the daylight hours of one day plus time enough to burn several of my precious candles. I began to catch something almost every trip, usually a mink or two, and then was thrilled to find a huge frozen lynx in one of my snares. This skin was worth more than I had earned in a week working for the Alaska Railroad. Soon I had to devote a day to making more fur-stretching boards with wood salvaged from the collapsed cache behind the cabin.

With daylight hours so few — less than four in late December — cooking and any work in the cabin had to be done by candlelight. To conserve my supply of candles I never burned more than one at a time. I had a portable radio powered by a dry-cell battery, and for a few days I was able to pick up KFAR in Fairbanks, usually to hear Al Bramstedt read the morning news and play "You Are My Sunshine." But the new battery quickly gave up the ghost, having probably lost the best part of its life in shipment or on the store shelf. For a few more days I was able to coax five or ten minutes of sound by heating the battery on the stove, and then I heard nothing more.

After breaking many miles of trail on snowshoes and with no new snow for some time, I began running the dogs on the trapline, which allowed me to cover much more distance and extend the trapline during the short days. Fox were a puzzle to me. In some places they would visit my most carefully prepared sets and defecate on the concealed traps; at other places, they would get caught in an exposed trap that was set in a cubby pen, a small bait-and-trap shelter for lynx. I could only conclude that there were some smart old animals and some young, hungry, unsuspecting ones. I stopped making much effort to catch fox because the last one I caught had rubbed flanks and was not worth much. But my interest in wolves heightened, perhaps because I had never seen one and because John Sagala had told me that white trappers never catch a wolf in their first year or two of trying. Catching a wolf lent prestige to a trapper; it also netted a thirty-dollar bounty from the Territory and an equal amount for the pelt if it was prime. But since I had seen no wolf tracks in the area, my prospects were nil.

One evening wolves howled for ten or fifteen minutes, a sound so captivating that I stayed outside the cabin to listen until I was chilled. It was impossible to judge how far away they were, one mile or five, but certainly they were much beyond the distance of those that had kept me company during the Kantishna Hills trek. There, caribou had offered abundant prey for the wolves; here, there were no caribou, and so few moose that attacks by wolves would surely guarantee their future scarcity. The following day I found where the wolves had met my trail and run close to it for more than a hundred yards. I backtracked the animals and found a place where a couple of them had passed between two birch trees. There I carefully hung one of my large snares.

I wasn't able to get back to this area for about four days. When I did, excitement surged as I saw that the wolves had again crossed my trail in about the same place. Leaving the sled and dogs on the trail, but taking my rifle, I walked back toward the snare in nervous anticipation. Sure enough, there was something large and dark where the snare had been hung, but no movement. I found an enormous black wolf curled around one of the birch trees and frozen solid. He had been caught around the neck and seemed to have died quickly for there was nothing chewed up and no other signs of a struggle.

I went back to bring in the dogs and sled and was surprised that the dogs refused to move toward the wolf. Their fear must have welled up from instinct, because they surely had never been threatened by wolves. I managed to drag and coax the dogs to the wolf. By laying the sled on its side, I was able to roll the carcass in and then right the sled. I would have to thaw the frozen animal before I could skin it. I dragged it into the cabin and got it partially suspended from the ridgepole. The wolf wasn't the prettiest housemate, and after two days it had barely begun to thaw.

Frank Justin arrived that night. He was on his way to Tolovana for flour, but had shot a moose that walked across the river in front of him a few miles upstream from my place. Frank showed real interest, even excitement, about my wolf and he believed it had thawed enough to skin. I knew I would be a lot more comfortable in the cabin if the wolf were out. That became a necessity moments later. Frank hefted the carcass, as though to judge its weight, and we heard the soft sound of air escaping under pressure. Suddenly the cabin filled with a foul, noxious gas that forced us outside. Once we got to fresh air, the incident seemed hysterically funny. After skinning the wolf, we found that its stomach was full of moose meat, generating the gas that released when Frank squeezed its rib cage.

Frank gave me a hind leg from his moose, and I agreed to help him haul the rest of it back to Toklat. I had been thinking about going there anyway to buy dog salmon from Joe Justin. At Toklat, Joe again invited me to stay with him.

Following dinner, a Victrola and some scratchy records materialized to the delight of the kids, who began dancing. Their mother had taught them dances she learned at the Eklutna boarding school. During this lively evening, there was a knock at the door and then, with a draft of frigid air, the James girl came in.

My surprise gradually turned to embarrassment when I saw she was wearing high-heeled shoes. In truth, she may have changed from moccasins just outside the door, but I assumed she had walked more than a hundred yards through a foot of snow in those shoes for my benefit. She spoke no English; she had never been even to Nenana, much less away to school. The girl danced with the Justin children, and the high-heeled shoes kept rolling on their sides. But everyone was happy, and it was one of my most innocent and enjoyable nights out.

THE NEXT MORNING was extremely cold. Joe said it was forty-five degrees below zero and suggested I not start home. But I knew the cold spell could last for days and perhaps get even worse, so I decided to leave. The snow was not slippery at such low temperatures, and with the load of frozen salmon on the sled, we didn't move easily. The dogs soon frosted up more than I had ever seen. The work of crossing portages warmed me, but a chill would set in while we traveled on the river, where I didn't have to work as hard and there was more exposure. The last several miles before home were on the river ice. There was little wind, but heat loss was so much faster in the open than in the woods of the portages that I had trouble keeping my face and hands warm.

I began to ponder whether to stop and build a fire or take a chance on reaching my cabin before getting into really serious trouble with the extreme cold. The way my hands felt, I dreaded even trying to start a fire, so I pushed on. When I arrived home, my hands seemed useless, the fingers like sticks. I was disgusted with myself for letting the situation deteriorate to the verge of disaster.

Thankfully I had been almost religious about leaving plenty of shavings and kindling by the stove for starting the next fire. My hands were immobilized, useful only as large tongs, but I managed to put the makings of a fire in the stove. Matches were something else. By spilling the box on the table, I could move a match to the edge with the striking head pointing inward and attempt to grasp the match with the edges of my hands. With no sense of touch, I had only visual control and failed repeatedly until most of the matches were on the floor and beyond hope of picking up. Whenever I was successful in holding a match and trying to strike it on the stove top, it dropped out of my grip.

I felt a low-grade panic building. I sat down, composed myself, and vowed to make every move very deliberately. On my next try I lit a match and, though the flame was against my skin, I awkwardly got it into the shavings, which ignited. The joy of seeing the fire start was quickly replaced by worry of irreversible damage to my hands and fingers. As they warmed and feeling gradually returned, the pain was excruciating, but so welcome. There were no adverse effects, so the tissue apparently had not actually frozen.

Years later I read Jack London's short story "To Build a Fire," both the 1902 version in which the protagonist survived and the 1908 version with a different outcome. The similarity between London's fictional narrative and my own experience was unnerving. Although I could never plagiarize Jack London's dramatic, eloquent prose, it occurred to me that if I ever wrote of my own struggle to light a fire, it would be suspect in the minds of some readers.

I was anxious to get back to trapping. A pack of wolves had found the location of Frank Justin's moose kill. The sign was so fresh that I decided they may have departed only when they sensed my approach. I returned to the cabin for two No. 4 Newhouse traps. Before leaving camp, I cut two toggles (small, short logs) and fastened a trap to each of them with wire, an extra dog chain, and staples. With a trap attached only to a toggle instead of to a fixed object such as a tree, a trapped wolf could still travel slowly but would not be able to pull against a fixed attachment and likely escape the trap, minus a toe or two. The wolves had not eaten much of the moose hide, so I used it to cover the toggles and concealed the traps next to it.

I checked these traps regularly. After two weeks, the wolves had not returned. A new snowfall caused me to think the traps wouldn't function even if an animal stepped on them, so I decided to pick them up. I didn't cross any wolf tracks as I approached the trap site, and I was startled to see it had been disturbed. I could see one sprung trap, but I couldn't find the second trap and toggle.

It was clear the wolves had approached from the opposite side and left the same way, one dragging my trap and toggle. The trapped animal left an easy trail to follow because wherever the toggle hung up in the willows, signs of a struggle were visible. My heart pounded as I advanced slowly through the brush with rifle ready. One worry was that the toggle would come loose from the trap chain, allowing the animal to escape with the trap. In that event, I would despair of tracking him down. Worse than losing the trap, I would be haunted by the image of the animal's extended pain before dying; much better if the wolf simply pulled free of the trap and escaped.

I studied a place where the toggle had hung up and the wolf had bitten through willows the size of my wrist. Then, not fifteen yards to my left, I saw the cowering animal, with a face that instantly reminded me of a big sled dog. A question flashed through my mind. Could it be a dog? But just as quickly, I dismissed that notion. The animal's eyes projected futility, not ferocity, and I ended its life quickly. There was relief in knowing its suffering was over but a feeling that this wild country had lost something important. What a magnificent animal it was. Only later in talking with experienced trappers did I learn that trapped wolves are so stricken with fear of humans as to be literally paralyzed.

The mixed sentiments I felt about the death of this wolf had bothered me before. It was puzzling that I could be motivated to kill something and then suffer a sense of remorse. Looking into the eyes of an animal whose life I was about to extinguish was somehow unsettling, though these feelings passed once the animal was dead. When a pelt was drying on a stretching board, I even felt pride in having produced something of real value.

I remembered a small lynx that had been caught in one of my traps. The lynx reminded me of a large domestic kitten as it pulled the trap under its chest as though trying to hide it. Its pelt wouldn't be worth much, and I wanted to release the trapped animal. I tried to hold the lynx down with a large spruce bough and a snowshoe while I opened the jaws of the trap. But the lynx fought me, and I couldn't free it. The death of this lynx, as with the wolf, kindled emotions I could not yet understand.

A FEW DAYS BEFORE Christmas, I received some guests: Roosevelt John, his wife, and three young relatives, driving a very large team, and Frank Justin and his family, with just a few dogs. I boiled moose meat and fried pancakes until everyone was full. They kidded me about needing a longhaired cook. My cabin was literally wall to wall with people that night. The floor was cold and their bedding consisted of only blankets and a few caribou hides, so I kept a fire going all night.

They had left Birch Creek, near Lake Minchumina, several days earlier and were on their way to Minto for Christmas and a potlatch. The Justin family joined the group at Toklat. Roosevelt John was an elderly man, blind in one eye—poked out by a broken tree limb while driving dogs many years before. He received some kind of government pension and was considered to be wealthy. His wife was young, in her late teens or early twenties, and I think the marriage was Roosevelt John's way of assuming responsibility for her and her family more than anything else. But I did marvel that a man over eighty, give or take a few years, could stand the rigors of such a long trail.

During the clear, cold days of late December and early January, I sometimes had the most perfect view of the Alaska Range and snow-covered, pink-tinted Mount McKinley to the south. What pure joy it was to experience the quiet beauty of that wilderness.

I was satisfied with the amount of fur I had been taking, particularly the number of mink. I had stopped setting traps for fox because the pelts appeared to be poor quality. I left several snares for lynx in promising locations because the larger lynx skins brought a good price. I always kept some snares out for snowshoe hares, too, because I enjoyed eating them fried the way my mother had fixed cottontail rabbits. What I didn't eat, the dogs happily accepted.

A weasel took up residence under the cabin, and the mouse problems ceased. The little animal would come up through a hole in the floor and nose around even as I sat reading at the table. Because I feared it would leave after killing all the mice, I put pieces of moose meat on the floor for it. Unfortunately it had bigger things in mind. One night it got on the table and tackled a piece of moose meat I had brought in to thaw and, not satisfied with just eating, tried to drag the whole thing away. I shouted at the weasel and things quieted down for a while, but then it continued with its scratchy, noisy, sleep-robbing project. After what seemed half the night, my affection for the little villain turned to wrath. The smartest move would have been to simply throw the piece of meat outside, but in my frustration I did the dumbest thing possible. I got up and set a steel trap by the moose meat.

I had barely fallen asleep again when the trap sprang shut, followed by the thrashing of the trapped animal. As I sat up, the potent musk stench sprayed by the weasel seemed worse than the gas that had escaped the bloated wolf. I crawled out of the sleeping bag, lit a candle, and put an end to the struggling of the weasel with a chunk of firewood. Then I rushed outside for air. I threw out all exposed food and scrubbed the table, utensils, pots, and floor, but the odor was still noticeable after several days.

When the Roosevelt John party returned in mid-January, they brought with them a teenage girl, a "longhaired cook," to leave with me. It was a delicate matter convincing them I couldn't allow the girl to stay. I'm sure they felt it would be to my advantage, and delight, to have a female companion. But I also knew that a major motive for the plan was to get some family out from under the burden of caring for a grown girl. She was thin and had a plain but attractive face with perfect teeth and a soft, easy smile. Yes, she caused a stir of hormones within me, but that couldn't override the practical limitations of my situation. I felt badly that these folks had created this dilemma based on a couple of joking remarks. However, they must have known there was some uncertainty about it all, because they happily took the girl with them, and all were in good spirits when they left. I never heard more about her.

Roosevelt John also brought alarming and somewhat confusing news about Japanese planes bombing Pearl Harbor in the Hawaiian Islands. I needed to learn more. The batteries in my little radio had long since died, so I quickly sought out Harry Martin, the trader at Tolovana who made such a point of keeping up on the news. From Harry I learned that, indeed, the Japanese had attacked the United States at Pearl Harbor — on December 7, 1941, more than a month earlier.

I started back toward my cabin in a snowstorm, in a confused, unsettled state of mind. With visibility near zero, the dogs held a perfect course down the Tanana River and up the Kantishna. Back home I was hit full force with a cold virus that had arrived at the cabin with the Roosevelt John party. About all I could manage for a week was to feed the dogs, bring in wood, and do a little cooking. As soon as my appetite and energy returned to normal, I went upriver to John Sagala's cabin to discuss the war situation with him.

I found John upset and worried. He had found a note where his trapline crossed the Diamond mail trail, left by trapper Slim Carlson at the request of the Nenana postmistress. It contained a military draft notice for John, with a reporting date that had already passed.

John and Ethel were busily packing to leave, and John asked if I would bring in a tent camp that was at the far end of his trapping area. He said I was welcome to stay at his cabin and trap beaver in the area. This sounded wonderful to me, for I had found only a few beaver houses in my area. John drew out a map locating all the lakes and beaver houses in relation to his trails.

I returned home to collect my furs and the few items I wanted to take, leaving the crosscut saw, utensils, and the traps and snares, except for the two No. 4 Newhouse wolf traps. I also took the small tent I planned to give to Joe Justin in gratitude for his hospitality. As I cleaned out the accumulation of spruce boughs and needles from the bunk, I thought about John Folger, who had ended his life there. I was sad to leave the little cabin, but proud of its spick-and-span condition, clean pans, and even a few long candles handy for the next visitor.

IN CONTRAST TO THE MOSTLY FLAT country in the lower Kantishna where I had been living, John Sagala's trapline traversed a rolling landscape with many small lakes. Marten tracks were everywhere, which surprised me because I had not seen a single one on the lower river. The season was closed for marten that year, or I'm sure that John would have had a fine harvest. Small groups of caribou were scattered throughout the area; I had no inclination to shoot one because John had left more moose meat than I could use. Despite a general scarcity of moose, everyone on the river seemed to have plenty of moose meat, though they weren't fussy about the sex of the animals (the law permitted the taking of bulls only).

The annual limit on beaver was ten per person, and I had easy access to more than twice that number of beaver houses, so I was soon spending much more time skinning, fleshing, and stretching beaver than in running the traps. But there were hazards along the way that almost ended everything for me.

Aspen is a favored food of beaver and a good bait for use in trapping them. I noticed a nice stand of small aspen just across a bend in the river from John's cabin, so I took the ax and walked over to the trees to cut a supply of bait sticks. I didn't wear snowshoes because the snow was hard-packed on the river ice. With a bundle of sticks under my left arm and the ax in my right hand, I started back across the ice. Suddenly I was up to my armpits in water, in current so swift that it pulled my body horizontally under the ice. By great luck, the bait sticks spanned the break and held me from sliding under and drowning, though it took strenuous and careful struggling to work my way out. A snowdrift had so insulated the ice that the water beneath had melted it away.

I also ran into trouble during one of the times I stayed at a little shelter cabin along John's trapline, a hut he called Sugar Bowl. Carl Hult and Fabian Carey had built it by excavating a square hole about a foot deep and seven feet square, and erecting over it an A-frame pole structure covered with sod. There was barely room inside for a small stove and a pole bunk across one end; the tiny door, with the hut's only window, measured about two feet by four feet.

By that time the days were growing longer and warmer, but the temperature still occasionally dropped well below zero. It was during one of these cold spells that I left Sugar Bowl on snowshoes to check beaver traps on a lake about a mile away. A few inches of ice had formed in the two holes I cut on the lake in order to set traps in front of a beaver house. As my ice chisel punctured the ice, water streamed up, flooding underfoot. My moccasins soaked up the water like sponges. By the time I removed a dead beaver from the trap and checked the second hole, my feet were turning numb, and I was getting worried. As I hiked back to Sugar Bowl, the moccasins froze solid.

Back at the hut, it was a long and laborious process to loosen the laces and get the moccasins off. My stockings were frozen to my skin. After working the stockings off, I crawled into my sleeping bag for a night's rest, hoping I had not permanently injured my feet. By morning, feeling had returned to my feet, with a vengeance; when I tried to stand up, it felt like stepping on red-hot coals and I fell back on the bunk. But after a while I started moving around, and there was no further problem. I had been lucky, but once again I felt disgusted with myself for getting too close to trouble.

Sugar Bowl was also memorable for another incident. One afternoon I pulled a piece of dried salmon from under the bunk where John had left a supply. Putting a chunk in my mouth, I quickly tasted something very different than I expected. Holding the fish to the light of the open door, I saw that the cuts across the flesh that are made to facilitate drying were packed with mouse feces. That ended my snacking; I left the whole lot for the rodent family.

FOR SOME TIME MY EVENINGS had been less than enjoyable because of toothaches. Breathing the warm air in the main cabin after a day on the trail, I would occasionally get a toothache that would soon subside. But they were becoming more frequent and severe, not responding to the cloves that I packed against the teeth. One night the toothache continued in a throbbing, unrelenting way. I considered harnessing the dogs and going to Nenana, but that would have taken three days, and the nearest dentist was still sixty-five miles beyond that, in Fairbanks. The night continued without relief and my desperation was building.

I got up, lit a candle, and started a fire in the stove, even though, as I expected, the warmth aggravated the toothache even more. With my small hand-mirror I examined the source of the trouble, two upper teeth on the right side. Both had cavities that had been filled, but the decay had apparently reached the pulp chamber or was very close to it. I resolved to try pulling the teeth out.

A rusty pair of pliers lay on a shelf just outside the cabin door, and I put them on the stove to warm. Then I tentatively positioned the pliers on one of the bad teeth with the aid of the mirror. The poor light of the single candle made it hard to see how to manipulate the pliers, so I lit a second candle and then a third. Time after time I got a light grip on the tooth, only to release it as the nerve warned me of worse things to come. The half-pint bottle of Everclear that I had brought to the cabin on the advice of John Burchard was still unopened. Don't touch it unless you need it, he had told me.

After a good slug of Everclear mixed with water and sugar, I tried again with the mirror and pliers. My hands were shaking so much that I couldn't get the pliers and tooth properly together. The Everclear may have bucked up my courage. Dispensing with the mirror, I positioned the pliers on the tooth solely by touch, took a light grip to avoid crushing the tooth, cringed, and pulled it out. Then I looked at the tooth and saw that it had no cavity. I had pulled the wrong tooth. At this point, there was no stopping. I pulled the next tooth that appeared to be an offender. Then I thought that the tooth next to that one might be the real problem, so it came out too. The toothache was gone.

THE SADDEST EVENT of the winter was yet to come. Several miles downriver from the cabin and about a mile west, I had set beaver traps near a house on a slough. As I had done before, I turned the sled on its side and left the dogs on the river while I snowshoed back to check the set. The wind was blowing a little, and while I worked with the traps I thought I heard sounds off in the distance. I listened carefully, thinking it might be wolves, but it didn't sound right. Walking back toward the river, I had an apprehensive feeling that something might be wrong with the dogs.

When I reached the riverbank I was horrified to see the dogs scattered, with blood spread over a large area. There had been a terrible fight, with three of the dogs apparently focusing their attack on one. Mutt had been viciously mauled, his ears chewed off, then let alone only when he was considered dead. But he was still alive. I righted the sled, put Mutt in it, untangled the harnesses, and tried to arrange the other dogs to pull the sled. They were strangely shy and seemed wilted, refusing to move. When I walked up and grabbed the tow line to start things moving, Mutt let out a moan.

Instantly the three dogs jumped on the sled and began another attack. I beat them off with a snowshoe. The idea of shooting the dogs then and there went through my mind, though I quickly realized it would leave me in an even worse fix. We managed to get to the cabin, and I carried Mutt inside. He lapped some water. As I tended the stove, he made a sound and died.

What caused the dog fight can't be known, but I suppose the potential was always there and closer to the surface than I realized. My guess is that some of the dogs decided to move and that Mutt got tangled in the tow line or harness; his barking and struggling might somehow have triggered the attack. The dogs were strangers to one another when I first brought them together; they were all males and probably competitive in certain respects. Ganging up on the underdog may be an instinctive behavior in dogs, but its unfairness surely provokes a deep sense of sadness in us.

I was devastated. Mutt had been the only dog that seemed to need my company and affection, and he had worked his heart out for me. I found the Everclear again, but it didn't help at all. I brought in all of the traps, secured John's cabin, packed the sled, and headed to town. It was the end of the season for me.

At the Diamond mail trail, we met an appalling sight. A train of Caterpillar tractors had passed, knocking down trees and destroying the lovely dog-team trail. I learned at Knights roadhouse that the tractors were going to Lake Minchumina to start construction of an airfield.

Jack Ferguson, manager of the N.C. store at Nenana, had been kind to me so I was happy to sell my furs there rather than send them to the Seattle Fur Exchange, as John Sagala had recommended. While I was in the store, the U.S. marshal, John Dwyer, approached me sternly and said I had better accompany him to his office. Puzzled, I went. He sat me down, got out some papers, and began asking questions. When he asked my age, I told him I was nineteen. He jumped up and shouted, "That's a lie, you're a draft dodger!" I was stunned and speechless. Fortunately I carried a copy of my birth certificate, which proved I was nineteen and not yet eligible for the draft.

He did an instant about-face, apologizing and insisting that I have lunch with him and his family at his house. I had not yet bathed, and I still wore my woolens. Mrs. Dwyer and the Dwyers' son and daughter were in the kitchen when we arrived, and it was hot. I could feel myself melting, and knew I wasn't radiating lilac perfume. The daughter, Catherine, was about my age, blond, and absolutely beautiful. All in all it was an embarrassing situation that I was greatly relieved to see end.

I still had three dogs to deal with. Patty and Seagram returned to their former owners, but Charley Shade didn't want Tony. Whiskey Jack seemed pleased to have him and that's where he stayed. Then I left by train for Fairbanks.

CHAPTER TEN

Fairbanks

THE MORE I LOOKED AROUND Fairbanks, the more I liked it. It radiated an aura of being at the end of the line, in the heart of a wilderness and in the center of gold country. Its vitality seemed enhanced by the presence of some modern concrete structures (the post office, the First National Bank, the Lathrop Building) and the dominance of wood frame houses over log cabins that spread out from the business center on First and Second Avenues. There were a large number of saloons, some having a round card table in the rear occupied most of the day by old-timers silently playing a card game called pan (panguingue).

A bar on Second Avenue, called the Fairbanks Cigar Store, featured a ragtime pianist. Several other bars had nickelodeons (jukeboxes) to liven the atmosphere. The red light district operated openly on Fourth Avenue, west of Cushman Street. Silver dollars were in common use, and it was rare to see paper currency in a denomination smaller than ten dollars. Although I discounted the notion, some folks thought the use of silver was a ploy by the banks and business community to discourage people from mailing money out for catalog purchases. The residents of Fairbanks were friendly, and most of them seemed proud to live there. Natives, mostly visitors from outlying villages, and whites mixed easily. There was genuine shared pleasure when I met Natives whom I had known in Nenana.

I needed to get a dental bridge because my missing teeth made me self-conscious and uncomfortable. At first, the dentist didn't want to believe I had pulled those three teeth myself. With the new bridge in place, I felt better about my appearance.

Weeks Field, the center of northern aviation, was only three blocks from the small house I was renting on Eighth Street. Frank Pollack, owner of an air service, hired me to work with his mechanic, Jim Hutchinson. The low pay and trivial duties—wiping oil and mud from the outside of airplanes and cleaning their cabins—were offset by the fascination of being near airplanes and pilots.

One day shortly after I began working at the air service, pilot Norm Weaver asked if I wanted to ride along as he test-hopped a Fairchild 24 I had just finished polishing. Inwardly a little frightened, but ecstatic over my good fortune, I climbed into the right-front seat. It was an exhilarating ride of fifteen or twenty minutes, and seemed to me a remarkable exploit. (A couple of years later, Norm Weaver was lost on a flight between Nome and Kotzebue. No trace of the airplane was found, and it's assumed he crashed into Kotzebue Sound.)

Although I failed then to appreciate their future place in history, many of the pilots I saw daily were true aviation pioneers. Noel Wien or Sig Wien sometimes stopped by to chat with Frank Pollack or Hutch. Jim Dodson's hangar was next door, and Harold Gillam's hangar was across the field. I became close friends with a fellow my age, Glenn Hudson, who worked for Gillam and often rode with him on mail flights from Fairbanks to outlying villages. It seemed a novel coincidence that I should meet the people who flew the mail plane over my trapline.

Then I got an opportunity to drive a freight truck for the Alaska Road Commission, a job that would triple my earnings. Although my interest in airplanes remained high, Hutch said it would take years for me to get a license as an airplane and engine mechanic. The possibility of ever actually becoming a pilot was almost beyond fantasy. I decided to change jobs.

Work had begun on the Alaska Highway in Canada, and surveyors were in Fairbanks to begin laying out a connecting route eastward from a point on the Richardson Highway that would later be called Delta Junction. The vanguard of this survey party was a group of cowboys from ranch country somewhere down south; their initial task was to catch some free-ranging horses that roamed between

Big Delta and Donnelly Dome. The men who owned the horses had leased them to the government — as is, where is — for use as pack animals. My first duty was to drive these cowboys and their gear from Fairbanks to the roundup site in a flatbed truck.

With the sideboards up on my truck, and loaded with saddles, tents, stoves, rope, food, and cowboys, we headed down the Richardson Highway and eventually took the ferry over the Tanana River at Big Delta. We unloaded most of the gear and people at Rica's Roadhouse on the south riverbank and drove on with a few men to look for horses. After sighting some of the horses in the distance, we returned to the roadhouse. The cowboys discussed tactics for catching the animals, but this didn't divert the conversation long from their favorite topic: rodeo riding.

By the time I arrived again from Fairbanks, transporting the survey crew, the cowboys had caught a couple of the horses. It sounded like a tough job. The horses had been left on their own for a couple of years and were wild, probably from sharing their range with bison, grizzly bears, and wolves. The next time I returned from Fairbanks, I found that all the horses had been rounded up and organized into a pack train that was heading east into the bush.

By late May the snows had melted from the higher mountain passes and it was time to move crews to the road maintenance stations. I carried crews to camps along the Richardson and Steese Highways and the Livengood Road (Elliot Highway) and drove resupply runs to the camps. These trips exposed me to some of the most beautiful country in the world. They raised curious questions as well, such as the puzzle of how clam shell fossils came to be on top of Eagle Summit on the Steese Highway. The explanation came years later when I learned about continental drift and plate tectonics.

My job with the road commission was enjoyable and satisfying, and not only because of the work itself. I bought a new fly-fishing outfit and usually found some excuse to stop for an hour or so when I reached an inviting stream. The willingness of grayling to take a dry fly, especially a black gnat, was thrilling. Adding to my good feelings was the friendly, almost gracious treatment I received from Frank Nash, the superintendent, his assistant Jack Warren, and a young engineer named Ben Stewart. Frank was a veteran of World War I and sometimes wore military breeches and wrap leggings on drives out on one of the roads. Jack Warren and his wife, Helen, treated me like a son, perhaps partly because they had no children.

Jack Warren's life rang of excitement. A big and gentle man with the nose of a pug, he said he had earned his ham and eggs as a professional fighter for many years before coming north. He was an airplane and engine mechanic having, he said, the second such license issued to an Alaskan. For several years he was involved in a salmon processing business in Cook Inlet. After that he managed a roadhouse at Teller, where his patrons included famed aviator Carl Ben Eielson and his mechanic, Earl Borland—and also the elite Alaskan and Canadian pilots who searched for the two men following their disappearance off North Cape, Siberia, on a flight from Teller on November 9, 1929.

The search effort depended on Jack and his roadhouse for living necessities and operational support. The search was frustrated by storms, low temperatures, and the long winter nights. Pilots and mechanics became impatient and irritable; Jack took great pride in pacifying and encouraging his guests without revealing his own stress. Joe Crosson and Harold Gillam found the fatal crash site in late January. The search for Eielson has been widely chronicled, but there has been little recognition of the important role of Jack Warren in its success.

Jack was once in charge of the Lomen Brothers' reindeer operations in Nome, before the federal government bought all non-Native-owned reindeer. He loved to tell stories of the old days, including this one about the reindeer business:

During the annual roundup of reindeer for marking and castration of bulls, the Lomen herders accidentally picked up some animals that belonged to Eskimo herd owners. When the Lomen herd was being returned to its summer range, one Eskimo owner cut out some animals to square his loss. Jack believed the man took too many, and filed a complaint in court. The Eskimo told the judge he had taken only his own reindeer. The judge asked the man how he could identify his animals. The owner replied: "Lomen mark deer with notch in ear; my mark, cut off ear."

AT JACK WARREN'S SUGGESTION I joined the Fraternal Order of Elks and made many new friends. I played poker with several of the Elks one night a week, and I was lucky to break even playing with those old foxes. With free time in the evenings and on weekends, I enjoyed wandering around Fairbanks. On a few occasions as I was walking or shopping, I recognized a face from Fourth Avenue, and I must say that the ladies were the epitome of discretion. They readily gave a nice smile and a crisp hello but nothing more, out of concern that someone might accuse them of soliciting—something they really had no need to do.

There weren't many young people living in the Fairbanks area except for students at the University of Alaska, who mostly lived in dormitories on campus. I never met any of the women students—and anyway, because of my limited schooling I would have felt ill at ease with girls who valued higher education. Usually on Friday or Saturday night I went to a movie or to the saloon that had a ragtime pianist. One evening I met Ethel Kokrines, John Sagala's trapline partner, and her sister Myrtle Burchard in the Nevada Bar on First Avenue. We were joined at a table by three of their Native male friends from Nenana. These fellows were feeling the effects of alcohol, and their initial friendliness quickly changed to nastiness. I wanted no part of a bad scene, so I excused myself and left.

The men followed me and came up close behind as I walked in front of the N.C. store in the next block. I had wanted to get along with them, but now it seemed I was in for a tangle. One of the men spat on the back of my head, and this was too much to take. I gave the closest man a right fist in the face, and he sat. The other two charged in to grapple, but they were awkward, perhaps too drunk to fight. I got a headlock on one of them and flipped him over my hip to the wooden-board sidewalk, with me on top. The third fellow jumped on my back and grabbed my hair with both hands. A few bumps of his head on the boards tamed the one under me. When I rose to deal with the hair puller, I realized he was in no condition to protect himself, much less hurt me. When I excused myself this time, no one followed. I was embarrassed at being involved in this kind of brawl, and glad that few people would know about it.

It was wartime, and during the spring and summer of 1942, Army personnel were arriving at Ladd Field in Fairbanks in considerable numbers, though they seldom came into town. A Territorial Guard unit was being organized in Fairbanks by Major M. R. Marston, and I signed up along with about thirty other men, all considerably older than I. Forbes Baker, a Linotype operator at the *Fairbanks Daily News-Miner,* was our local commander. We met twice a week in the evening at a schoolyard, learning close-order drill from two noncommissioned officers of the 4th Infantry at Ladd Field. At first we were issued sticks to carry in lieu of firearms, but we soon received Enfield rifles.

About this time my superintendent at work, Frank Nash, asked if I would be interested in learning to operate bulldozers, carry-alls, and other heavy equipment. It would mean a raise in pay and a chance to develop new skills. It was an easy decision. Tractors and other construction equipment had been brought in for upgrading the Richardson Highway and building a larger bridge across the Salcha River and a bridge over the Tanana River at Big Delta. I packed my seabag and moved from Fairbanks to a tent camp at Salcha. I had worked as a pearl diver, a gandy dancer, and a grease monkey; now I would be a cat skinner — a person who operates Caterpillar tractors or other heavy equipment.

I shared a large wall tent with three older men, one being a great practical joker and raconteur named Denver Lane. In the evening Denver would hold forth with unending stories, sometimes making me the butt of a far-fetched yarn. I found a little frog one evening and brought it into the tent just as Denver was about finished passing around a bottle of whiskey. I took a swig, then quietly slipped the frog into the bottle. No one noticed, and Denver put the cap on the bottle and stowed it under his cot.

That seemed to be the end of it. But then one evening when we were in the tent enjoying some food treats, Denver asked: "Jim, did you eat that piece of apple pie?" I said yes. "Well, then," he said, "you got your frog back." And I had thought it was simply seeds or part of an apple core I had chewed.

On my twentieth birthday, August 6, 1942, Jack Warren came to see me with a box of cookies Helen had baked. He also came on business: he was a Selective Service registrar and a member of the draft board. I had been thinking seriously about military service, especially since the Japanese attack on Dutch Harbor in Alaska's Aleutian Islands in June. Because I was in the Territorial Guard and because my work in highway construction was considered helpful to the war effort, the draft board was not required to call me into active duty right away. I told Jack I would like to finish out the month at my job, take a short hunting trip, and then enlist in the Army Air Corps.

A replacement cat skinner arrived and I was again assigned to drive the freight truck to the maintenance camps. I was surprised when Frank Nash asked if I had a rifle to take along because caribou were migrating across the Steese Highway northeast of Fairbanks. He mentioned that two elderly men who did light work around the headquarters yard could use some meat. It became clear his plan was to make several people happy at once. I saw the hand of Jack Warren in all of this.

In driving out the Steese Highway the next morning, I encountered a car that stopped as it saw me approaching. Not until the driver introduced himself as a Game Commission agent did it occur to me that I didn't have a hunting license. He was happy to sell one to me, while describing the migrating caribou crossing the highway farther on. After unloading the truck at a construction camp, I was anxious to go after the caribou that were moving in small bands on the opposite mountainside. These were stragglers of the main migration that had been passing here for several days but which now was well along toward the Forty Mile or upper Chena River country.

Tommy Olson, a University student employed at the camp, was also eager to bag a caribou or two, so he joined me in the chase. There wasn't much hunting to it; we separated just a short distance and tried to position ourselves so the moving animals would approach within rifle range. Tommy soon made two clean kills, while I killed one animal and wounded another. I discovered I had brought only the few cartridges that were in the magazine of the rifle, and these were now spent. Fearing the crippled animal would escape before Tommy could come near enough to help, I dropped my rifle and chased it. Catching up with it, I jumped on its back and was able to reach its throat with my hunting knife.

That was a messy way to take a caribou, but I felt great relief in not letting it get away to suffer a lingering death. As viewed by Tommy from a distance, it was an unforgettable escapade, for I later heard him recount it with excitement in his voice and eyes. Some days later, I drove my Model A pickup to the Chatanika River and killed a young bull moose. I gave moose and caribou meat to the old-timers at the Road Commission headquarters and other friends who cherished wild meat but were unable to get it. The time had come for me to hand in my Enfield rifle to Forbes Baker and enlist in the army.

CHAPTER ELEVEN

Army Pilot

AT LADD FIELD IN FAIRBANKS I met army recruits from throughout the Interior. The local men reflected the varied social and economic colors of Fairbanks, while those from the bush were mostly miners; ages ranged from about twenty up to forty-four years. My friend Glenn Hudson was among the new soldiers. There were now enough Alaskan recruits to mount a basic training program at a barracks called Camp Reindeer. I became acquainted with many fine men, but also met a few fellows who regarded themselves too highly, in my opinion. These latter, it seemed, usually described themselves as heavy equipment operators.

After boot camp Glenn and I were assigned to the 439th Squadron, on the crew responsible for the ground handling of airplanes being transferred to Russia under a lend-lease program. As newcomers in a squadron that had come up fully established from the United States, we Alaskans occupied the lowest ranks. Our lot was pulling kitchen duty two or three times a week with little chance for promotion. We towed airplanes around, tied them down, heated them, and fueled them.

U.S. pilots flew the airplanes, P-39 Airacobras and A-20 Havocs, to Ladd Field where Russian pilots picked them up and flew them on to the Soviet Union. The Russian noncommissioned officers, who were learning about airplane maintenance, ate in our mess hall. We assumed they had all seen action against the Germans, but the language barrier made it difficult to learn much about them. At meals, when an interpreter was present, they were happy to engage in chitchat, though they refused to discuss the war. It was clear they had been instructed to avoid the subject.

I was trying to learn the Russian language, and I talked with the Russians whenever opportunity offered. I mentioned to them at lunch one day that we were eating hot dogs. They stopped in mid bite and stared at me in speechless, dreadful apprehension. I instantly grasped that they had taken me literally. Not even the interpreter was able to persuade them to continue the meal.

Glenn Hudson taught me how to play chess, which proved to be an enduring source of pleasure. However, I was becoming increasingly disenchanted with my army duties. While the war was raging, surely I could do something more helpful for my country than peel potatoes, scrub the mess hall floor, or tow airplanes around and heat their engines. I certainly had done more menial things and enjoyed them, but now my attitude was different, helped along by one incident that was especially aggravating to me.

I had never been able to see a motion picture on the base because the theater line was always too long when I got off duty. One time I arranged with the mess sergeant to get free early and then dashed to change into my class A uniform and arrive at the theater in time to get in. What a nice feeling to walk into the theater at last. But I was only a few steps past the ticket taker when I was stopped by a shouted "Hey, you!" I turned around. A buck sergeant then demanded to know "Where is your belt?" In panic, I felt my waist and found no belt. He ordered me out.

In mounting frustration I asked our squadron commander for a transfer to a combat unit. He said the best he could do would be a transfer to Company E, 4th Infantry, which handled guard duty on the base. This sounded even worse. I couldn't tolerate sitting out the war in this situation; something had to happen, and a bizarre scenario developed in my mind. I would stow away on the Russian transport plane that ferried Russian pilots to Fairbanks and then returned empty to Siberia. When I got off the plane in Siberia, the Russians would welcome me as someone who wanted to go to the fighting front.

On the verge of actually doing it, I forsook the plan when I realized it would amount to desertion and result in loss of my citizenship, something almost sacred to me. It wouldn't matter to U.S. authorities that I had acted out of patriotism, and I would bring shame on my family. After the eleventh-hour decision to stay put, I felt fright and relief at how close I had come to making a grave mistake.

THEN A WONDERFUL THING happened: I saw a poster on the library door that showed a young man wearing a white scarf and flying helmet, with the words "You too can be an aviation cadet." A written test would be given on the base for applicants. I rushed to tell Glenn Hudson about it, thinking he would be excited too. To my surprise, Glenn was not interested. Although he loved flying, he was reasonably content and didn't care to join me in an uncertain venture.

I knew my lack of a high school diploma reduced my chances, but I was desperate enough to lie about that. I found a couple of fellows in the squadron who had taken the exam earlier and failed, and I quizzed them on what to expect. Then for three weeks I crammed: algebra and vocabulary mostly, but also current events in copies of *Time* magazine. Strangely enough, *Esquire* magazine was the most help. In each article, I found several words I didn't know. I would find the definitions in the dictionary and memorize them. The exam left me in a nervous state. Part of it was straightforward and I felt good about that, but other parts were confusing to me—particularly the ink blot questions, a psychological screening technique that directs you to state what images you think you see in the abstract black shapes.

I did OK, because about two weeks later I was called to the orderly room and given printed orders for aviation cadet training. What a thrilling moment! It got even better: I was not given KP duty again before my departure. I took a train to Seward, then boarded a small freighter to Seattle. My rank as a private didn't serve me well on the ship. I was assigned to periods of daytime work in a stifling hot galley, and to guard duty on deck for part of the night. All I was given to guard was an outside cabin door that separated me from an intermittently screaming man. From what I could learn, a Chinese crew member, having exhausted his opium supply, had gone mad during the withdrawal ordeal. The ship was blacked out to avoid submarine attack and it pitched hard in heavy seas, adding to the eeriness of the fellow's periodic moans and screams.

At Fort Lewis, Washington, I was immediately granted a furlough that allowed a wonderful visit with my family in Detroit. While my letters had kept the family generally informed of what I was doing, they also provoked a hundred questions. Family friends were called in to listen to my yarns, and everyone got to bed late. The cadet training program then took me to a succession of different places: basic training in Utah, a training detachment in Arizona, then classification and preflight training in California. The classification procedure was an ordeal of tests that determined whether a cadet would be trained as a navigator, bombardier, or pilot. I felt lucky and pleased at being selected for pilot training. Discipline was strict during preflight training at Santa Ana, with demerits for infractions. Each demerit was worth one hour of parading in front of the barracks with a broomstick on your shoulder—a little humiliating for future eagles, but it taught attention to details. I once carried the broomstick for three hours because the edge of an envelope showed at my hip pocket during a Sunday parade.

Primary training followed at Dos Palos, California, in Ryan PT-22s, in which I soloed. These airplanes were so easy to fly and had such wide landing gear that almost anyone with a few hours of instruction could get them safely up and down. Shortly thereafter, Stearman airplanes were brought in—which was a blessing, for we really had to learn to fly a demanding machine. Almost a third of my class washed out in these airplanes, mostly I think for ground looping—dragging a wingtip on the runway and spinning around to a quick stop—as a result of not learning to correct for sidewise drift in crosswind landings.

We were introduced to aerobatics—spins, loops, chandelles, snap rolls, barrel rolls, and the more demanding slow rolls. We were told the Stearman had such built-in stability that it would right itself from any position if you simply released all control pressures. I resorted to that knowledge when I was attempting my first solo slow roll and suddenly found myself upside down and totally confused. I released the controls—but I failed to close the throttle and quickly went into a dive, with the engine roaring and the ground approaching very fast. I pulled back on both the throttle and the stick to stop the dive, and my vision blacked out, but I was conscious enough to keep pressure on the stick until the nose was back up to the horizon. It was a close call.

Basic training in BT-13 airplanes at another base introduced night flying, and advanced training in twin-engine AT-17s followed at yet another base, where we learned formation and instrument flying. Before graduation we were asked what type of airplane we would like to fly. Here again, *Esquire* helped me out. I had seen a full-spread picture in the magazine of a B-24 Liberator, an awesomely beautiful airplane. I got my choice, and I went for training to Albuquerque's Kirkland Field. We trained in early-model B-24s that had returned from battle in the Pacific as newer airplanes became available to replace them. Most of them carried a record of their missions in the form of bombs or Japanese flags painted on the fuselage ahead of the cockpit. I felt a reverence for the old planes, imagining the trials they had weathered.

Tragedy struck during training when a B-24 caught fire in the air and blew up, killing my instructor and my student partner. I was not aboard because I was recovering from food poisoning. It was the only training flight I had missed.

After qualification as a B-24 first pilot, I was assigned a nine-man crew and sent to a training unit in South Carolina, where we practiced formation flying, bombing, gunnery, and navigation. We were sent to Batista Field, Cuba, for several days to finish high-altitude bombing training, and it was like a vacation: warm weather, sunny skies, and overnight passes to Havana. The passes issued to officers had two addresses printed on the back, and I suspected their significance without asking. I suggested to one of my crew members that we check out the addresses, and he agreed. One address led us to a place called Casa Del Mar, where we encountered two huge locked doors and a person who opened a small, sliding peep door to ask for our passes. My companion asked me, "What kind of place is this?" When I told him it was a sporting house, and apparently a monitored and approved establishment, he backed away as if in fright. We parted then, and I thought that he must have had a proper upbringing and was saving himself for a future wife. But it proved not to be quite this way. Several days later he came to me with a terrible problem. He had met a lovely Cuban girl, and yes, he had a dose of clap. Our many VD movies, lectures, and short-arm inspections hadn't saved him.

FROM SOUTH CAROLINA we went to Mitchell Field on Long Island and picked up a new B-24, fresh from the factory. It was then on to Bangor, Maine, where bomb-bay auxiliary fuel tanks were installed and the airplane was loaded with bales of GI blankets for an unknown destination. On December 22, 1944, two years after taking the examination at Ladd Field to qualify for army flight training, I took off from Bangor with instructions to fly an east heading for one hour before opening a sealed manila envelope containing orders. The men of the crew counted the minutes until I could open the orders and learn where we were going. The orders told me to report to the 460th Bomb Group, 15th Air Force, in Italy. The B-24's intercom came alive with chatter as the crew began thinking aloud about wine, Italian women, spaghetti, operas, Pompeii, and so forth until the navigator, Bill Anderson, told everyone to shut up.

The flight leg from Bermuda to the Azores was memorable, to say the least. At fifteen thousand feet we were in light to severe turbulence, and rain intermittently pounded the airplane. It was too bumpy to use the autopilot, the navigator couldn't see the stars, we didn't know the winds, there were no radio aids, the glow of static electricity known as St. Elmo's fire ringed our four propellers, and I expected lightning strikes at any moment. Then we lost power on a starboard engine.

I instantly shoved the control column ahead to hold airspeed and tramped hard on the left rudder to stop or slow the plane's right yaw (its swing to the right). I would have to feather the propeller of the bad engine, but first I had to determine which engine it was. Before I could figure this out, we started losing power on a port engine. This made it easier to control the yaw, and also told me that we had a more general problem.

My flight engineer, Sergeant Maclyn Abbot, was not at his usual station between the pilot seats. I suddenly recalled that only minutes before, Abbot had asked me if it was all right to transfer fuel from the bomb bay tanks to the wing cells, and I told him to go ahead. This must be our problem. On the intercom, I told him to turn off the fuel transfer pumps and put all of the valves back to their original positions and then turn the fuel booster pumps back on. The engines regained power and the crisis passed. The airplane lost a few thousand feet in altitude, but we kept it under good control. Air or vapor locks in the fuel lines had caused the shutdowns. We went to a lower altitude, where we transferred fuel with no problem.

A short time later, the directional gyro showed that the airplane was slowly going off course to the left. But at the same time, I sensed that we were turning right. In fact, it felt to me like we were banked so steeply to the right that I was about to fall out of my seat. From my training, I realized that I was suffering from a vertigo phenomenon called the leans—and that the instrument was correct and my own senses were lying to me. But I still couldn't bring myself to respond to the instrument indications.

I watched until the gyro showed us drifting off course about thirty degrees to the left, then asked copilot Alvin Hougnon to take over. He quickly turned the B-24 back on course. I attributed my vertigo to fatigue. Because of a poker game, I had slept only a few hours the night before leaving Bangor. Out of the following twenty hours, I had flown for about twelve, mostly on instruments.

As we arrived over the airstrip at Goia, Italy, I could see dust flying through the air and I heard from the tower that there was a 45-mile-an-hour crosswind from the left. The landing strip, covered with steel matting, was narrow and less than five thousand feet long. I held an extreme crab angle on final approach and then lowered the left wing enough to sideslip, removing lateral drift before letting the wheels touch the runway. The landing was one of my best — but before we parked, two B-24s that followed us both ground-looped and were badly damaged. While my crew sometimes bragged about my flying to other crews, I felt this time they had reason.

Two lieutenants met us and said they would be flying us to our bomb group base at Spinazzola. I had developed an attachment to the airplane by this time and felt a little put out, but the group commander promptly took possession of that new airplane. I never flew it again.

IN ITALY I WAS DISAPPOINTED to be assigned as copilot with another crew, rather than continuing as a first pilot in command of my own plane and crew. With all our training, I had perfect confidence that we could perform with the best. My missions as copilot included an especially difficult bombing run against railroad marshaling yards at Vienna. When we were still about fifty miles from Vienna, we could see a dark cloud ahead. It was caused by exploding anti-aircraft shells, and they seemed to have our altitude bracketed. On our straight and level course to the target, we got jolted hard several times. But we were aboard one of the lucky aircraft; our bomb group lost several planes.

After the Vienna mission and the loss of the airplanes, I was assigned once more as first pilot, again flying with my own eager crew. When word reached us in April 1945 that President Roosevelt had died, we were stunned and saddened. He was the only president I had known since being ten years old. By this time the war was clearly winding down on our front. Our bombing missions encountered less opposition and they were short, mostly to Brenner Pass on the Austria/Italy border and to targets just north of Italy's Po River. Senior officers and even the group commander seemed to like these missions. My crew and I felt that these officers were simply trying to build their combat record, because some of them now flew every other day while newer crews were not called for duty. In any case, we were fortunate in having no serious problems or injuries before the war ended. My crew was the only one in our bomb group to return home with its original ten members, although that was due partly to the short length of our tour during the late stage of the war — from January 4, 1945, until May 8, 1945, celebrated as the day of Victory in Europe.

After VE Day we flew to Goia again and were assigned to test-fly airplanes that had seen combat, to make sure they were in shape to be flown back to the United States. Here I was pleased to again fly the stout old plane that carried the scars of my bumpy Vienna raid.

We flew a B-24 back to the United States by the so-called southern route. It was like a rich tourist's dream: we landed at Marrakech, Morocco; Dakar, Senegal; Fortaleza, Brazil; Georgetown, British Guiana (now Guyana); Boringuen Field, Puerto Rico; and finally Savannah, Georgia. While we awaited reassignment, the war in the Pacific ended. I had been blessed with the finest group of crew members that anyone could have prayed for; we had bonded as closely as any family. Parting with those fellows when I was separated from service in September 1945 left me with a sad sense of loneliness. My wonderful family in Detroit again welcomed me home, but knew that I would soon head north. My mother and father planned a trip to visit me in Alaska, but to my deep sorrow, their poor health frustrated those plans.

CHAPTER TWELVE

Romance and Other Adventures

A PRETTY GIRL CAUGHT MY ATTENTION soon after I began classes at the university. After I met her and we had a chance to talk, she dominated my thoughts. Her name was Bertha Mae Jane Schaeffer, a girl from Kotzebue, Alaska, who was part Inupiat Eskimo. Her Schaeffer family, brothers and nephews, would later emerge as Alaskan political, business, and military leaders. When I learned that she had declined invitations to a dance in the hope that I might ask her to go, my interest really soared.

We both lived in university dormitories, so courting Bertha mainly consisted of long walks on the few roads around the campus. On weekends we would ride the bus to town to take in a movie or sip a cocktail in the Mecca Lounge. Bertha was to graduate at the end of the semester with a degree in education and intended to sign a contract to teach in a remote village school. The move would mean painful separation. Bertha decided not to sign the contract because I proposed something different. We got married when the semester ended. I decide to delay my further education until we were better able to manage it financially. Meanwhile I would take a pilot's job I had been offered with Dillingham Air Service, in Bristol Bay on the Bering Sea coast.

I had met Robert Dennis Fenno, half-owner of the air service, when he and his wife, Betty, visited the university, where Betty's father, Howard Wilcox, was dean of the School of Mines. Dennis had flown B-17 bombers in the Eighth Air Force; we enjoyed talking together and soon became friends. I discussed the job offer with Bertha, who told me that Mrs. Wilcox didn't hold Dennis in very high regard. It seems that Dennis and Betty had married against the wishes of her parents. Just before Dennis went into the service, he and Betty had eloped, with Dean Wilcox in hot pursuit. Dennis's father, Pete Fenno, who was the U.S. Commissioner at Dillingham, married the couple just moments before the dean arrived in a chartered plane.

Bertha left it to my judgment, and I took the job. With my military file in hand, I hurried to see a Civil Aeronautics Administration flight official and was issued a commercial single and multiengine pilot license after a physical examination, but without a written examination or a check ride. A few weeks later, after a check ride, I got my seaplane rating, and later an instrument rating.

At Dillingham I discovered that only one of the company's four airplanes was ready to fly. The army-surplus Noorduyn Norseman was not yet certificated for commercial use, the Waco was being rebuilt, and the Curtiss Robin had a worn-out engine, leaving only a Stinson Junior floatplane to support the business. On the positive side, Bertha and I rented a nice, new small house on the bluff overlooking Nushagak Bay.

Dennis's partner Matt (Red) Flensberg wasn't even flying at the time because his license had been suspended after several people reported him at the controls of an airplane while intoxicated. Flying in the Stinson, Dennis showed me how to get around from Bethel, north of Bristol Bay, to Ugashik in the south and points in-between. I had a lot to learn. Dennis introduced me to the ins-and-outs of flying a floatplane and how to deal with the water and weather conditions of this stormy region.

I learned especially quickly one dark and windy night when we had to fly the Stinson off the intertidal area in front of Dillingham to the calm safety of Wood River. Dennis had already taught me the tricks of landing at night on glassy water—but he had shown me these techniques during the day. Now he would demonstrate at night. He let down into the blackness of Wood River, upstream from an old cannery, and gently bounced off the water a couple of times before hearing a small *click* on the left side.

"Shit, I think we hit a boat," Dennis said.

The outboard left wing strut had barely touched an anchored fishing boat. As we beached and tied up the airplane, the frightened and riled Native fishermen on the boat came over to us. Dennis knew them, calmed them down, and before long they were all laughing about it. Beyond what I learned about night landings on water (avoid them), I discovered that Dennis had an extraordinary talent for cajoling people into believing that everything was going wonderfully well, despite appearances. This was indeed a charismatic quality; no matter how the troubles mounted and involved others, Dennis remained popular and well liked, except by competitors.

In Bristol Bay, the big business is commercial salmon fishing and processing. In the summer, many people move between villages and salmon canneries, with enough traffic to keep all of the local bush pilots busy. It was vital that we complete the rebuilding of the Waco as quickly as possible to take advantage of this seasonal business, so Dennis and I both pitched in to help whenever we could. Mechanic Mike Korhonon, assisted by Al (Swede) Aaberg, a cabinetmaker, had done a beautiful job on the plane. New star clusters—the joints of tubing prone to stress cracking—had been welded in, and all of the tubing had been flushed with oil and primed for corrosion protection. They had fabricated a new firewall, engine mount, and stronger gear attachments. The fabric and paint job were gorgeous. Our spirits soared as we mounted the plane on reconditioned, tight pontoons and started the airplane's Jacobs engine, which came from a surplus AT-17 that Dennis had flown up from Arizona in the spring.

With Dennis flying the Waco and me at the controls of the Stinson, business began to look more promising. Bertha was happy too, taking care of the company's office, which was in a tiny hexagon-shaped building sitting apart in the center of town.

Business slowed way down during the fall, so part of being a pilot was hustling customers. Competition was intense, with Kenny Armstrong, John Walatka, Don Wren, and the Ball brothers operating out of Dillingham. Every night Dennis checked into Billy's Bar, where the owner, who was

Mike Korhonon's uncle, tried to steer patrons to us. Dennis's father helped too. As manager of Felder's Store, he directed people and freight our way. These supporters partly offset the advantage of Don Wren and the Ball brothers who, Dennis thought, recruited from the Seventh Day Adventist congregation. Still, there was not enough money coming in to meet the payroll, and only the credit line assured by Pete Fenno at Felder's Store kept the employees of Dillingham Air Service going.

MORE THAN A FEW of the people who flew with us from Dillingham back to their home villages showed carry-over signs of celebrating, and we had to be pretty tolerant of their condition. I didn't suspect the trouble in store when I loaded a tipsy, talkative Native, Alex Trefon, for a flight to Nondalton on Lake Clark. It was November, with the weather getting nasty, although water in the rivers and larger lakes still allowed the use of floatplanes. We encountered occasional snow showers that gradually formed a solid front as I flew low to keep the ground in sight.

I was on the verge of turning back to Dillingham when Alex said, "Take my number." He had unbuckled his seat belt and was fumbling with a wallet. Soon he held out a Social Security card and hollered, "Someday I pay you." Realizing that he wasn't going to pay for the ride anyway, I told him we were going back to Dillingham. He became highly excited, shouting that he had to get home because he had food there that would freeze. When I shook my head no, he swung a haymaker that hit me in the ribs under the right arm. Although the blow wasn't hard, more a threatening gesture, it startled me and caused my hand to jerk back the throttle, slowing the engine. We were already flying slowly at an altitude of no more than a hundred feet, so it was a critical moment.

Fortunately, Alex again resorted to shouting and didn't throw another punch. I had time to gain some altitude, and also to get the brass fire extinguisher from under my legs, ready to bash him on the head if he continued to be violent. To calm him, I claimed we were going on to Nondalton, and we got his seat belt fastened good and tight.

As things settled down, I smelled smoke; Alex's cigarette must have fallen into his lap. The circumstances seemed to justify letting him burn a little, so I waited, saying nothing. The smoke got worse, with no indication that Alex felt anything. I realized the fire was in the seat cushion, and I alerted him. Flying in bad weather didn't scare him, but the fire did; he began tearing at the cushion, tossing smoldering kapok around the cabin.

That was the end of the fire, but then I had to land—and Alex would see that we were at Dillingham, not his home village. I was apprehensive, fearing how he might act, but during the landing he was perfectly docile.

Apparently Alex had become a serious nuisance around Dillingham, because the Bureau of Indian Affairs gave us a government travel request for his trip home the next day. Once again I faced some tense flying before my round-trip flight was over, but this time it wasn't Alex's fault; he was sober and spoke politely. We met snow showers, but skirted them to the south and got to Nondalton. Alex was happy, and upon my inquiry, assured me that his food would be OK, not frozen.

As I started the return flight, I was encouraged by decent visibility to take a direct heading for Dillingham, though I knew that snow showers were moving across from the north. Soon I was flying in snow, and forward visibility dropped to zero. I slowed the airplane and dropped lower and lower so I could keep the surface in sight out the side window, hoping things would improve. They got worse, and I was constantly switching my attention between the magnetic compass and the side window. I thought of turning back, but it seemed likely to be as bad behind me as ahead. I had no radio, but this didn't matter since there were no radio aid facilities near enough to be useful. I could probably land on the snow-covered tundra, but that would surely damage the Stinson and put Dillingham Air Service in a deeper hole than it was in already. In considering my limited options, an old Air Corps admonition popped into mind: fly the airplane, no matter what.

The daylight was failing fast. I was flying at less than fifty feet, and I knew there were some low, meandering ridges along my course. My peripheral vision picked up something on the right. Looking over, I saw a snow surface with vegetation poking through, just off the wingtip. I pulled the wheel back a little to gain altitude, but instantly lost sight of the surface. So I eased the wheel forward a bit, until I could see the snow surface on the left side.

Trees and then water finally appeared, the Nushagak River. I banked sharply left, chopping the power to drop to the surface before reaching the far side of the river, which wasn't visible. On touching down, visibility improved slightly, and I saw boulders and rapids just ahead. I added power, lifted over the hazards, and settled down beyond them. What a relief it was to run the airplane to the riverbank and tie up for the night. My training, focused attention, and youthful reflexes helped me through this flight, but judgment had failed me. I should not have flown into the snow showers in the first place.

With the annual freezeup of the rivers and lakes, we put the planes on skis. Matt Flensberg's pilot license was restored and he occasionally flew the Waco. Business slowed, and we sometimes resorted to illegal use of the Norseman, which still hadn't been certificated for commercial use, for a big load of freight or cash-paying passengers. A below-average fishing season prompted the Department of Agriculture to send surplus food, mostly cheese and beans, for distribution to villages around Bristol Bay. Payment for delivery of this aid hardly paid for the gasoline, and the people really didn't want food they weren't accustomed to eating. But to stay busy, we moved quite a lot of it anyway, hoping it would generate other business.

On one such flight in early January 1947, Dennis and I landed the ski-equipped Norseman on the river ice at Koliganek, on the upper Nushagak River. As was usual at the villages, a crowd of people quickly appeared when we landed. The chief, Anton Johnson, escorted us to his large cabin. It was spotlessly clean, with very few furnishings. The interior was covered in broad red, white, and blue-striped wallpaper that ran up the walls and around the ridge-poles. The only places that escaped the paper were the floor, windows, and the single door. Dennis and Anton were still engaged in lengthy greetings when a terrible commotion erupted outside. Guns fired and people yelled. I was petri-fied, wondering what terrible thing was happening. Anton opened the door, and it seemed the entire village was pa-rading by, shooting into the air and spinning colorful crepe-paper wheels. We had walked into a Russian Christmas cel-ebration—at least the noisy part of it.

Dennis was a master at influencing people, if there was gain in it. When Anton mentioned that a young couple was interested in getting married, Dennis soon promoted that circumstance into a wedding party. He decided we would take the betrothed couple, and whoever else wanted to attend the wedding ceremony, to Dillingham in the big plane. I had trouble counting the number of people Dennis urged on board. It really wasn't the number that mattered, but rather the bulk or mass. He knew we were tail heavy, and before takeoff he commented that we would have to be careful.

We roared a long way down the snow-covered river, along straight stretches, around bends, and again down straight stretches until the airplane finally flew. Our passengers must have thought we were going to taxi all the way to Dillingham. Dennis was careful not to slow the airplane much until the skis touched down on landing. Most of the landing area disappeared behind us, and only the steerable tail ski saved us from bouncing over the road at the end.

Carlos Carson, the ever-alert Game Commission agent, whose front-room window overlooked the frozen pond where we landed, later told me how confused he was. He saw the plane land, but unaccountably when he looked up a minute later, a huge crowd had materialized. Counting Dennis and me, there were sixteen souls aboard, plus two dogs. The Norseman was rated as an eight-passenger plane.

IN SEPTEMBER AND OCTOBER of 1946, I made a number of flights to Bethel, over Togiak Lake and the Kilbuck Mountains into the Kuskokwim Valley. Aside from the spectacular scenery, I was struck by the large flocks of migrating ptarmigan that appeared almost as small, white clouds moving across the landscape below me. There were certainly thousands of birds moving mainly in a southerly direction. I suspected it to be an uncommon phenomenon, perhaps related to extraordinarily high populations over a wide area. This notion later seemed to be supported by the great abundance of willow ptarmigan that appeared around Dillingham that winter.

The myriad of game trails cut into both the rocky and vegetated alpine slopes of the Kilbuck Mountains also piqued my curiosity. I looked carefully, hoping to spot caribou or Dall sheep but saw only moose and a few bears. From what I could learn, it seemed unlikely that sheep ever occupied this region, at least in historic times. Reindeer or caribou were better possibilities. Pete Fenno, who was in charge of the government reindeer herds that had been brought to the Bristol Bay region, said the reindeer range allocations were confined to the valleys and the coastal plains where, indeed, I had seen brush corrals in unexpected places. But reindeer herding didn't catch on; by 1946 no deer remained.

I made many inquiries of the pilots, old-timers, and Natives who claimed some familiarity with the Kilbuck country and none had seen sheep or caribou there. However, Frank Waskey, a scholarly elder trader (and the first delegate to Congress from the Alaska Territory, 1906-07), told me he had traversed the Kilbuck Mountains by dog team and said the game trails undoubtedly were made by caribou. It was intriguing to me that the high alpine areas that now seemed so lonely could once have been alive with caribou. I later learned that major long-term caribou herd shifts between regions are common in Alaska.

IN MID JANUARY 1947, Matt Flensberg left Dillingham in the Waco with four passengers aboard, bound for nearby Togiak. He showed no obvious signs of drinking. The weather was fine, and we expected him to return within a few hours. He didn't show up the same day, and our worrying intensified when a blinding two-day blizzard struck.

We couldn't communicate with him because none of our airplanes had radios.

After the storm, it became clear and cold. Dennis and I heated the Norseman and flew off toward Togiak. The strikingly beautiful countryside appeared to contrast with the deep apprehension we felt. We saw no sign of the Waco en route, or at Togiak, so we turned up the Togiak River. Something dark seemed out of place in the distance. Approaching, we discovered two wings projecting vertically from the Waco fuselage, which lay on its side. Matt and the four passengers popped into sight as we circled. They were all drunk. We took the passengers to Togiak and returned to Dillingham with Matt.

After sleeping it off, Matt explained that he had landed on the frozen river near a driftwood-and-sod hut, or barabara, to pick up some *piivaq*, a Native-made alcoholic drink created by fermenting potatoes, beans, or certain other foods with some sugar. While still moving fairly fast on glare ice during the landing, the airplane began to turn toward the bank, sliding sideways. It hit a rough spot, wiping out the gear and folding the wings on one side.

Though contrite, Matt tried to see humor in the accident. When the airplane stopped, he was hanging from his seat belt with his face just inches from the right-seat passenger, who was the chief at Togiak. Jammed against the window, the chief looked at Matt and said only, "Wing broke." This accident further worsened the company's financial state, though we all felt a strange loyalty and continued working in hopes that things would improve.

Mike Korhonon silently examined the Waco and planned its next revival. This had to be a disheartening exercise for Mike because he and Swede had labored for months to totally rebuild the airplane. The fabric and paint job had been superb, creating a showpiece that was the envy of the Dillingham flying community. Now the airplane lay still, bent and torn, on the frozen Togiak River like a big shot bird.

Everything on Mike's list of things needed to repair the Waco was available in Dillingham and could fit into the Norseman, including a new propeller. Mike and Swede, disdaining the nearby barabara, set up shop and camp next to the airplane in two large wall tents. These men took pride in undertaking challenging work and seemed inspired by Dennis's optimism and encouragement.

Under these difficult conditions, they lifted the airplane, removed the damaged parts, cut and welded tubing and fittings, reinforced the wing spars, and repaired ribs and fabric. Mending this airplane to basic flying condition in three weeks was the bush-aviation version of "wooden ships, iron men." Dennis flew Mike and Swede in the Norseman and I flew the scarred Waco in loose formation back to Dillingham.

Because of my great fondness and sympathy for Dennis, it was hard for me to concede that my job with him held no promise. I had not been paid for three months. If Bertha and I had stayed until our money was gone, we would have been stuck in an even worse situation. John Walatka was aware of Dennis's problems and had earlier mentioned to me that he, Ray Peterson, and some other air service operators in Dillingham were talking about merging to form a company to be called Northern Consolidated Airlines, and they could use me. But when I considered Dennis's good intentions and the effort he had invested in teaching me bush flying, the idea of competing with him was obnoxious.

Tom Gardner, who headed the local fishermen's union, told me I could fish for salmon commercially if Bertha and I decided to stay in Dillingham, despite their rule that only three-year residents of Bristol Bay be allowed the privilege.

But I knew it was time to leave. We reluctantly said good-bye to friends and flew to Anchorage.

Dennis struggled on with the business for almost ten more years. The name changed from Dillingham Air Service to Bristol Bay Airlines. Matt Flensberg dropped out. The Norseman was sold, still without certification, and was replaced by a Bellanca Pacemaker. With a new airfield at Dillingham, Dennis got a variety of airplanes including AT-17s and single-engine Cessnas. A succession of pilots followed me, all eventually leaving as I did. Finally the Internal Revenue Service closed in. Dennis had failed to forward income tax withholding from the employees for an extended period. He fled abroad. His wife, Betty, got a divorce and remarried. Dennis found flying jobs in various parts of the world. John Walatka told me that he ran into Dennis at the Okura Hotel in Tokyo in the mid-1960s. He was working for an airline, flying between Taiwan and Japan. I heard through other friends that he had married again, this time to a wealthy woman.

Dennis died in Catania, Italy, in 1991. He had an adventurous, trying life, managing always to keep pain and humiliation under a deep veneer of good spirits. In many ways he seemed to me innocently, almost innately, oblivious to responsibility. With the right kind of hardheaded business manager Dennis might have been successful.

In any case, he was a true war hero, among the first B-17 pilots in the Eighth Air Force to survive thirty missions and rotate home. He was awarded a Silver Star, a Distinguished Flying Cross, and the Air Medal with two oak leaf clusters. Somehow, Dennis arranged to have the Silver Star presented to himself in a ceremony at Ladd Field, Fairbanks, which must have pleasantly confounded Dean and Mrs. Wilcox.

CHAPTER THIRTEEN

The Eskimo Way

OUR NEXT HOME WAS AT THE ESKIMO VILLAGE of Wales on the Bering Strait, a couple of hundred miles southwest of Bertha's hometown of Kotzebue. We were hired to run the weather station at Wales. My interest in meteorology stemming from flying and Army Air Corps training had led me to the U.S. Weather Bureau office in Anchorage, and an immediate job offer to Bertha and me.

We received a week of familiarization training at the weather office and a briefing by a military intelligence officer; Wales was just across Bering Strait from Siberia, and the Cold War with the Soviet Union was under way. We flew to Nome in a DC-3, and from there, Jack Whaley flew us to Wales in a vintage ski-equipped Wien Airlines Pilgrim. I perked up when Jack mentioned that his brother, Frank, had a Piper J-5 Cub for sale. It was something I would check on after we got settled.

It was mid-March and the region was still in the grip of winter. The couple then running the Wales station planned to leave as soon as Bertha and I were sufficiently trained. Although skilled and devoted employees, they had not involved themselves in the community and were anxious to return home to New York City after a lonely year.

About 150 Inupiat Eskimos lived at Wales. The Inupiat people occupy arctic coastal regions from Alaska's Seward Peninsula to Greenland and speak a common language. With isolated exceptions, they share a hunting culture based on marine mammals ranging from small ringed seals to massive bowhead whales. The Inupiat are relative latecomers; the Eskimos south and east of the Seward Peninsula are Yupik, thought by anthropologists to have arrived centuries earlier.

From violent episodes dating back more than half a century, the Wales people possessed at least remnants of a reputation for being hostile. Now that we were here, Bertha admitted to hearing as a child in Kotzebue that the Wales people were intimidating, or words to that effect. Bertha could still converse in the Inupiat tongue, and as she became acquainted with the older folks in the village, they described to her firsthand some of the troubling conflicts of the past.

However this might be, in all of our associations these people proved to be absolutely trustworthy, wonderfully friendly and cheerful. To Bertha's delight, they also shared with us some of their native foods such as seal oil, dried seal meat, and tomcod. Except for the flimsy structure of their dwellings, their culture seemed more intact than that of Interior Athabaskan Indians or the many Yupik Eskimos who showed the influence of travel to Bristol Bay for commercial salmon fishing or work in canneries. It was fun and stirring to walk through the village, meet people who came out to greet us with a quiet smile, and see things like a polar bear hide stretched to dry in the wind, racks holding the huge walrus-skin-covered boats called umiaks (pronounced OO-me-aks), and freshly killed ringed seals in the vestibule entries to the little frame houses.

In the sand dunes about a quarter-mile north of the village, a large white cross marked the mass grave of some eighty people who died during the influenza epidemic that ravaged Eskimo villages in 1918. At the turn of the century, the population of Wales numbered about four hundred. The marked decline since then has been due mainly to introduced diseases such as smallpox, tuberculosis, and the influenza disaster.

A WHITE MARBLE GRAVE MARKER stands prominently on a slope just south of the village as another reminder of past tragedies. The story as told to us by villagers and as I subsequently verified through documented accounts is a grim one.

A disastrous encounter in 1887 with white traders may well have conditioned the atmosphere within the village for subsequent violence. The brig *William H. Allen*, under command of Captain George Gilly, anchored at Wales in that year with an interest in obtaining baleen, the long, bonelike strips that hang from the upper jaw of certain whales. A large party of Wales men approached in several umiaks. Without firearms, they went aboard the vessel to trade, their principal interest being alcohol.

No one knows just why violence broke out, but at some point Captain Gilly ordered his crew to shoot the Eskimos. Thirteen of them were killed outright and others drowned trying to escape. Such a slaughter surely intimidated the Wales people, while stirring thoughts of retribution in the minds of some. This state of mind may have provoked further trouble a few years later.

In July 1890, missionaries Harrison Thornton and William Lopp arrived at Wales. With the help of carpenters from the Revenue Cutter *Bear*, they erected a mission and school building. In the fall of 1891, Thornton returned temporarily to the United States. His intention was to improve conditions for the Wales people by seeking, among other things, whaling paraphernalia and breech-loading rifles to help their hunting. He also wanted to advance the idea of importing reindeer from Siberia as a source of food and livelihood for the Eskimos. Beyond this, and perhaps not the least of his objectives, was to find a wife for himself, and perhaps one for Lopp as well.

Thornton was successful in marrying Neda Pratt in the spring of 1892 and in recruiting a social worker, Ellen Kittridge, to accompany them back to Wales that summer. Three weeks later, he presided over the marriage of Thomas Lopp and Miss Kittridge. The Lopps were then persuaded by the Rev. Sheldon Jackson, Alaska's general agent for education, to take charge of the new reindeer station at Port Clarence. About this time, liquor had been reaching Wales, precipitating aggressive and frightening behavior on the part of some village men. When the *Bear* arrived to take the Lopps to Port Clarence, Thornton appealed to its captain to lecture the Wales people against any actions to harm him or his wife.

On the night of August 19, 1892, Thornton made a voice response to a knock on their door. At that instant a whaling gun dart was fired through the door, killing him. Neda Thornton waited until the light improved and was then able to summon a friendly neighbor named Kitmesuk, who protected and comforted her. Then he left to consult with other villagers about dealing with the crime.

Several days later, Kitmesuk and several other men who had resolved to punish the murderers returned to the mission dragging two bodies. A third man involved with the murder, a known troublemaker named Titalk, was wounded but escaped. When Titalk returned to the village, he was told that he must die; he could choose to be shot, strangled, or stabbed. He chose to be shot. Titalk was ordered to lie down in a shallow grave next to the place Thornton was buried, and the execution was carried out. A few years later, friends of Thornton from the United States erected the marble monument.

NOT LONG AFTER ARRIVING at Wales, Bertha and I were invited to a dance in the *kasgi*, the men's communal house, a semi-subterranean structure. Bertha was familiar with Eskimo dancing, but it was all new to me; I had no idea what to expect. Passing through a low, excavated passageway, we entered a large room. It was stifling hot, reeked of seal oil, and was lighted only dimly and unevenly by two kerosene lanterns and a fire in an open-door, oil-drum stove. The senses were further assaulted by sporadic drumbeats emanating from indistinct figures sitting on a bench along the opposite side.

The floor was crowded with sitting forms, whispering and coughing. They wriggled around to make room for Bertha and me to sit down. The drums were hoops, about eighteen inches across, covered with membranes from the walls of walrus stomachs. The drums were tuned by splashing water from a small can onto them and tapping the edges with switches. When the drummers were satisfied, two men, sweating heavily, stepped to the open area in front and ceremoniously donned fancy gloves. This done, the drummers sounded off together, accompanying the beat with vigorous chant singing. Being totally new to all this sound, it struck me as an awful din with a strange, only somewhat musical quality. The dancers began a rhythmic stomping and arm waving. Sweating now myself and half nauseous from the foul air, I could never have imagined such a scene. Time might have been turned back to ages preceding Native contact with Europeans.

After this abrupt, spine-tingling introduction, Eskimo dancing was never again so rousing to me. With more exposure, I came to enjoy the music and even learned to dance and sing a little.

Wales had a subsistence economy; little money entered or left the village. The people depended on seals as their main food, augmented by walruses and lesser amounts of polar bear meat, fish, birds, willow leaves, salmonberries, and a few items from the village store. Their heating fuels were seal oil, unrendered seal blubber, and most important, driftwood, but cooking was mostly done with portable "Swede stoves" — brass, round-shaped, kerosene-burning stoves imported from Sweden. People in Wales kept a total of about forty sled dogs, a small number for a village this size. Dogs required the same basic food as the people and were burdensome. They were used mainly for hauling driftwood and tending fox traps along the beach but only in a limited way for hunting on the nearby ice.

The Wales men and boys carved walrus ivory, which they traded at the federally sponsored and loosely supervised Wales Native Store for tobacco, coffee, pilot bread, flour, sugar, dried fruit, needles, cartridges, and other essentials. The carved ivory, a few white fox pelts, and an occasional polar bear hide were sent to the Alaska Native Service, which sold them to pay for the store inventory that was delivered annually by the government vessel *North Star*. Dried sealskins, rawhide line, and raw ivory were also traded at the store, but rarely escaped local use. Alfred Mazona, the store manager, maintained a soiled notebook record for each family showing their debts or credits. The postmaster, Dwight Tevuk, and our maintenance man, Ernest Oxeorok, were the only other villagers who worked for wages. If we hired a man to do a little job at the station, he would invariably refuse money and ask for coal or something from our commissary that was not available at the store.

Bertha and I took weather observations and transmitted them to Kotzebue, hourly during the day and every three hours through the night, seven days a week. If the clouds permitted, we also released one helium-filled balloon each day, tracking it with a theodolite to record winds aloft. This was the only duty requiring both of us at the same time. We could arrange our schedule so that one or the other would have lengthy periods of freedom.

IN THE LATE SPRING with loosening of the ice pack and appearance of the open-water channels called leads (pronounced "leeds"), the men of Wales launched two umiaks to begin hunting for walruses and bearded seals, and for ducks if the sea mammals were not around. This was the time of the northern migration of eider ducks, an enthralling spectacle. For several days, large flocks flew low over the water. Although old-squaw ducks were present in fewer numbers, their calls were the dominant sound of the season. I developed a loving appreciation for the noisy old-squaws as the harbinger of spring and new life, as I did when I was a boy for the red-winged blackbirds returning to the marshes of Peach Island in the Detroit River.

Not all of the Eskimos had shotguns, and shells were expensive, so I was a welcome member of the hunting crew. I was advised to take plenty of shotgun shells. Duck hunting was easy because the ducks didn't recognize the umiaks as dangerous until we were within easy range. Then it was flock shooting, with several birds raining down with each fusillade. We shot until our shotgun-shell bags were emptied.

When we returned to the shore ice, the dead birds were tossed into a big pile. Under guidance of the boat owner, the *umaluk* (OO-may-luk), one man would divide the ducks into smaller piles corresponding to the number of crew members. Then the umaluk would signal each man to a certain lot of the birds. Most were king eiders, with Pacific eiders next in abundance, followed by spectacled eiders. We didn't shoot Steller's eiders, old-squaw ducks, or harlequin ducks because they were too small.

In 1947 the vagaries of weather and ice conditions carried the walrus herds through the Bering Strait mostly beyond the reach of the Wales hunters. Only a small number of walruses were harvested during the spring, and a few more in the fall, all being shot while swimming. Unfortunately, unless the animals can be killed while they are out of the water and on the ice, the loss through sinking is very high—except for adult females, which tend to float. I felt bad about the number of walruses I saw lost. Additional animals might have been saved if the boats had carried more harpoons, which were thrown into an animal that had been shot so the body could be retrieved by hauling on the harpoon's line. But here the hunters respected tradition: two harpoons were the proper number in each boat. Except for a small, metal cutting-blade on the tip of the detachable toggle head, the harpoon design and structure probably dated to the dawn of the Inupiat marine-mammal-hunting culture.

The split-walrus-hide coverings of umiaks must be replaced every few years. However, their wooden frames seem to have perpetual life, though various parts need periodic replacement. There were no blueprints, only an existing model. Worn or broken parts were used as templates to fashion replacements from driftwood. It is likely the continuous use of particular umiaks at Wales dated back centuries. During our time at Wales, Bob Tokiana, assisted by a few others, began rebuilding an umiak from a long-collapsed frame that had lain near his house since the death of its umaluk many years before. Bob had long watched for and collected pieces of driftwood for the reconstruction. His quest was prolonged because wood suitable for longitudinal members and keel were rarely found and then, unfortunately, were sometimes spotted first by firewood gatherers. But Bob persevered. Eighteen months after work started, the frame was finished and several women sewed the walrus-hide covering over it, increasing the village's umaluk population to four and its seagoing capability by a quarter.

Whaling gear — relics of the Yankee whaling era, consisting of a brass shoulder gun and a darting gun with harpoon, line, and sealskin floats attached — was always ready in the bow of the umiaks. We saw many bowhead whales, and got prepared a few times when one seemed headed in our direction. Generally, however, the hunters didn't make a spirited effort to go after them. In fact, the last whale that had been landed here was taken by Arthur Nagasruk and his crew in 1935, though some had since been struck and lost. Many bearded seals, *oogruks*, were taken, however,

which fortunately provided a good supply of the most favored meat and skins.

Hunting bearded seals required special care, and a good
measure of luck seemed associated with every one taken.
During passage through the Bering Strait, these seals seldom hauled out on the ice. They were frequently heard before they were seen, because they vocalize under water. By
holding the blade of a wooden boat paddle in the water with
the other end to your ear, you can hear their singing. The
intensity of the sound varies with distance. If a singing seal
is very close, the sound seems to rise weirdly from the water all around the boat.

When a bearded seal was sighted, the hunters tried not
to shoot at its head since, if killed instantly, it would sink
and be lost. But in the act of diving, this seal raises its back a
little above the water's surface; this is the target. A hit on
the body disables the animal so it can be harpooned before
dying. Shooting open-sighted rifles from the boat didn't
make for accurate shooting; a fusillade of bullets gave the
best chance of hitting the animal. The seal, in these waters,
probably faced little danger before firearms were introduced.

BEFORE COMING TO WALES I bought a military surplus sheep-
skin parka called a DVG, designed by Colonel Dale V.
Gaffney while he was commanding officer of Ladd Field
early in World War II. Bertha had a muskrat parka made by
Laura Wright in Fairbanks. The Inupiat women were curious about these garments, even to the stitching. Their own
parkas were made of reindeer skins (ground-squirrel skins
for children's parkas) and showed the effects of long wear.
They told us that until recent years, they always had plenty
of reindeer but now they were all gone.

In the 1890s, reindeer (domesticated Eurasian caribou) were introduced from Siberia to improve the life of Alaska Natives. The animals thrived on the Seward Peninsula, including the vicinity of Wales, and soon spread widely. By the mid-1930s, there were some 650,000 reindeer in more than a hundred herds scattered along the coastal region from Barrow to Kodiak Island. Given such abundance, it was unimaginable that they could disappear, but they did so at Wales and other areas in the late 1930s and early 1940s.

Why did the early promise and success of the reindeer introduction go awry? One cause was that the Inupiat people are village dwellers and hunters by tradition and preference, rather than herdsmen. The first coming of reindeer offered benefits without demanding much lifestyle change. Reindeer husbandry at Wales began in the 1890s and continued for half a century as a bountiful supplement to the hunting of marine mammals. After an early period of rapid increase, the herd stabilized, declined, scattered, and then disappeared altogether as the virgin forage of lichens and sedges in the vicinity was grazed off. The Inupiat men put the blame on too much killing of the reindeer, by both humans and wolves.

Federal officials largely ignored possibilities of incorporating reindeer into the Natives' subsistence lifestyle, and instead promoted maximum production for commercial enterprises. This strategy required constant herding of animals to new grounds and a nomadic existence for herders. The Natives weren't inclined in that direction, but white entrepreneurs were. The Lomen Corporation in Nome owned several herds, hiring local whites, Natives, and even Lapps from Scandinavia as managers and herders. Lomen exported large quantities of hides and meat during the late 1920s and 1930s, but when markets faltered, the federal government in 1940 bought all reindeer owned by whites and conveyed most of them to Natives. In the pattern seen at Wales, these herds withered away.

Several hunters at Wales commented to me about their shareholdings in the now defunct Cape Reindeer Company and seemed to entertain a forlorn yearning that reindeer would return. But the occasional stray animal that wandered into the area, probably from the Topkok herd at Teller, was shot as wild game. The people's continued dependence on reindeer skins for parkas, bedding, and sinew for sewing was mostly satisfied with the help of the Alaska Native Service in arranging transfer of these products from a federally owned herd on Nunivak Island and from a few remaining small herds in other areas.

By good fortune, some reindeer-leg skins, cherished by the Natives for mukluks, became available during our time at Wales from an unusual source. On a chilly, drizzly morning in late June 1947, with scattered ice still in the Bering Strait, two wooden whaleboats powered by outboard motors, each carrying twelve Siberian Eskimos, arrived at Wales. Because of Cold War tensions, only a few of the village men ventured down to greet the visitors; most others were cautious until they could learn the nature of their trip. It was a trading expedition on its way to Nome.

Percy Ipalook, the Presbyterian minister, invited the Siberians to stay in the school building, empty for the summer. I reported their arrival to my military intelligence contact before Bertha and I went to meet them. Some wore fragments of uniforms—hats and tunics—but otherwise they certainly didn't look military. Speaking the Inupiat language, the lone woman in the group told Bertha that she had not wished to come, because she was pregnant and had to leave a large family behind. The authorities at East Cape, Siberia, had ordered her to make the trip anyway, perhaps thinking that a woman's presence would convey the benign nature of their visit.

These traders wanted liquor, and when they discovered none was available, asked whether they could get it at Nome. When told yes, they became quite stingy with their goods. But they were tempted by cigarettes and canned fruit from our pantry, offering a few reindeer-leg skins in exchange. They showed quantities of colorful fossilized walrus ivory, commonly picked on beaches or along sloughing banks, but the Wales people wanted reindeer skins above all else. Ersatz fossil ivory produced by soaking new ivory in coffee or tea served the Wales carvers well enough if the real product was scarce. The Wales store manager obtained several bundles of reindeer-leg skins in exchange for coffee, sugar, and canned condensed milk. The Siberians went on to Nome, returning in early July, presumably with a different cargo.

I SENT WORD TO FRANK WHALEY that I was interested in buying his Piper J-5 Cub, and one day he landed it on the sandy beach in front of the village. The airplane looked good and the price was fair, so I bought it. Bertha and I now had freedom to get around the region as well as an independent means of transport in an emergency. Beach-combing became a favorite recreation, and I landed on many interesting beaches. Dead walruses were common, and attracted fox and wolverines. These animals would usually scurry away as the airplane approached, although one wolverine decided to hide inside a well-decomposed walrus carcass, peeking up at us as the airplane circled. This poor fellow might have been well fed, but he would certainly need a bath after his feeding orgy.

Most of the walrus carcasses were headless, probably from encounters with King Island or Little Diomede hunters who were after ivory, because the Wales people didn't abandon carcasses of the relatively few walruses they were able to get that season. I collected two nice sets of tusks, though it was a stinky chore to chop them free of the skull.

Whenever I flew to Nome, I carried a list of things to pick up for the village store or individual Eskimos, but I drew the line on sacks of coal. The Eskimos were delighted I had the little J-5 Cub; they not only knew it could help them in an emergency, but seemed to think it elevated the status of the community.

After freezeup, I put the airplane on skis, which opened an even wider choice of landing places. Roy Snyder, a Civil Aeronautics Administration mechanic who was half Eskimo and an avid hunter and fisherman, came to Wales periodically to service our generators at the weather station. He was always eager to fly with me, beach-combing or looking for a stream containing arctic char. We found superlative fishing, catching char weighing up to ten pounds in Mint River, a fifteen-minute flight from Wales.

During our talks about hunting, Roy told me that Bill Munz and Jack Whaley had both shot wolves from their airplanes. Munz landed on the tundra near the wolves and shot them with a rifle, but Whaley carried a gunner who shot the animals with a shotgun from the air. Roy was trying to whet my interest, but was too polite to actually suggest we hunt wolves. Nevertheless, on his next visit in November, he brought along a few boxes of twelve-gauge buckshot loads just in case I might have use for them.

Blanche Peterson operated a store in Teller, and we communicated with her regularly over our radio. When I asked whether the reindeer herders there had been troubled by wolves, she said yes. Just the previous day some men had left Teller to help find reindeer from the local herd, which had been scattered by marauding wolves. This was exciting news for prospective wolf hunters. Roy and I loaded a couple of extra cans of gasoline into the J-5 and headed toward Teller, just down the Bering coast southeast of Wales, with wolves on our minds.

On reaching the main reindeer herd, we flew in ever-widening circles looking for wolves or wolf tracks. We saw tracks in abundance, but on closer inspection, they always proved to be those of reindeer. We directed our search northward, toward home. As we approached the foothills, I saw several dark spots in a line that looked unnatural. We had found a pack of wolves, and they were already racing for the rough terrain ahead. As we approached them, I slowed the airplane and descended to no more than thirty feet above the terrain so that Roy could shoot out of the right side. When we were almost even with the animals, two of them turned under the airplane and the others swung away from us. Roy shot and missed by several yards. I isolated one wolf, and after several passes, Roy scored a perfect hit in the head, neck, and shoulder, killing the animal.

Back in Wales the dead wolf created a stir. It seemed that everyone able to walk came to the weather station to examine and touch it gingerly, the first wolf most of them had ever seen in one piece. I didn't claim the bounty because it would have required sending the skin to Fairbanks or Anchorage and, furthermore, I didn't have a current hunting license. Bertha and a woman from the village tanned the pelt, which was then transformed into parka ruffs, one of which still does service on my snowsuit. A few days later, we bagged a second wolf near the reindeer herd. Roy took this trophy pelt with him back to Anchorage where he presented it for the bounty, which now amounted to fifty dollars.

Pressing our luck a bit too far, Roy and I came very close to ending it all one late afternoon after an unsuccessful search for wolves. We stopped at Teller, fueled the airplane, and bought a half reindeer carcass before starting back to Wales. On the way home we saw a wolverine on the gentle slope of a mountain. Wolverine skins are highly valued for parka ruffs because frost is easily brushed off. We attempted to shoot the animal from the air, and planned then to land and pick it up.

Roy missed three or four shots, and the animal burrowed under the snow. This should have alerted me that the snow was quite deep. I landed the airplane upslope, and we stopped with the right wingtip almost over the hole where the wolverine was hiding. The wolverine burst out of the snow, and Roy shot it from his seat.

Only then did I realize conditions were not good for getting airborne again. The snow was dry, light, and so deep that the aft part of the fuselage and the horizontal stabilizers were resting on it. We got the airplane turned to face downhill, but with our load, it wouldn't move down the slope. Straight ahead of us the slope, at an angle of about fifteen degrees, continued and steepened slightly for nearly half a mile—then ended abruptly in a cliff above a deep, narrow ravine with a steep wall beyond.

We were able to get the airplane moving with Roy jogging alongside, pushing on the wing strut. Once under way at four or five miles an hour, Roy climbed aboard, and we began to accelerate. When I could lift the tail and feel the skis riding up on the snow, I tried slight back-pressure on the stick, which only caused the tail to drag again. We continued to move down the slope toward the cliff.

The next time we approached flying speed, I let the airplane decide when it wanted to fly. We were flying in ground effect, supported by that little extra lift gained with the wings near the surface, when we ran off the cliff. I felt an awful sinking sensation and pushed the stick forward to restore lift to the stalled wings. We were diving into the narrow ravine with the opposite wall looming ahead. With a turn left, down the ravine, we were safe. I silently resolved not to cut it so close again. Roy was a fearless passenger with total faith in me. Just minutes later, we saw wolf tracks and he was ready to go again, but I wasn't.

IN NOVEMBER 1948 we witnessed an unusual wildlife passage. A great mass of southward-migrating spotted seals appeared in front of the weather station. There must have been many thousands; they passed for hours in a tight, narrow band. The seals were accompanied by many killer whales, as singles or in small groups, cruising leisurely close among them without raising any fuss. Probably the great predators were already satiated and the seals somehow sensed they were little threatened. Perhaps, too, an individual seal's security rested on being a small unit in a large mass. Trying to flee the whales could have destroyed its best defense.

During our first winter at Wales, I began going on the sea ice to hunt ringed seals, initially with others, and then alone. Two of the men, Willie Senungetuk and his half brother Andrew Seetuk, would stop by the station and invite me to go with them. The method of hunting was to sit by a strip of open water (a lead) and wait for a seal to surface near enough to be shot in the head. Ringed seals, being always fat, float well after they are killed. If a dead seal didn't drift to the edge of the ice, it could usually be retrieved with a seal hook, a gourd-shaped piece of wood having sharp, bent-nail-like projections, attached to a throwing line. When I shot a seal, I would give it to Willie or Andrew.

These two also fished for seals under the ice at night, using a large mesh net made of thin rawhide, similar to the *babiche* used for snowshoe webbing by Natives of the Interior. They would take their net and ice chisel on a sled in the afternoon, cut holes in the ice, and with the aid of thin driftwood poles, string the net under the ice between the holes. Then, through the hours of darkness, they sat in the shelter of snow blocks waiting for a seal to be caught, detectable by jerks of the net line. It was a cold vigil, and I suggested to them one afternoon that we build a domed snow igloo as a place for us to wait. They had seen pictures of them but indicated only a skeptical interest.

I had studied the construction technique in Vilhjalmur Stefansson's *Arctic Manual*. With good snowdrifts handy, we picked a spot and began cutting blocks with our butcher knives. Stefansson recommended using a snow saw, but we did all right without one. Willie and Andrew could cut and bring the blocks to me as fast as I could trim and set them. In a little over two hours, the spiral of blocks was up and I fitted the last one in place at the top. We patted snow in the cracks, built a tunnel entrance, and crawled inside to sit on the snow bench. Light penetrated, making it bright, and it seemed warm right away. Willie and Andrew were thrilled, laughing and giggling like kids. The net line was led into the igloo and the hunters sat in comfort.

For several days, that igloo was an attraction. Every local hunter looked it over, inside and out. Many boys went out to see it, actually crawling on top, for it was amazingly strong. But when a south wind came, bringing thawing temperatures, the igloo went through a weird change. It slowly involuted, the central part bending inward until it touched the floor without ever breaking. The Wales men were too conservative to embrace such a cultural curiosity; I don't think another domed igloo was ever built.

CHAPTER FOURTEEN

Medicine Man

OUR SECOND SPRING and summer at Wales were delightful. I enjoyed going along in the umiaks, and the walrus
hunting was more productive than the previous year. On
two occasions we went to Fairway Rock, some fifteen miles
out in Bering Strait, and gathered murre and gull eggs. There
we met a group of hunters from Little Diomede who were
doing the same thing. These hunters from the American island on the U.S.-Russia border had several walrus heads in
their umiak, but no meat. I had heard of their head-hunting,

taking only the heads for the ivory and discarding the meat, but seeing the evidence was sobering. I knew that the people in Wales could use a lot more walrus meat than they had.

Bertha loved to go berry picking and socialize with the women of Wales. In July the small herd of reindeer at Teller was herded into a corral for marking and some butchering. I flew there to bring back fresh meat, and fawn skins to be made into parkas. All was going smoothly for us, but having developed a closeness to the people, our serenity was to be affected by events that didn't at first concern us.

Bad news that arrived with the supply vessel *North Star* caused an ominous stir in the village. Alaska Native Service officials came ashore, met with the village elders, but avoided us. They told the villagers that there would be no teachers at Wales in the coming year, and implied it was their fault because of the way they had treated the last teachers. That, we knew, was nonsense, even malicious. These teachers had never experienced life outside of a city, with its cultural and social support systems, and they simply couldn't adjust to the isolation of a remote Eskimo village. Not wanting to admit this fact, they concocted other excuses for leaving. This situation meant, in addition to no schooling for the children, that many of the village problems the teachers normally handled—such as dispensing first aid and medicines, arranging evacuations for the ill, and counseling—would fall to me and Bertha.

TWO BOYS ABOUT TEN YEARS OLD, while wrestling in a house, fell on bedding and the blade of an unnoticed pair of shears punctured one of them in the back. The accident wasn't reported to me until the boy became very ill. I examined him and got a sinking feeling on seeing a large swelling between his shoulder blades and a smaller one at the base of his spine. He was feverish and only semiconscious. The weather was terrible, with no hope of flying out or of getting an airplane in from Nome or Kotzebue. Over the radio, I explained the problem to Dr. E. S. Rabeau at the Public Health Service hospital in Kotzebue. He judged the boy's condition critical and told me immediate action was necessary. First, he said, get penicillin from the school supplies and inject staggering unit numbers.

This I could handle. But next I had to incise those large pus sacs. Dr. Rabeau must have known how that would hit me, because he quickly added that it had to be done and he would take the responsibility. He told me to boil razor blades, slice the pus sacs open, and apply hot towel compresses, changing them often. I got everything ready and went back to the patient, who lived with his mother and sister.

I approached the task with a trepidation that was greater than when I pulled my own teeth. At least then I could feel what was happening; here I didn't know what to expect when I started cutting. After cleaning the boy's back with rubbing alcohol, and with a good grip on the razor blade, I made a firm cut about four inches long. Nothing much happened. The skin was so tough, it felt like cutting sandpaper. It simply spread apart, showing the white connective tissue of the deeper dermis layers. I put more pressure to it on the next try and opened a mess that threatened to gag me, not from smell but from appearance. I finished the job and then left a stack of clean towels, with instructions for them to be changed every hour.

Early the next morning I was dismayed to find the mother and sister asleep when I knocked. The mother must have tended the boy through most of the night and then dropped off to sleep from fatigue. The sick boy had rolled over on his back; reindeer hair from his bed was matted and dried in the wounds. Draining had stopped. We got the incisions cleaned up and draining again, but his fever still raged. The following day, the weather improved enough to allow the mail plane to get in and take the boy to Kotzebue. Dr. Rabeau reported that the boy would recover. He came home in a couple of weeks, full of life and stories of his unexpected visit to Kotzebue.

Villagers increasingly came to the weather station seeking help. With access to the school's medicine chest, I could sometimes help them. Aspirin was my only prescription for the many earaches. I had striking success with two young men, recently returned from Nome, who were experiencing a burning sensation when they urinated. From the many VD lectures I had heard in the army, I recognized gonorrhea; sulfa and penicillin recommended by Dr. Rabeau cleared it up quickly.

Pulling teeth was one thing I dreaded and refused to do. I told people they would have to wait for the mail plane and then fly to a real dentist. Alfred Mazona, an enormous Eskimo, pleaded with me on several successive days to pull a tooth. He refused to go to Nome. I finally recognized he seemed to have an abscess that began involving his sinus. His face was badly swollen. I agreed to try to pull the huge upper molar. As I got the pliers closed on the tooth, it just fell out. I loaded Alfred with penicillin, and made a friend for life.

My community service role even extended to counseling the Presbyterian minister, Percy Ipalook. The influence of religion in the lives of the Wales people was hard to gauge, and Percy worried about it. After killing a polar bear, there was a custom that the men gather in their communal house, the kasgi, where the lucky hunter would perform a strenuous dance until overcome by exhaustion. The dance assured that no offense was meant toward the animal and the hunter might again expect to kill a bear. Percy frowned on the practice, which he thought was an expression of superstition not supportive of his religious teachings. A polar bear had recently been taken by Bob Tokeina, an elder in the church, and Percy told Bob that the bear dance was unnecessary and should not be performed. Bob replied, "Yes, but I have big family; can't afford to take chances." I didn't help Percy much, and maybe aggravated his problem, when I noted that Bob Tokeina killed most of the bears taken by the Wales hunters.

During our second winter at Wales, I felt reasonably competent as a hunter myself, having gone alone out to the open-water leads and taken ringed seals many times. Mainly, though, my intention in going out there was to see a polar bear, and if conditions were right, to bag one. During one of these solo ventures, as I was some two miles out on the ice northwest of the Cape Prince of Wales, a snowstorm with winds of extraordinary fury suddenly struck. I was nearly blinded by the blowing and ground-drifting snow; the strength of the wind made anything but crawling impossible.

To say I could see six feet ahead would be an exaggeration. I knew the wind came from the southeast when it first began, and this was my only reference. I crawled until the light failed without recognizing anything, but I knew that if the wind direction didn't shift, I should eventually come to the mountains behind the village. Finally, something dark showed under my mitten, and I focused on it, brushing the snow aside. It was a brick, then I found two more, then another. I knew there were bricks next to one of the buildings at the weather station. Turning left, I crawled ten or twelve feet and was home.

ON JANUARY 6, 1949, hunters Lawrence Mazenna, Raphael Patunac, and Gregory Ayak, following fresh polar bear tracks, moved onto drifting pack ice near King Island, in the Bering Sea south of Wales. They were experts in judging whether it was safe to hunt on moving ice, but they neglected their usual cautious assessment in the heat of tracking the bear. An open-water lead opened in the ice and it was impossible for them to return to the island. They drifted away.

The men were swept north atop the floating ice, past the Diomede Islands and into the Chukchi Sea. Aerial searches failed to find them. After almost three weeks of drifting and wandering on the sea ice, Gregory Ayak found himself back on snow-covered land. His tracks were discovered by an Eskimo trapper, Arnold Olanna, and followed to a shelter cabin thirty miles northeast of Wales. Gregory, the lone survivor, was taken to a nearby hunting camp. His hunting companions were never seen again.

Arnold's brother, Elliot, with his dog team raced to Wales, bringing me a long note Gregory had written to his mother and a Jesuit missionary. I immediately transmitted the note to King Island over our radio. It told the story of the three men's ordeal.

> One man just found me yesterday at 12 p.m. at this Sinrazat shelter cabin after I had slept four days through. I stop here after I walk for three days out in the country. I got to land on 17th last week. When we first got away from Island we were in good all of us. And next day comes it was snowing and damp and that day and then night come we got all wet and heavy. And when the third day comes Lawrence couldn't walk much longer. His end of left leg start to hurt and his stomach and so we got very slow. And that day he is going to left his

stuff behind. And so I start to drag his hunting bag for him. Take all the heavy stuff off. And that night when my shoulders start feel tired took it off and stop to have little sleep. And fourth day he couldn't walk and he told us to go on to try to get to save place. And covered him with little snow, and he tell us to say prayer for him. After we left him and say our prayer for him and we start out again. We didn't want to left him behind. He told us to go on and start walk as young ice is moving. Very cold day. And on the fifth day I start to feel my left foot freeze and so does Raphael start to feel his feet too and his hands. And no longer he couldn't keep up with me. And finally he couldn't even stand up. I let try three times. He said he couldn't make it and start to cry. Told me to go. He said he will pray for me to get to save place.

Only Son
Gregory Ayak

With his frozen feet, Gregory required medical attention as quickly as possible, the nearest professional help being at Nome. Unfortunately, daylight was fast fading and my airplane was in storage for the winter in a Quonset hut at the station, with the wings off. Several men were at the station to hear me talk with the teacher at King Island, and when I told them I could use some help with the airplane, everyone eagerly volunteered. It took us all night to shovel snowdrifts away from the building, get the airplane out, put the wings on, connect the aileron cables, and fill the fuel tank.

At the first break of morning light, the engine was heated, and I started my takeoff on a freshly frozen lead in front of the village. Crystals that had formed on the ice surface had the effect of sand or grit as the aluminum skis moved across it. This extra drag kept the airplane from accelerating, and with the fixed-pitch propeller, the little engine would not turn up to full power. At about twenty miles per hour, the drag and thrust seemed equal. I must have poked along almost a mile before the airplane began to accelerate further, and just in time, for I could see an ice pressure ridge ahead coming closer. Just at the point where I had to either abort the takeoff or fly, the airplane mushed into the air.

I quickly located the hunting camp and landed roughly on a section of the hard, wavelike snowdrifts known as sastrugi. Arnold Olanna and I put Gregory in my emergency sleeping bag before taking him to the airplane and loading him on for the trip to Nome. The flight became agonizingly slow as we encountered an increasing headwind. An ambulance was waiting at the airstrip.

After retrieving my sleeping bag at the hospital and wishing Gregory a good recovery, I hastened to fuel up and start back to Wales. I never received the message Bertha sent to me, advising me to stay at Nome because winds at Wales had increased to near hurricane force. Instead I flew toward Wales, pushed by the strong winds that were now at my tail; it was exhilarating to see the peaks whizzing by.

I stayed on the upwind side of the higher mountains to avoid downdrafts, but encountered turbulence and updrafts that carried me ever higher into colder air with the engine at idle power. I applied full carburetor heat to discourage ice from forming and choking off the fuel flow, and I worried that the fickle little engine would stop, as it was known to do, if it got too cool. Approaching Wales, I was still above three thousand feet. By the time I completed my turn in preparation for landing, the wind had blown me miles out over the Strait.

The J-5 Cub could fly as slow as thirty miles an hour, but no faster than seventy-five. Descending steeply to keep the propeller windmilling and hoping the offshore wind would lessen at lower altitude, my airspeed generated sounds from the wings and fuselage I had never heard before. At an altitude of about three hundred feet, it was an enormous relief to have the cold engine respond to full power and see that I was slowly clawing back toward the hazy, distant coast. Now my problem was to land and secure the airplane.

I considered landing just in the lee of the station buildings, but when I got close enough, that looked too dangerous. There were sand dunes within a few yards of the station in the direction of an approach, and I was afraid of turbulence there too. So I landed on the sea ice in front of the station. Nearly full engine power barely held the airplane in place.

I saw figures struggling out on the ice toward me. One was Ernest Oxeorok, our maintenance man. He was carrying an ice chisel for use in cutting ice bridges — short trenches connected at the bottom — for securing tie-down lines. But then, I was horrified when a person moved in front of the plane. He was fighting to keep from sliding right into the propeller. I had to lift off quickly, back into the air — which was necessary anyway to let Ernest cut ice bridges. I must have hovered for a quarter hour before the ice bridges were ready and I could land again. Three men moved in from each side and grabbed the wing struts. I cut the engine, jumped out with the lines, and we got the airplane safely tied down.

That done, someone hollered a warning, and we saw an oil drum tumbling and bouncing toward us from the direction of the village. We could only hold our position by leaning acutely or going to all fours, so it was impossible to dodge, even if we could anticipate which way to go. The fast-moving drum went under the right wing, missing us, but hitting the wing strut, bending it upward.

From the first word of Gregory Ayak being found, it had been thirty-six hectic hours. Dazed from lack of sleep, I still felt a glow of relief and satisfaction. I recounted the whole event to Ed Fortier, publisher of the weekly newspaper *The Forty Ninth Star*, and he was able to talk to Gregory. Later he wrote a small book about the incident, titled *One Survived*.

ONE CLEAR AFTERNOON in early March of 1949, a Taylorcraft landed on the ice and parked next to my J-5 Cub. I went out to meet the pilot, who was Dr. Terris Moore, director of the Boston Museum of Science. He said he hoped to fly to Little Diomede Island, in Bering Strait twenty-seven miles west of Wales. He accepted my invitation to stay overnight with us.

Moore had flown his little airplane across the continent during the previous couple of weeks. Beyond the pure adventure of the flight, his purpose was to meet with the Board of Regents of the University of Alaska to be interviewed for the position of university president. (This encounter would occur during his return trip—and he got the job.) When we told him that Bertha and I had both attended the university, Moore enjoyed conducting his own interview well into the evening, asking us about the university and our experiences there.

In the morning I accompanied Moore to Little Diomede in my J-5. The flight was beautiful on a clear, windless day, and we were warmly welcomed by villagers who came out on the ice to greet us. Okpeoluk invited us into his one-room home, which we entered by way of a short tunnel and then up through a hole in the floor. The roof, with a small skylight in the center, was supported by the jawbones of bowhead whales. A bench was built around three of the four low walls, and a flat, stone, seal-oil lamp burned with an oval ribbon of blue flame. When a bit of yellow flame appeared in the lamp, Okpeoluk's wife simply touched the moss wick with her fingers, restoring the perfect blue burn.

We had a pleasant visit with a group of elders. Our hosts served coffee, pilot bread, and dried seal meat in oil. Moore skipped the latter, though I genuinely liked it. I felt real pride in the Little Diomede Eskimos for showing such hospitality and revealing a facet of Alaska to Moore that few outsiders would ever see.

Terris Moore wasn't the only one who had his eye on joining the University of Alaska. My infatuation with wildlife and hunting and fishing had led to thoughts about conservation. It was alarming that past excessive exploitation of bowhead whales and later of walruses by the American whaling fleet was likely still affecting the life of the Eskimos. I visualized other wildlife being subject to similar abuses. The Alaska Game Commission and a handful of agents, most of whom I had met or read about since my first days in Alaska, had long focused on hunting and trapping restrictions without knowing much about the actual condition of the animals themselves. It seemed to me wildlife management would become ever more necessary in Alaska. Despite this growing interest, I had only a vague notion that career opportunities might be available to me in this field. Nevertheless, after more than two enjoyable and rewarding years at Wales, I needed to seek a different career than was offered by our life in a remote Eskimo village. Bertha and I decided to move back to Fairbanks so I could resume studies at the University of Alaska. This decision meant selling my beloved J-5 Cub. I temporarily became a ground gripper, a derisive Army Air Corps term applied to nonflyers.

TOP LEFT: Summer vacations to farms of relatives in Ohio were the happiest days of my youth. 1929. TOP RIGHT: A Fourth of July picnic in 1926 at Belle Isle in Detroit was the occasion for this photograph of me and my younger sister, Hazel. My costume probably reflects my father's liking for maritime things. BOTTOM LEFT: Dogfish sharks caught from the CCC *Wanigan 12* in Naha Bay, June 1940. I was more than a little proud when sending this photograph to my family in Detroit. These monsters dwarfed anything I had caught in Lake St. Clair or the Detroit River. BOTTOM RIGHT: Basic flight training in the BT-13. Merced, California, 1943.

TOP: A copy of this photo taken on the Chatanika River a few days before joining the Army Air Corps in September 1942 remained in my wallet and stirred happy memories throughout my tour of duty. MIDDLE: This fuzzy snapshot at John Salaga's Kantishna River cabin survives because I included it with a letter to my sister Hazel in the spring of 1942. BOTTOM LEFT: Carl Hult with sled dogs arriving at his Sugar Bowl cabin, 1930s. BOTTOM RIGHT: A free day in Spinazzola, Italy. April 1945. From left, navigator William Anderson, pilot Jim Brooks, and bombardier Arnold Hanson.

TOP: This veteran Piper J-5 stayed in Nome when we returned to Fairbanks in 1949. The plane had a top speed of 70 mph, but was light in weight and could safely venture into places that would be problematic for Super-Cubs. MIDDLE: Wales Inupiat hunters pulled their umiak through an ice pressure ridge to the safety of shore-fast ice after an unsuccessful day of hunting bowhead whales in the Bering Strait. April 1947. BOTTOM: Dr. Francis H. "Bud" Fay observes the objects of his life-long-scientific research during our expedition to Round Island in Togiak Bay, June 1958. The animals were tolerant of our presence if we moved slowly and quietly.

TOP: Soviet Eskimos departing Wales in June 1947. They wanted liquor, but on discovering none was available, ended up trading their reindeer-leg skins for coffee, sugar, canned milk and fruit, and cigarettes. UPPER MIDDLE: The arrival of an airplane at Little Diomede would bring a welcoming committee and invitations to homes for *coopiak* (coffee). Soviet-controlled Big Diomede Island is two and a quarter miles distant. The author's J-5 Cub, March 1949. LOWER MIDDLE: Inupiat hunters on the shore ice near Cape Prince of Wales wait for their coffee water to heat and for walrus to come into view. May 1948. BOTTOM: Eskimos departing Little Diomede in quest of Walrus, May 1953.

TOP: For an instant, I didn't know whether this ram fell to a bullet or a lightning strike. BOTTOM: Wooded Island sea lion rookery occupied by breeding bulls, females, and recently born pups. June 1958.

ABOVE: This large beluga disappeared quickly as Native women carried it away as fast as it was butchered. The skin was relished as food for humans, though much of the flesh went to happy sled dogs. In earlier times, belugas were an important subsistence resource in Bristol Bay. May 1954. With the development of commercial salmon fisheries, Natives became less dependent on marine mammals. Levelock on the Kvichak River, May 1954. OPPOSITE TOP: Sea lion pups are perfectly docile. We marked most of the pups by attaching cattle-ear tags to their front flippers. Only one tag was seen again, that being on a live pup found on the beach in Homer. The crew of a halibut-fishing vessel had taken the animal aboard at the rookery and released it near Homer. OPPOSITE MIDDLE: Clear of Hinchinbrook Entrance and headed across northern Gulf of Alaska to the Wooded Island sea lion rookery. June 1957. OPPOSITE BOTTOM: The night-marauding brown bear where he fell just outside our cabin door. October 1956.

TOP LEFT: A special scale allowed weighing polar bears by lifting them with the helicopter. This four-year-old male weighed 425 pounds. Pilot Joe Soloy, biologist Sterling Eide. TOP RIGHT: Despite the frost, clear days on the Chukchi Sea made for easy aerial tracking and handling of polar bears, March 1971. BOTTOM: We numbered polar bears with indelible dye to avoid recapture. Such markings also protected the bears from guides and their trophy hunters who complained bitterly.

TOP: Juneau offered great opportunities for a boy to learn the joys of the great outdoors. Here son Lewis happily poses with his first king salmon. Harris Harbor, Juneau, 1959. BOTTOM: The author with a sow polar bear and twin cubs that are about twenty-seven months old. They are tranquilized and can be measured and ear-tagged without risk. Chukchi Sea, March 1971.

TOP: Our cabin at Farragut Bay was built in 1953 and used only infrequently. Wildlife came to consider it part of the natural environment. When we were inside, Canada geese, moose, wolves, and bear commonly appeared in the front yard, taking no notice of the airplane. 2002. BOTTOM: The mountains and forests surrounding Juneau beckoned Christa. She hurried to hike every trail and search out the berry patches and mushrooms, reliving the delights of childhood.

TOP: On top of Mount McGinnis with Lynn Canal in background. Wife Christa led the way and took photographs to validate our conquest. July 1977. BOTTOM: Farragut Bay Tootsie, a noble and biddable Chesapeake that never asked for or received a harsh word. Always a house dog, yet under the toughest conditions she would retrieve a jacksnipe or a large goose without ruffling a feather. She showed an uncanny empathy with her human companions through the spectrum from jubilant feelings to depression. August 1998.

CHAPTER FIFTEEN

Flying with the Birds

AT THE UNIVERSITY OF ALASKA, I was elated to learn of plans to introduce a curriculum in fish and wildlife management within a year or two. In the meantime I registered in the pre-medical curriculum to get relevant biology courses. Druska Carr (later Schaible) was head of the small Department of Biological Sciences and taught most of the courses. It was my good fortune to have such a demanding and inspiring teacher early in my academic efforts.

The same year, Neil Hosley arrived on campus to establish a U.S. Fish and Wildlife Service cooperative wildlife research unit. In 1950 three additional teachers arrived: Jim Rearden to head up a new Department of Wildlife Management, and John Buckley and Brina Kessel to teach courses in biology with Druska Schaible in the Department of Biological Sciences. I switched my major to wildlife management.

For the first time, I was in contact with a group of non-Native people who shared my interests in wildlife and the natural environment. Close friendships developed quickly with professors and many fellow students.

I WAS HIRED IN 1951 to fly support for a waterfowl banding project on the Yukon River Delta. The operation involved placing aluminum leg bands on molting adult and nonflying juvenile geese and brant for the purpose of tracking their migrations and other information from bands later recovered and returned by hunters. I got the summer work after I talked with Clarence Rhode, Alaska regional director for the U.S. Fish and Wildlife Service, and he learned I was a pilot and was involved in wildlife studies. After being checked out in a Stinson Station Wagon on floats, I was instructed to fly alone to the village of Chevak, on the Kashunuk River near the Yukon Delta. The banding crew was waiting.

At Chevak there was no sign of people—only a frame building, a tent, and what looked like four or five small barabaras. I landed in a slough adjacent to the village, and four Yupik Eskimos —an elderly man, a woman, a teenage boy, and a small girl—came out of the tent to greet me. None spoke English.

I took off and flew in ever larger circles, hoping to find the banding crew or their camp. Instead I discovered a village with many new frame houses several miles to the west, a community that wasn't on my chart. I landed and learned this was New Chevak, a village recently relocated from the old site. The mystery deepened: no one knew anything about my wildlife people. It was late in the day, and I accepted the hospitality of Father Hargrieves for the night. He was an avid chess player and required that I stay up half the night playing against him.

The next morning I launched the search again, and found an outboard-powered skiff with waving men aboard near the mouth of the Kashunuk River. They were my party of bird banders: biologists Sigurd Olson and Edward Chatelain, physiologist Raymond Hock, and Mattie Peterson, a Yupik helper and guide. I had flown over their olive drab tents the previous day, but from the air they had blended into the tundra.

Chevak—Old Chevak, that is—was indeed the base of operations; supplies were cached in the frame building I had noticed on my first stop. On our return there, Sig Olson found an old *Outdoor Life* magazine in the building and was delighted to see an article in it written by his father. The pecking order in our group was affirmed when Ed Chatelain, with smiling majesty, insisted on reading it first.

Chatelain decided to hire Louie Friday, the teenage boy who was staying at Old Chevak, to help catch the flightless black brant and cackling geese for banding. Back at camp that night, we found that Louie had no bedding. He seemed unconcerned about it and lay down on a piece of corrugated sheet metal, with only a mosquito net as a blanket. This seemed to pain us more than it did him. I got a sleeping bag for him from the airplane's emergency gear.

Louie didn't understand much English and had no idea what we were doing. On his first outing, he eagerly helped round up the birds. After herding a large number into our net, which was staked in a U shape, we closed it, trapping the birds. Then working together as fast as we could, each bird was examined for sex, a numbered band placed on its leg, the data recorded, and the bird released.

Louie was excited by the initial catch; it must have looked like hunger would never come again, with all these succulent birds in our net. After the first bird was processed and released outside the trap, it went flapping away across the tundra, with Louie in hot pursuit. He caught it after a good chase and brought it back, thinking it had escaped. That we would catch these birds only to free them again surely confused him. He certainly had a right to wonder about us, since we were eating mostly military surplus rations in the presence of these tasty fowl.

ON DAYS WITH DECENT FLYING weather we handled fewer birds because Ed Chatelain always wanted to fly somewhere. His excuse was to survey waterfowl; his intent was to beachcomb. I enjoyed it too. We visited most every place between Bethel on the Kuskokwim River and Sheldons Point on the Yukon. Once I made the mistake of pointing out a dead walrus, and Ed insisted that we slog across a quarter-mile of muddy tide flats to chop the tusks out of the most bloated, putrid animal I had ever touched.

On one clear but windy day, Ed decided we would go to Tanunak, a village on Nelson Island, noted for the fine grass baskets that are woven there. We encountered moderate turbulence as we approached the north side of the island. I suggested we try again another day. Ed didn't want to turn around, and he talked me into continuing. The turbulence became severe.

Suddenly we were rolled almost upside down, with the nose dropping sharply; everything loose in the airplane fell to the side windows, windshield, and even the ceiling. I hadn't experienced such an unusual flight position since aviation cadet days, but I managed to right the plane almost as a reflex. We lost more altitude than I'd like to admit. This startling incident changed Ed's attitude and, with pale face and large eyes, he allowed that we might turn back. But by then we weren't far from Tanunak, so I went on and landed toward the beach. The tide was in and I taxied close to the village. Ed headed for the store to buy his grass baskets while I stayed with the airplane.

Soon the floats were hitting bottom because of the receding tide. I worked up a good sweat pushing the airplane out toward deeper water, but it was a losing proposition. The beach here was obviously very flat. Several village men saw my problem and came out to help me. Just as it was certain we would get ahead of the falling water and free the airplane, the church bells rang. My helpers heeded the call and deserted with hardly a good-bye, even though it wasn't Sunday. Ed returned about an hour later with his load of baskets, and then we waited for another seven hours for the tide to return. This gave him plenty of time to grouse about my letting the airplane go dry.

In the evenings, Raymond Hock entertained us with tales of his research dealing with mammal hibernation and temperature regulation. In his Anchorage laboratory he monitored several physiological parameters of a captive, semihibernating black bear. This required crawling into the bear's lair and, among other things, inserting a thermometer in the animal's anus. On one occasion the bear shook off its torpor and began to examine its roommate. Ray escaped, with the placid bear sniffing at Ray's buttocks as he crawled out. The experience led him to pioneer new (and safer) instrumentation for that kind of data gathering.

When we left Ray alone at camp, he made forays on the tundra to set snap traps for rodents and live traps for arctic hares. Sometimes he forgot the locations of his traps, and we had to help search them out. Three live traps set for arctic hares were never found, which launched Ed Chatelain on a continuing discourse about the eccentricities of (other) scientists.

By the time young birds fledged and the adults were through the molt, we hip-booted biologists had banded more than two thousand black brant and cackling geese, testimony to how really abundant they were. Mattie Peterson told us the Natives shoot a lot of geese in the spring and later collect eggs for food as well. It appeared to us that this subsistence harvest could never be detectable against a background of such plenty. Probably unknown to most people hereabouts, the springtime goose shooting was illegal, but at this season enforcement agents always found duty in distant places. In earlier years, the Natives sold breast down taken from goose nests to the trader at Mountain Village. The trader told us he quit buying down, which he purchased by weight, when he found stones hidden in it.

A decade after my bird-banding experience, the numbers of black brant, cackling geese, and emperor geese declined alarmingly, due primarily to storm tides inundating nesting grounds, and then worsened by shooting. Attempts to help bring them back have been confounded by any number of roadblocks: Natives' assertion of subsistence rights, a larger human population, lead poisoning, politics, the bureaucracy. But in the summer of 1951, having coexisted with the Eskimos and their unique technologies for millennia, the clouds of waterfowl on the Yukon and Kuskokwim Deltas were an avian spectacle almost beyond comprehension.

CHAPTER SIXTEEN

With the Walrus Hunters

ON ST. PATRICK'S DAY 1952, Bertha gave birth to our son, Lewis. This new responsibility added seriousness to getting on with my education. I started course work at the University of Alaska toward a Master of Science degree even before receiving my bachelor's degree. My research subject was the life history of the walrus, and it would take me back to a familiar region and people, for the northward spring migration of walruses through Bering Strait.

I traveled back to Wales, where the villagers welcomed me like a returned family member. I began going out again in the umiak with my old hunting crew. As the men brought in the walruses they killed, I took various measurements. I also collected the bacula (penis bones, commonly called oosiks) from the males and a tooth from all of the animals, for use in trying to determine their age. With females, I also recorded whether they were carrying an unborn calf. The stomachs sometimes contained clams, which were eaten with gusto by the hunters, who said they were already cooked by the stomach. I too thought they were pretty good. During one of these plain seafood meals, it occurred to me that it was graduation time back on campus: I had received a Bachelor of Science degree in absentia that very day.

As the ice and the walruses moved northward, I went on to Wainwright and Barrow, where I continued my observations and specimen collections. At Wainwright a gentleman named Waldo Bodfish invited me to stay at his house. He was the son of a Yankee whaler who married an Eskimo and stayed at Wainwright after commercial bowhead whale hunting had ceased. Waldo himself was captain of an Eskimo whaling crew that caught one or more bowheads almost every year. He was generous in conveying a wealth of information about the manner of taking and utilizing marine mammals, but he had little knowledge of how often the various animals bred, how long they lived, or what the trends in their abundance might be. Such information was simply not evident because most marine mammals appear only briefly during seasonal migrations and their local abundance varies widely from year to year.

In late summer, with ill-concealed nervousness, I read a preliminary report of my walrus investigations at the Alaska Science Conference held at the Mount McKinley National

Park Hotel. The substance of my presentation was flimsy — mainly just counts of walrus killed and retrieved, size measurements, and some few data on calf/cow ratios — but new and interesting to many. It was memorable to me that the renowned Scottish ecologist F. Frazer Darling sought me out to encourage me in my work. Conscious of my earlier life as a hobo, gandy dancer, and trapper while others my age were attending high school and college, I was surprised and pleased to find acceptance by the academic community.

A Ph.D. candidate at the University of British Columbia, Francis H. (Bud) Fay, was also conducting research on the Bering Sea walrus, working on St. Lawrence Island. Bud was extremely helpful in giving me information, foreign translations, and a more scientific bent to my efforts. I was much better equipped for my second season of field research — but it got off to a rather scary start.

LITTLE DIOMEDE ISLAND, anchored right in the middle of Bering Strait, was the best place to examine a large number of walruses. I arranged to leave school early and arrive there in mid-April 1953, while the sea ice still allowed a ski-plane landing. After flying from Fairbanks to Kotzebue with Wien Airlines, I hired a young, well-respected bush pilot named Bill Levy to take me to Little Diomede in his Stinson Station Wagon. We flew into whiteout conditions where the diffused light caused the snow surface and low clouds to merge, wiping out the horizon — the milk bottle effect. Bill continued beyond the point where I felt comfortable, so I told him to turn back. Bill had no training in flying on instruments alone, so there was every likelihood we would crash if he lost visual contact with the snow.

We tried again the next day with the same result, except that Bill pushed farther into the bad weather, making me even more nervous. On our third attempt we were successful in reaching Little Diomede, though the weather was pretty nasty in places. Despite a penetrating cold wind and blowing snow, the entire population of the village seemed to appear on the ice as a welcoming committee.

I strongly urged Bill to delay his return flight to Kotzebue to await better weather. He declined, saying that he had to report in two days for induction into military service. It was his last flight. He crashed on the bleak north coast of the Seward Peninsula, where his wrecked plane was located two days later. Bill Levy was a precocious nineteen-year-old — a commercial pilot, owner of two airplanes and the Kotzebue movie theater. When Bertha and my friends at the university heard the airplane was missing, they had great concern for my safety; only after the wreck was found did they learn that I wasn't aboard. On Little Diomede, we belatedly heard of the accident on a radio news report.

ONE HUNDRED AND TEN Inupiat lived in the village perched just above the water on the steep, rocky west side of Little Diomede Island. Food resources were seasonally bountiful, including walruses, four species of seals, beluga whales, an occasional polar bear, fish, king crabs, and a multitude of seabirds. Despite the good nutrition these people enjoyed, mortality was high and the population had remained nearly stable for decades. Tuberculosis claimed two people shortly after my arrival. The coffins joined many others in various stages of decay, setting on the surface in the Inupiat tradition (an adaptation to living on permanently frozen ground), just a stone's throw above the village. The grief was deep, but outwardly brief. Orphan children were quickly adopted into the families of relatives.

A few very ancient, partly subterranean houses, made of stone, driftwood, and bowhead whale jawbones and ribs, with a tunnel entrance opening through the floor, were still in use. These were warm, dry, and easily heated with seal oil lamps. Other houses, built of lumber and tarpaper, were less comfortable and harder to keep warm, though better ventilated — which may have been a virtue, given the prevalence of tuberculosis.

The village store was similar to the one at Wales, operated by the local people, with the inventory purchased and shipped by the Alaska Native Service. In addition to nonperishable foods, there was a range of items from walrushide harpoon lines to a sweatshirt bearing the words "Diomede Alaska." A popular brand of twist-leaf chewing tobacco, Black Bull, was given away free. A large supply had been obtained some years before with the idea of trading it to the Siberians for reindeer skins. This trade ceased, and the tobacco speculators couldn't use it or even give it away since the Eskimos smoked only cigarettes or chewed plug tobacco. Jars of horseradish were also free for the taking; Father Tom Cunningham, the Jesuit missionary, was the only one who would touch it.

Each summer the people of Little Diomede traveled in their umiaks to Nome or Kotzebue, where they camped under the umiaks or with friends during July and August. This was a time for carving ivory and trading or selling surplus ivory. Their sled dogs were left behind on the island, turned loose and expected to forage on the nesting seabirds and their eggs. Pups born during this period were so wild that the Eskimos, upon returning, sometimes had to set fox traps to catch them.

In previous years I had become acquainted with most of
the men of Little Diomede during their visits to the mainland and my flights in the J-5 Cub to their island. Now, three
of them asked me to stay with their families. I declined because David and Bernadette Trantham, the schoolteachers,
invited me into their household and the spacious housing
unit in the school building. A tall, pleasant North Carolin-
ian, David came to Alaska with the Army and fell in love
with the country and with Bernadette, a full-blooded Eskimo
and a student at the university during my first year there.
David had organized a National Guard unit on Little
Diomede and served as the recruiting sergeant, medical officer, drill instructor, and keeper of the telescope.

A serious duty of the National Guard members, and the
only one I noticed, was using the telescope to scan for activity on Big Diomede Island, the Russian possession only two
miles away. People on Big Diomede, thought to be Soviet
soldiers, manned an observation post opposite Little
Diomede village. Men could be seen there at times, but the
only significant intelligence gained was that the island perimeter was occasionally patrolled by a motor launch, and
their building didn't have indoor toilet facilities.

The people of Little Diomede were extremely wary, even
frightened, of the Russians, and for good reason. In 1948,
the year following the visit of Siberian Eskimos to Wales
and Nome, a group of Little Diomede Islanders attempted
to go to East Cape, Siberia, stopping first at the old village
site on the west side of Big Diomede. They were met by
military personnel, and they learned that the former Eskimo
inhabitants, some of their relatives, had been evacuated. The
Little Diomede group was held for several weeks before
being released. Two people died shortly afterward from the
effects of their captivity. The islanders now were extremely

careful not to cross an imaginary line centered between the two islands.

I experienced their concern about Big Diomede during a hunting trip. I was riding in Albert Iyahuk's umiak along with two elderly men, Frank Koyuktuk and Tom Iyapana, and three of Tom's sons. We traveled many miles south of the Diomede Islands in search of walruses. South was the favored direction, because the current would carry us back toward the islands while the animals were being butchered or if the outboard motor failed.

Unexpectedly we found ourselves in a dense fog. This excited nervous discussion, and we headed in the direction of home. Albert, the helmsman, took direction from slight shoulder movements of Tom Iyapana, sitting just ahead, who watched a gimbaled compass between his feet. An error of just a few degrees in our course could put us on either side of the islands if we didn't escape the fog.

After more than an hour, Albert stopped the outboard motor and everyone listened intently for the many-pitched drone emitted by the thousands of seabirds that had recently returned to the island rookeries. We could hear them distantly, and with each stop thereafter their sounds grew louder. Anxiety was building and was very evident on the men's faces and in their now-whispered voices. They didn't want to blunder into Big Diomede Island and an encounter with the Russians.

I couldn't help wondering how the Russians would treat me, a white man snooping around in the fog claiming to be studying walruses. Finally, a quick but slight tipping of the boat by a sharp-eyed crew member signaled that something had been sighted. Albert again stopped the motor and the men studied the dim darkness of a shoreline. Paddles were then used to sneak closer in an effort to identify the land. It was Little Diomede. The men showed relief and joked about the prowess of our navigator, old Tom Iyapana, and the accuracy of his marine compass, a relict from the days when New Bedford sailing ships plied these waters in quest of bowheads.

On reaching the village, excitement stirred again when we found that three other umiaks, containing the rest of the able-bodied men in the village, were still out in the fog. An ancient foghorn, a square box affair with a handle sticking out the side, quickly materialized from somewhere, and the men took turns pumping it. The horn belched out a low-frequency, raw-throated groan that must have carried well. One by one the boats arrived, to the great relief of all. It was cause for celebrating with an evening dance. The children surprised me with a special performance, singing and giggling their way through several verses of "Old MacDonald Had a Farm."

AS THE BROKEN ICE PACK DRIFTED north, it carried migrating walruses past Little Diomede. Four crews in their umiaks hunted whenever weather and ice conditions permitted. The National Guard issued ammunition to the men for training purposes, so there was no thought of conserving it. My previous hunting with the Eskimos of Wales had not prepared me for what I would witness while with the Little Diomede hunters. The following account of a hunt is rendered from my field notes.

I accompanied Albert Iyahuk and his crew on a hunting trip that lasted a day and a half. We killed two bearded seals shortly after leaving the island; these were skinned, butchered, and taken aboard. It was legal for me to shoot seals but not walruses. Soon after, we encountered walruses, and the men saved only the heads of the several taken. The walruses were being hunted solely for the value of their ivory tusks. More walrus herds appeared nearby and the shooting continued. With so many heads, the bearded seal meat was jettisoned to lighten the boat. Soon the seal skins were also discarded. Still more walruses were shot; we stopped at a large piece of ice, where the hunters chopped the tusks from the heavy skulls to again lighten the boat enough to safely continue. After a shooting episode, the men would make coffee, eat pilot bread, and occasionally boil some meat. Then followed some quiet talking and catnapping, but with at least one fellow always alert and on the lookout for animals. The decision to return home came when we ran out of coffee.

These men, as far as I could understand, didn't believe they were doing anything wrong or even wasteful in their mass killing of walruses. The discarded carcasses were going back to the place where they were created, and would be made over into some kind of new life. But if the men brought home something, perhaps bearded seal meat, and left it where dogs could get it, that was frowned upon. Their focus was on conservation of their own energies, not worrying about other living things. Dogs were only labor-saving instruments, and their maltreatment was painful for me to see. The dogs were without shelter, tied on short chains all winter, and were still happily ready to serve man, though the Little Diomede mushers seemed to think a continuous fusillade of thrown ice chunks was necessary to bring out the best work.

I saw ample demonstration that an indifference toward the lives and suffering of birds and animals was taught at an early age, perhaps as an imperative in a culture based on hunting. Children only three or four years old were given live birds, usually crested auklets, as playthings. The inevitable death of the birds sometimes caused the children to cry—not out of sympathy, but in disappointment that their toy was no more fun.

Boys were introduced to hunting at the age of six or seven. When a cow walrus is killed, its calf remains close to it, and a young boy would be told to shoot it in the head with a .22-caliber rifle. When Albert Iyahuk's young son, Glenn, was told to do this, he was confused and didn't really know what to do. With the help of his father and two other men, the crying boy succeeded. Before the walrus season ended, this boy witnessed a great amount of shooting and killing of walruses, and was himself happily shooting walrus calves.

I could understand why such dispassionate attitudes toward birds and animals would be a necessary part of a pure hunting culture. For millennia, in trying to satisfy their essential requirements for life, these Eskimos had to face the uncontrollable whims of nature. Even their best efforts commonly didn't bring in enough of the birds and animals they depended on for food and for the materials used in fashioning clothes, shelter, boats, tools, and works of art.

This was no longer true. The coming of outboard motors, rifles, and almost inexhaustible stores of ammunition multiplied their hunting power many times over. But expecting people raised in such an environment to understand and adopt a conservation ethic in a relatively short period of time poses difficulties for everyone.

I thought about this problem when I read, forty years later, that Glenn Iyahuk—the reluctant child—had been convicted of illegally taking and trafficking in walrus ivory. In this case, however, there were aggravating factors, related to trading in drugs, which undoubtedly warranted the charges and penalties.

When the walrus spring migration ended at Little Diomede in 1953, I tallied a retrieved take of 507 animals by the four crews. Judging by the number of headless walrus carcasses on the ice drifting up from the south, the King Island hunters were also killing in large numbers. The ivory taken far exceeded what the carvers could utilize; this excess was sold in its raw state. Some found its way to other villages where it was needed, but much of the ivory ended up in the hands of whites with small return to Eskimos. I was told by Eskimos that a saloon in Nome, a place called the Board of Trade, acquired large amounts through purchase and trade.

Although I didn't know whether the overall walrus population was trending up or down, I was convinced that wasteful hunting practices needed change. There was certainly plenty of room for change that still satisfied the meat, hide, and ivory requirements of the Eskimos. I thought about being an instrument of change, but didn't have very concrete ideas about how to go about it. Federal law reserved the taking of walruses to Natives, and there wasn't much knowledge in wider circles and therefore not much concern for the status of these animals.

CHAPTER SEVENTEEN

Walrus Islands

TO MEET THE WALRUS AGAIN, I went to Barrow, the northernmost community in Alaska. There I stayed with Eddie Edwardson, an Eskimo with whom I had become friendly while we worked together for the Alaska Road Commission eleven years earlier. He asked his wife to serve me an Eskimo delicacy, sliced-up seal intestine laced with seal oil. I appreciated the gesture, but would have settled for apple pie and a slice of cheddar.

I was invited by Eben Hobson to go along on his motor launch while he and his crew hunted walrus. Only bull walruses commonly reached Barrow, and in relatively few numbers compared to their seasonal abundance in the Bering Strait. The female and younger animals favor the Chukchi Sea, to the west of Barrow. The Barrow hunters were highly efficient; every bit of the walruses killed was salvaged. This thoroughness assisted my own work in studying the animals; the hunters even set up a tripod composed of floorboards from the boat and helped me weigh a walrus, piece by piece.

Here I finally encountered polar bears, after my many futile efforts at Wales. Most of the time I stayed out of the way by sitting on top of the boat's cabin, scanning with my binoculars as we motored along the edge of the ice pack. One day I saw two polar bears about a half mile back on the solid ice. I asked if I could go along with the men to hunt the bears. Eben said, "You saw them, you go and Max Ungaruk can go too."

So Max and I left the boat and stalked the bears. As we got closer, they appeared pretty big. Both were feeding on a large bearded seal. A low remnant of an ice pressure ridge gave us cover to within a hundred yards of the bears, and there was no wind to worry about. We shot the bears and they died quickly. All of the meat was saved as food by the Eskimos. The bear I shot proved to be the fourth-largest polar bear on record at that time; his skull is in the University of Alaska Museum. Since adult male polar bears cannibalize cubs, I told myself that killing some of them should have a positive effect on the population. But except in self defense, this would be the last polar bear I ever wanted to kill.

THE WALRUS ISLANDS IN TOGIAK BAY, an offshoot of Bristol Bay, remained the only place in Alaska where walruses regularly hauled out on land. My effort to go ashore on one of them—Round Island, where these animals concentrate—was unsuccessful in the summer of 1952 and no more fruitful in 1953. I had to settle for aerial observations that allowed an estimate of their number and confirmed the animals were all bulls.

Earlier that summer the Cooperative Store in Dillingham had bought forty walrus tusks from Yupik Eskimos who lived at the nearby village of Togiak. Jim Downey, the store manager, told me the Natives killed the walruses at Round Island while en route from Togiak to Dillingham for the salmon fishing season. He had been buying ivory from them for years, paying a dollar and a half a pound and selling it for considerably more to non-resident fishermen as souvenirs.

This occasional disturbance of the walruses had not caused them to change their habit of spending the summer and fall on or near the Walrus Islands. This could change. Any big increase in hunting could bring the risk that the walruses would forsake the islands, as they had done at several other haul-out sites in Alaska and along the Siberian coast. How they might disperse and relocate would be anyone's guess, though the Togiak people would not benefit. I concluded that if any unique wildlife area deserved preservation, the Walrus Islands should be the top candidate.

I spent two summers studying the walrus and its use by Eskimos, gathering material for my university degree thesis. But I urgently hoped that my studies would not amount to a mere academic exercise. In the thesis, I included a batch of ideas for reforms in the way the walrus population was managed in Alaska, and later I fought for these changes.

Protection of the Walrus Islands was number one. We also needed a limit on the killing of cow animals and their calves. I also called for legalizing the hunting of a small number of walrus bulls by non-Natives, who would have to employ Eskimo guides. I believed this proposal would bring new money to Eskimo communities, temper the intensity of ivory hunting, and responsibly satisfy the desires of trophy hunters.

It would take an act of Congress, literally, to allow any walrus hunting by people other than Natives. I wrote to Alaska's delegate to Congress, E. L. (Bob) Bartlett, asking whether action on this idea was feasible. He replied with a request for more information and suggested that I propose language for a bill. I knew next to nothing about drafting legislation, but I sent him my reasoning and he found it convincing. He had a bill drafted, found a sponsor, and the legislation quickly became law.

Although Bartlett had no vote, he was the conduit between Alaskans and a Congress not in the habit of consulting beyond him on matters that affected Alaska. It turned out that Eskimos benefited from guiding white trophy hunters, but otherwise they were unconcerned about the new law. This exercise in lawmaking, my first taste of achieving something as a wildlife manager, brought a good feeling. Professors Jim Rearden and John Buckley seemed proud of my work, and I received the Master of Science degree in the spring of 1954.

It wasn't until June 1958 that I actually set foot on Round Island in the Walrus Islands, this time in the company of fellow biologists Francis H. (Bud) Fay and Karl Kenyon, both of whom became renowned in the world of marine mammal science. In our rush to get ashore and set up camp, we challenged a nasty surf and split a couple of planks in our borrowed rowboat. Several hundred walruses were hauled-out on two narrow cobble beaches, with hundreds more in the water. I thrilled at being so close to these massive animals.

During the next five days we attempted to count the walruses (impossible), observed their behavior, and tagged several of them. Bud Fay's interest in describing walrus anatomy in scientific detail kept us all busy with the careful, tedious dismemberment of three animals. We estimated that the walrus herd numbered between fifteen hundred and two thousand. There were thirty-three headless carcasses on the island, the work of Togiak village hunters seeking ivory. Before retiring in the evenings we enjoyed a touch of spirits as we mused over designating the Walrus Islands a federal wildlife refuge.

BACK IN 1954, finished with my university studies, I faced the world again. It was almost like leaving home the first time, or getting out of the army. I had to think about a career. I discussed my prospects with Jim Rearden, who was so optimistic about my chances that I shamelessly conceded my intention to become the head of Alaska's fish and game program. Jim had his own ambitious plans. He intended to resign from the university to devote all of his time to journalism. He was already writing and selling articles about Alaska to a variety of magazines, and he became only more successful in future years.

Employment options for me were essentially limited to the Territorial Department of Fisheries or to the U.S. Fish and Wildlife Service, where Clarence Rhode had put together a team of wildlife biologists I liked and respected. Their efforts to upgrade Alaska's wildlife programs were beginning to show progress, although they were somewhat hindered by the federally appointed Alaska Game Commission, five great Alaska gentlemen doggedly determined that the foundation of Alaska's wildlife program would be predator control, protection of female animals, and restrictive bag limits—and no need to adjust regulations with changing abundance of game, since that would supposedly balance out over time.

Talk of statehood was everywhere in the air. Fish and Wildlife Service biologists seemed uniformly opposed to statehood, and I realized I might not fit in well with this group. Besides, I still harbored a generalized sourness at the treatment of Alaskans by the federal government. I strongly resented the paternalistic, abusive, or misguided treatment of Natives. I was disgusted with the fiasco of the reindeer program, and with the federal default of jurisdiction over salmon fisheries to the politically powerful Alaska Packers Association. My heart was with the Territory and aspirations for statehood.

I accepted the offer of a permanent job with the Territorial Department of Fisheries. My first assignment would be to learn whether beluga whales feeding on salmon in Bristol Bay were hurting commercial fishermen by reducing their catches. Some people thought so, but the question remained unanswered. I was excited about the work. As the only biologist trained in wildlife management to be employed by the Territory, the job offered a chance to show what I could do, while letting me in on the ground floor in the event Alaska achieved statehood.

About this time, I heard that a Cessna 170 flying commercially out of Talkeetna had crashed. The pilot's name was Glenn Hudson. My Fairbanks buddy, chess teacher, and fellow buck private, the friend who decided not to accompany me to air corps pilot training, had died with three others in his own small airplane.

CHAPTER EIGHTEEN

Whale-catcher

AS I PREPARED TO LEAVE for Bristol Bay, I again felt regret and uneasiness about leaving Bertha and Lewis alone in Fairbanks for several months, although we understood that such absences were an unavoidable part of my career choice. My baggage for the trip included a lot of paraphernalia for catching belugas, since it would be necessary in my research to look into their stomachs. Among the gear was a large, heavy-twine net and a toggle-type harpoon head to be mounted on a throwing shaft. I had bought a naval line-throwing gun equipped with line and barbed darts, and packed my trusty old .30-06 Model 70 Winchester as well. This armory reflected imagined circumstances rather than beluga-hunting know-how.

During my bush flying days in Bristol Bay, I had looked with fascination at belugas surfacing and blowing in the muddy waters. Later in the Bering Strait and Kotzebue Sound I had seen Eskimos harvest belugas. Just a year earlier in company with John Schaeffer Sr., Bertha's brother, I helped catch and butcher a beluga near Kotzebue. I knew that a major part of the beluga population is highly migratory, spending the winter in the Bering Sea and moving through the Bering Strait and dispersing widely along the arctic coast during the summer. Other groups remain south of the Bering Strait throughout the year, being common in the larger bays and estuaries south of Norton Sound. But for the most part, what I knew about the biology of these small white whales came from books in the library.

I arrived at Dillingham with barely a clue about how to start the investigation. In talking with local people I learned that belugas are occasionally caught in salmon nets, and that killer whales sometimes come into Nushagak Bay, at the north end of Bristol Bay, and prey on them. Beluga hunting by local Natives for subsistence had dwindled and then stopped altogether with the development of commercial salmon fisheries, a changed lifestyle, and perhaps the effects of the 1918 influenza epidemic. A few of the older Yupik Eskimos remembered stories about belugas being hunted by groups of people in kayaks, and they knew that the skin, flukes, and flippers were good to eat.

Without a clear path to getting my work under way, I left Dillingham and went to Levelock, a small village on the lower Kvichak River, which flows into Kvichak Bay, which in turn adjoins Bristol Bay. There I got lucky. While standing on the riverbank musing and watching the turbid water flow upstream with the rising tide, a Native in an outboard-powered skiff came ashore. I approached and tried to engage the man in conversation, but found him a reluctant speaker. He gradually loosened up and showed some interest when I asked about belugas. He gave his name as Charlie Wilson. When he understood I was interested in hiring him, boat included, to try to catch belugas, his eyes lit up and he agreed to start work the next day. Charlie informed me that plenty of belugas ascended the river on each flood tide, passing Levelock before retreating to Kvichak Bay as the tide receded.

I sampled the river with a dip net, finding spawned-out rainbow smelt on which I suspected the belugas were feeding. If so, fine; no one worried about smelt. Charlie said the seaward migration of juvenile red salmon (smolts) from Iliamna Lake had not yet reached this far down the Kvichak River, but ought to appear soon. I was pleased with the situation; it appeared my beluga food-habit study was really getting started.

Neither Charlie nor I knew how to go about catching belugas, although we did know that a dead beluga, however killed, would sink. The next day at high tide the belugas appeared as Charlie predicted. We went out on the river and harassed them around with the skiff, not getting within harpoon throwing range before they dived. In the fashion of the Eskimos farther north, I decided to try shooting, hoping to wound an animal and harpoon it before it died and sank. I failed to hit any.

The water was too muddy and deep to see the submerged belugas, but I threw the harpoon many times, guided only by the slight surface disturbance caused by their swimming action. Just as my tired arm told the futility of this technique, the harpoon struck a beluga. The harpoon line flew out of the boat along with its buoy. I felt a spike of excitement, not knowing what to expect next. We soon picked up the buoy, and when the beluga surfaced in front of the skiff, I shot it.

People at the village observed and wondered about all the commotion. By the time we beached the beluga, a curious crowd had gathered. It was a male, eight feet long, and may have weighed close to a thousand pounds. Charlie and I butchered it under many watchful eyes; several women went to get pans or pots to carry meat and skin back home. On examination, I found the beluga's stomach well-filled with smelt and an uncountable number of their backbones from an earlier feeding period.

Hunting during the next few days resulted in nothing other than discouraging the belugas from coming up the river as far as Levelock. Our attempts to use the large beluga net were a waste of time, as Charlie had predicted. He said he had watched schools of belugas move through a maze of salmon nets, sensing their presence and avoiding them.

We moved down the river into Kvichak Bay, staying at an abandoned cabin at Copenhagen Creek. Here Charlie found he could haze the animals out of the deep channels; one or two could then be separated from the group and forced toward ever-shallower water. I learned to throw the harpoon quite accurately by judging the location of the submerged swimmer relative to the surface wave it created. With calm water, our technique was surefire. We caught and examined several more belugas. When the migration of salmon smolts from Iliamna Lake appeared, these became the dominant prey of the belugas.

In June, Charlie had to prepare for commercial salmon fishing, so I went back to Dillingham, hoping to catch and examine some belugas in Nushagak Bay. The superintendent of the Pacific American Fisheries cannery volunteered the loan of a skiff and outboard motor. Everyone was at work in the fishery; the only helper I was able to hire was a diminutive, gentle Finlander, Walfry (Whitie) Kivi, whose big taste for liquor seemed to disqualify him for work on a fishing boat or even in a cannery. With me, he demonstrated a great will to please and confirm my trust. I cut short our first day on the water when I realized that Whitie was shivering badly due to skimpy clothing which, it turned out, was all he owned. After I outfitted him with warm gear, he tried his best. I developed a genuine fondness for the man who did a fine job for me, amazing a lot of people who had expected that he wouldn't last a day.

Jim Rearden came to Dillingham in July to give me a most welcome hand. As a novice harpooner, he obviously suffered moments of high excitement. Jim saw serious adventure in our beluga investigation, which he recounted in a December 1954 article in *Outdoor Life* magazine. While the belugas themselves were harmless, there was ample opportunity to generate our own trouble. Maneuvering a speedy skiff in the dangerous waters of Bristol Bay, usually far from any assistance, posed considerable risk. Fortunately we avoided trouble and still caught a few belugas.

When the salmon runs ended for the season, I temporarily discontinued the beluga collecting. My examination of their stomachs revealed a shift in diet from smelt to salmon smolts to adult salmon as the availability changed. But I still had only a rough estimate of the numbers of beluga and not enough stomach samples. In the following few years I continued seasonal studies, trying to accurately gauge the beluga impact on the salmon fishery.

At one point, the Fisheries Department's great photographer, Amos Burg, joined me for a couple of weeks to document the beluga investigation with his movie camera. His film, perhaps too vividly, conveyed proof that belugas kill salmon. The movie, which Amos insisted I narrate, was widely shown in Alaska's schools for several years. But gradually, exposure to the raw realities of birth and death, showing blood and all, came to be deemed appropriate only in theaters and on television, not in schools. The film was relegated to the archives.

Finally, my investigations were close to providing an answer to the question of whether the quantity of salmon consumed by belugas amounted to a significant economic drain or was of little consequence. At this juncture, I gained the help of Cal Lensink, a former colleague of mine at the University of Alaska who was now completing his Ph.D. degree at Purdue University. Before long our work proved that salmon eaten by belugas amounted to a minuscule fraction of the fish available and had no detectable effect on the world's largest red salmon fishery.

Our attempts to mollify skeptical fishermen, however, were not made easier by the belugas' size and numbers, and the proven fact that they preyed on salmon. So we began experimenting with sound generators to discourage the animals from swimming into the confines of the rivers where they preyed on dense concentrations of seaward-migrating salmon smolts. This exercise stirred interest among fishermen, but otherwise did no more than shift the belugas' feeding areas. After six years of messing up their lives, we found the belugas innocent of bad behavior and left them in peace. It appears the commercial fishermen generally agreed with this decision, because their complaints all but ceased.

IN THE COURSE OF THE BELUGA STUDIES, we were distracted by a query from the director of the Fisheries Department,

C.L. Anderson, who wanted to know if we could catch some belugas alive to satisfy requests by a couple of zoological parks. Charlie Wilson, Cal Lensink, and I decided the best chance to catch belugas unharmed would be to somehow entangle them in a net. Our idea was to separate a beluga from the school and maneuver it into shallow water, where we would encircle it with a salmon net that we payed out from the speeding skiff.

The idea resulted in some fruitless water hauls, with the belugas changing direction and avoiding the net, or simply swimming under it. After several attempts we caught a small beluga and managed to get straps around it and lead it ashore. Using a body litter borrowed from the Levelock schoolteacher, we slid the animal about twenty yards across the tundra to a one-acre freshwater pond. The next day we got another one. The two belugas seemed to behave normally, so I contacted Carlton Ray of the New York Aquarium. He showed up in a few days to direct the air-shipping of the belugas to the aquarium. Somewhat later we heard the disappointing news that the belugas had died en route to New York, a painfully sad event for Carlton, who could not have been more devoted in caring for the animals.

Later in the summer we tried again to catch live belugas for the New York Aquarium and for Pacific Ocean Park at Santa Monica, California. Carlton Ray, along with two professional marine mammal catchers and dealers, the McBride brothers, arrived with a large pile of foam and air mattresses, straps, and slings. We planned to again use the perfectly placed small pond adjacent to the beach for holding captured belugas. With the encircling net we quickly captured an old, pure-white male, much too large to consider for the parks, so we released him.

Following several days of storms, we got a small beluga in the net and finally into the holding pond. The next day a second beluga was added to the first in the pond. The third capture was rather exciting. We tried to maneuver this beluga into water suitable for using the net, but even though we could approach the animal closely, it refused to move where we wanted. Driven by frustration, Darcy McBride took off his jacket and dived off the bow of the skiff, landing on the animal's back. He slipped back and managed to wrap his arms around the beluga's peduncle, the small part of the body just ahead of its flukes, but he was taking a good thrashing. When Carlton saw this, he too dived overboard, holding a strap.

With the animal struggling, water flying, and much hollering, Darcy and Carlton held on and got the strap over the beluga's head, bringing it under some degree of control. With the help of the skiff, we moved the turmoil into water where Darcy and Carlton could touch the bottom with their feet, and the battle was won.

The three healthy belugas were soon on their way to their new homes. Two remained in California, where they became great attractions and performers at Pacific Ocean Park. Carlton's beluga had the misfortune of a travel delay in ninety-degree heat at the Chicago airport, which probably weakened it. The animal refused to eat at the New York Aquarium and died about a month later. After this, Alaska's fish and game professionals had no further involvement with exporting wildlife, with the exception of musk ox and orphan bear cubs.

DURING OUR WORK with the belugas, Charlie Wilson and I spent a lot of time together, sharing meals, clouds of mosquitoes, some terrible weather, and a lot of satisfying small successes. Once Charlie realized that I truly enjoyed hearing him talk about his life experiences, he proved to be a pretty good storyteller. He told me where peregrine falcon aeries are located, where and when whitefish spawn, and where rainbow trout can be caught by the tubful. He loved to describe how the cannery owners favored their seasonally imported Italian fishermen, mostly from San Francisco, over the local resident fishermen. The locals looked for ways to get even. For example, the Red Salmon Cannery at Naknek required that any food issued to boats operated by residents, if not consumed, had to be returned at the end of the season. When the fishery ended, these folks jogged their boats in front of the cannery and summoned the owner, Winn Brindle, to bid good-bye. Then they called "Here's your grub, Winn, come and get it," and tossed the food into the river. Charlie was proud of this daring and gratifying act of defiance.

On one high tide we ventured up Copenhagen Creek with the skiff to look at some old collapsed buildings, a former saltery. There I found a book titled *The Collected Works of Lord Bulwer Lytton,* which included the story "Last Days of Pompeii." This classic probably gave comfort to someone tired and bored with butchering salmon. I found the book wonderfully entertaining. Charlie listened carefully as I described the momentous events in long-ago Pompeii, but his real delight was comic books, a reflection of his limited worldly exposure and not of his bright mind.

When time and tide allowed, we walked south for miles along the beach looking for whatever flotsam might have found its way there. Finding part of a mastodon skeleton with ivory tusks, exposed by a sloughing bank, was especially exciting. We developed a trust and friendship that grew stronger until Charlie prematurely passed on some years later.

CHAPTER NINETEEN

The Hunt

THE CRISP AIR and blaze of coloring leaves on a late August in Alaska always stir intense memories of the wonderful hunting days in Michigan with my father and brothers-in-law. A major gratification of being in Alaska has been the chance to satisfy this passion for hunting, despite ambivalent feelings about the sport that seemed to increase as the years went on.

At the University of Alaska I had found a fellow hunting enthusiast in Professor Jim Rearden. We also shared a common need for meat to stock the larder. On one memorable occasion, Jim and I left Fairbanks in my pickup truck with a canoe for a moose hunt on the Kenai Peninsula. We drove to the town of Kenai and then down the peninsula toward Homer, but we were quickly diverted from serious moose hunting by the marvelous steelhead fishing in the Ninilchik River and Deep Creek. As for moose, the most we saw were some weathered droppings.

On the return trip we resolved to make a last effort for moose, so we put our canoe into the peninsula's Upper Trail Lake. Paddling to the head of the lake, we sighted mountain goats on a slope a little above timberline to the east and decided to switch our quarry. We left our camp at dawn to struggle up a steep mountain through almost vine-like alders laced with bear trails; in steep places the alders provided handholds. Breaking into the alpine area six hours later, we found the goats, made a successful stalk, and each bagged one. The easy part of the hunt ended there.

Our strength and luck were sorely tested in getting those animals off the mountain, down through nearly a thousand feet of dense alders and finally the last several hundred feet of spruce forest. At one point we found ourselves on the edge of a vertical drop of two hundred feet or more. The alders were so dense that dragging the goats back uphill and around the cliff was beyond us. We had no choice but to shove the goats over the edge and hope to find them again somewhere below.

Jim found a small opening to one side where he could watch with his binoculars as I pushed the goats off the cliff. He could see the alders moving far below as the first goat tumbled down; the second goat took what appeared to be about the same course. We then traversed above the cliff, dropped down several hundred feet, and worked our way back in the direction of the goats. Though the light was getting poor, Jim found a white hair on an alder. This discovery led us to more hairs and finally the goats. This was akin to finding two needles in a haystack. When we reached camp several hours later in pitch darkness and hung the carcasses from tree limbs, we were exhausted to the point of staggering. Somehow the goat meat showed no evidence of damage from the pounding, and was superb on the table.

ALMOST ANYTHING I BAGGED while hunting had value to me beyond its worth as food; it was a trophy. I believe my father helped instill this respectful attitude in me as a novice hunter by taking two birds I had shot—a red-shouldered hawk and a barn owl—to a taxidermist. How proud I was of those birds displayed on the parlor mantle. But he cautioned we had no room for others, so I shouldn't kill any more birds that we would not eat.

As for trophies, I came to view the Dall sheep ram as supreme. The sheep season in Alaska in late summer and early fall can expose a hunter to all manner of treacherous weather conditions. But if you're lucky with the weather, the mountains can be a wondrous place, so uplifting to the senses and spirit that hardships and even periods of misery are forgiven if not forgotten. I cherish a couple of extraordinary sheep hunting adventures, fraught with unexpected encounters with game animals.

With a University friend, Burt Libby, I hunted sheep on Victoria Mountain, nestled in the White Mountains north of Fairbanks. Dick McIntyre, flying a float-equipped Cessna 180, dropped us off on Beaver Creek at the base of the mountain, and we spent most of the day climbing in a cold rain with poor visibility. In late afternoon the clouds lifted momentarily and we were thrilled to see a group of rams on the north peak. They were about a half mile away and only five or six hundred feet above our elevation. Then we saw two rams much closer. One was a beauty, with at least full-curl unbroomed (not broken) horns.

The clouds descended suddenly, hiding the animals but affording us an inviting opportunity to approach within shooting range. The visibility was so restricted, however, that we couldn't judge exactly where we were in relation to the sheep as we advanced. The clouds blew away and we were caught standing in the open, in clear view of the sheep just a hundred yards away. They bolted instantly. I got the larger ram in my scope sight and rolled him with a perfect shot in the shoulder. It was a beautiful animal, a trophy to thrill the heart of any hunter and whet the palate of a gourmet.

Burt decided to stalk the north-peak rams. I had finished field-dressing and carefully skinning out my ram's cape and head when I heard Burt shoot. With the binoculars, I could see that he had a ram. By the time he descended with the head and cape of his sheep, the light was about gone. I had our little tent erected and our gear sheltered from the rain, which continued to fall. We were two very fatigued but happy hunters who ate a cheese and hardtack dinner by candlelight while lying in our damp sleeping bags.

We awoke in the morning to beautiful weather and the howling of wolves. Our worry was that wolves or bears might get to our sheep carcasses before we did. Through the binoculars, the carcasses seemed undisturbed, so we aired and dried our clothes and sleeping bags before setting out to finish butchering the animals and begin packing meat. Burt started up the north peak while I headed for my sheep in the south saddle of the mountain, only about six hundred yards away. Then I saw movement near the carcass; two wolves were approaching it. I didn't want to lose the meat. To get their attention I fired a shot in their general direction, and they departed at a full run. But this merely changed the nature of my problem.

As the wolves fled, a sow grizzly with three cubs appeared. The sow went straight for the carcass. I shot into the air a couple of times but she paid no attention. Hoping she might be frightened and leave if she saw me, I walked rapidly toward her, hollering loudly to no effect. The cubs were now also eating. At a hundred yards, the bears still refused to take notice of me, though I knew I was entering ever more hazardous territory. I feared loss of the meat, but I didn't want to fight over it either. It was at this critical juncture that I heard a new sound: the *clap, clap, clap* of a helicopter's rotor blades. Just a hundred feet above us a helicopter roared by. The bears ran in high gear, by chance directly away from me, and I hurried to take possession of my sheep. Most of the meat was undamaged.

The helicopter continued toward the north peak of the mountain, where it circled and persisted in chasing a band of rams, undoubtedly the same ones Burt had stalked the previous day. The pilot then spotted Burt and landed next to him, which wasn't the smartest thing to do since they had just violated antiharrassment game laws. They told an irate Burt that they were geologists, and Burt allowed they were other things as well. They refused to give Burt their names and hastened to get on about their geology. Still, the noisy overflight of the helicopter had gotten me out of a ticklish spot.

IN COMPANY WITH BURT the following year on the same mountain, I was again startled by the unexpected. We spotted a lone ram, carrying full-curl horns, on a distant ridge, across a large ravine. The flip of a coin selected Burt as the hunter, and I got comfortably situated as I watched events unfold. It suddenly became evident that Burt had blown the stalk, because the ram bolted, running down into the ravine toward the main mountain where I was located. As the animal descended out of my sight, I felt a surge of excitement. It was possible he would reappear near to me.

When I next saw the ram, he was climbing a small pile of boulders, level with me and no more than two hundred yards away. I put the scope crosshairs on him as he stood scanning the area. What a magnificent animal, I thought, but probably too old to survive another winter. I began to squeeze the trigger when I was startled by a bolt of lightning that flashed out of the clouds directly to the sheep. At this very instant my gun discharged. The ram lay dead.

The lightning came from a thunderstorm some miles distant across the Beaver Creek valley; it did not actually hit the sheep, as it so clearly appeared to me. Still, I was shaken by the coincidence. I'm not superstitious, but this astonishing event—improbable beyond calculation—would forever haunt me.

I set the self-timer on my Leica, perched it on my packboard, and took my own picture with the ram. After butchering the animal, I cached most of the meat under boulders and packed the cape, horns, and some meat to our campsite. Burt arrived late, tired, and dispirited. I did elicit a pained, feeble smile from him when I commented that one good turn deserves another and I expected he would lend a hand in getting the rest of the sheep meat to camp in the morning. This chore presented us with some anxious moments.

From our camp to the meat was a short hike in open country, so we left our rifles and took only our packboards. When we were about four hundred yards from the boulder pile where I had left the meat, we saw a large grizzly bear to our left—quite obviously with the same destination in mind. The bear was no more than two hundred yards from us but moving faster.

Without rifles we knew that we couldn't contest possession of the meat. I suggested that Burt fire a few shots into the air with his .22-caliber pistol to reveal ourselves to the bear, which might then flee. So Burt fired the gun, but the effect was not what we hoped. The bear came running hard directly toward us. Burt said, "What now?" I replied, "Shoot some more." Which he did.

The bear stopped instantly and stood up straight, with its nose to the sky, testing the air. Then it turned and ran away, to our great relief. We concluded that the bear had mistaken the first pistol shots for rolling rocks dislodged by caribou or sheep. It had been rushing to see whether or not the banquet table was set. The second series of shots caused the bear to question what we were, and it got an answer when our scent drifted to him. Bears seem to detest the human bouquet.

MY CHERISHED HUNTING experiences have long presented a dilemma: whether to hunt, in order to feel the excitement and satisfaction it brings, or to put the gun down, in order to avoid the remorse and melancholy that can sometimes come with taking the life of a vibrant living thing. When I killed that trapped wolf during my youthful winter of trapping in the Interior, I felt I had made the wilderness somehow poorer. It's a feeling I've never been able to shake.

Natives pursuing a subsistence way of life have long since reconciled such conflicts through cultural rituals. Some of my friends admit to confused feelings about killing game—feelings that intensify with passing years. Others with qualms about killing shun the hunt altogether, even sparing spiders in the sink. But hunting connects and attracts some of us willingly, possibly innately, to a primitive past where survival itself was at risk. And hunting still yields food and prestige, to say little of pure fun. What hunter could deny the extraordinary rush that comes with the flush of a grouse?

The complex nature of hunting increasingly generates contentious issues: pro-hunting versus anti-hunting, unhindered gun ownership versus strict gun control, industrial development versus environmental quality, and so on. My hunter friends, all of them now younger than I, often express regret at not experiencing Alaska in earlier, simpler times.

I was schooled in the tradition of sportsmanship and moderation in taking game, though my mentors never spoke of compassion. For me, that notion seemed to evolve internally, perhaps from a germ implanted by my sisters. Without it, I doubtlessly would have killed more. I'm reminded of an effort to get fresh meat while living at the village of Wales, when Bertha and I were getting tired of canned foods. Swans occasionally flew along the edge of Lopp Lagoon, by an old reindeer corral that made a perfect hunting blind. One of those birds would provide extended feasting. After some chilling hours in my hiding place, scanning the horizon, a distant flock of swans appeared, bringing a tingle of anticipation. Were they on course toward me? They were. I double-checked my shotgun, making sure it was fully loaded and the safety was off, and adjusted my position for action. Soon I could distinguish color—a pair of white adults and three gray juveniles. A young bird would be the best eating. They loomed larger by the second, soon approaching to within ideal shotgun range. Then they were directly overhead, with swishing wings; I had let the perfect moment pass. As they peacefully continued on their way, I felt both chagrin and relief. For some reason—aesthetics? compassion?—my killer instinct failed me.

Despite reservations about killing, I enjoy being a successful hunter. As the years add up, however, I engage in more substitutes. Trapshooting, fishing, exercising our Chesapeakes, and even berry picking sometimes allow a layer of dust to collect on the hunting guns.

CHAPTER TWENTY

Dynamite

EARLY IN MY CAREER with state fisheries, I got a new title, a small raise, and an assignment I didn't much care for. After my first season in Bristol Bay with the belugas, department director C. L. Anderson called me to his office and said he was establishing a new division of predator investigation and control and would like me to take charge of it. Managing the department's seal control program, about which I knew nothing, would become my responsibility.

245

Harbor seals, the only species occurring in central and Southeastern Alaska, had a terrible reputation among some commercial fishermen because the marine mammals stole their catch. The seals went after salmon that were entangled in gill nets or caught by trolling gear, and halibut hooked on longlines. In Southeastern Alaska the program amounted only to hiring a couple of seal hunters, expert riflemen, to seasonally work in the Stikine and Taku rivers gill-net fisheries. Loss of catches from nets, particularly of king salmon, cut deeply into a fisherman's earnings. Our modest activities seemed cost effective and were highly lauded.

The seal control program at the Copper River Delta was an altogether different operation. Here seals were being destroyed in great numbers with dynamite depth charges. When I learned about this, I felt rather queasy, but it was necessary that I go to Cordova to size up the operation when it resumed in the spring of 1955.

What a surprise to discover that the person who had conceived and was managing the seal bombing campaign was my old CCC partner and fishing captain, Harold Hansen. It was truly a heartfelt reunion. Harold explained that when the Japanese attacked Pearl Harbor, he had enlisted in the Navy, where he specialized in depth charges. After the war he settled in Cordova and was now secretary and full-time manager for the Cordova District Fishermen's Union.

His fondness for spirits had changed from periodic binges to a daily, reasonably paced indulgence. Within the stable community of Cordova, especially during the winter, imbibing brought more cheer than problems. I was assured that it tuned the whistles of the barbershop quartet, raised bowling scores, and anointed social relations. Harold had landed in a good port.

Sympathizing with the complaints of his fishermen about seal depredations, Harold had contrived warfare tactics to resolve their troubles. The fishermen loved this seal control program, which they partly financed, and they were obviously proud and fond of Harold. When he introduced me at a union meeting as an old friend and explained my job, there was an embarrassing ovation. Thereafter, I could not leave Cordova without my airplane ticket being upgraded to first class. This treatment was disconcerting because I was already silently intent on finding an end to the seal killing, no matter how popular and cherished the program might be. But first, I would have to establish myself as knowledgeable, someone who knew exactly what was going on.

I accompanied a seal bombing expedition to gain acceptance and firsthand knowledge. A seine boat under contract served as the logistic base and for scouting. The fishermen executing the operation plied me with stories of their past activities, telling me how they killed literally thousands of seals, and very nearly killed themselves a few times.

Success depended on locating seals in large numbers while they were hauled out on beaches or sandbars. I rode along as an observer during one operation. An outboard-powered skiff (Harold's version of a small destroyer), loaded with a dozen or more twenty-five-pound charges of 60 percent gelatin dynamite, sped toward the seals. The animals lurched into the water and stayed beneath the surface. The men tossed the charges among the seals as the boat passed by.

The dynamite was detonated by a blasting cap rigged with an eleven-inch fuse (twenty-eight seconds burn time) and a pull-wire fuse lighter. The charges detonated in fast sequence, with muffled booms in deeper water and louder blasts where the water was shallower. The shallow-water explosions sent up tons of water in a geyserlike column. Shock waves jarred the skiff. Two hundred seals died in a matter of seconds. The crew chased down animals that were injured and finished them off with shotguns.

I WAS MANEUVERED into more active involvement in a later bombing. The fishermen were vexed that seals had found something of an autumn sanctuary on sandbars at the mouth of the Seal River, down the coast toward Yakataga. Harold prepared for an attack. He hired men to set up a base of operations in a patch of timber a half mile up the Seal River. In addition to a comfortable little cabin, the base included a skiff, outboard motor, and a powder magazine stocked with dynamite.

My visit to Cordova coincided with reports of several hundred seals at Seal River. Several fishermen almost demanded that Harold do something about it. Unfortunately only one man was available for the undertaking, a fisherman named John Gorus. Somehow the focus and pressure turned to me, as though I were being tested. I soon found myself with John Gorus on a flight in a Grumman Widgeon, bound for Seal River. Our expedition literally erupted with the unexpected.

On the first day, we launched the skiff down a ramp cut through the steep riverbank, loaded the dynamite, and prepared for the next day's undertaking. The old Johnson outboard left at the cabin did not want to run, leaving us with only the outboard we had brought down in the plane.

Next morning, John walked ahead of me to the skiff, carrying a shotgun for dispatching seals that might only be injured by our depth charges. As he started down the ramp, the shotgun fired, startling me. I assumed it was an accidental discharge. Walking closer, I saw a black bear lying at John's feet. It had been nosing around the skiff. When John appeared, the bear had a choice of swimming or running up the narrow ramp, and it made a fatal decision.

With time to spare waiting for the right stage of tide, we field-dressed the bear and found its stomach full of wild strawberries. Thanks to this delicious feast, it seemed to me that if a black bear should ever be good eating, this had to be the one. I decided to take it home, so we skinned the animal and hung it from the limb of a dead spruce tree about thirty feet in front of the cabin.

A large group of seals lay on a beach at the mouth of the river. With the skiff heavily laden with armed dynamite charges, our single outboard engine gave us only a modest speed down the river. John ran the motor and instructed me in when and how to throw the charges. The seals saw us while we were more than two hundred yards away, and they moved into the water By the time we reached the place they had been, I was standing with a bomb in my hands, though it appeared obvious that most, if not all, of the seals had swum safely away. Nevertheless, John shouted, "Now," so I pulled the fuse lighter and tossed the charge off the left side. As it left my fingertips, the outboard motor quit and the heavy boat instantly slowed.

I watched the charge hit the water about fifteen feet from the boat and slowly sink. John was pulling on the engine's starting cord as fast and as hard as he could. We said nothing. My first reaction was to simply stare at John. Then my eyes focused on the gas line; it left the tank and lay in the bottom of the boat. It wasn't connected to the engine. I told John, and he quickly made the connection.

The engine started, but it was too late. Twenty-five pounds of dynamite exploded within thirty feet of us. A violent blast of water accompanied a tremendously hard and loud jolt. In anticipation of the blast, I put my fingers in my ears, but John must have been thinking only of survival. We were badly shaken and soaking wet, and John was temporarily deaf. But we weren't injured. We beached the skiff to bail out several inches of water in the bottom, but found no damage. Nor did we find any dead or injured seals.

We did learn that our bomb run was foredoomed because the water adjacent to the haul-out site was much too shallow for the depth charges, causing the energy to blow out vertically. As far as John and I were concerned, the seals did in fact have a sanctuary at Seal River.

THE NEXT MORNING REVEALED that a large brown bear had visited during the night and carried off the black bear carcass. Out of curiosity and with all senses on high alert, I tracked the brown bear into a dense alder thicket, knowing it was a stupid thing to do even with my .30-06 rifle at ready. The thicket was ominously dark, dank, and so silent that the chronic tinnitus in my ear sounded like a stuck train-whistle. With each cautious step I felt closer to disaster but also felt a chilling inner thrill, an acute awareness of risk-taking.

My better judgment or survival instinct surfaced, and I backed out without incident. The bear now had food enough for several days, so it shouldn't have any reason to bother us again. But it returned the next night and carried off the black bear's viscera. The following night it noisily rummaged around the cabin, even testing the door. It ignored the black bear hide I had salted, rolled up, and stuffed into a wooden gasoline crate. We were becoming uncomfortable with the brownie's persistent presence. Our usual call of nature during the night became a little spooky, too. I rigged an alarm by tying one end of a spool of strong twine to the black bear hide and ran it to the cabin, under the door, and to my bunk.

That night I was awakened by a sharp pain. Something was pulling the twine; with the spool tangled under my sleeping bag, the line was biting into my neck. I got up, felt for my rifle, and opened the cabin door. The light was barely enough to show the dark outline of a large bear some yards away. At such close quarters, I didn't wait for the bear to make the next move. I pointed the rifle at the front part of the animal and pulled the trigger. The muzzle flash temporarily blinded me.

John was startled awake, shouting to know what happened. When I got him calmed down and my night vision began to return, we could discern the bear, apparently dead. We lit a Coleman lantern and moved a few steps toward the bear, with John in front. At that point two moving green eyes shined back at us. John said, "It's alive!" and bolted back to the cabin with the lantern. I hesitated briefly, staring into absolute darkness, thinking that if the bear was coming, it would be better to face it with the rifle than be caught from behind.

As I turned toward the cabin the lantern light went out; John had slammed the door. Stumbling in the darkness, seeking the cabin door, it occurred to me, and not for the first time, that he didn't seem greatly concerned about my safety. When I got inside, we doused the lantern and waited about ten minutes for our night vision to recover before checking again. The bear was dead, and he was indeed a giant of his race, with a beautiful hide. His skull resides in the University of Alaska Museum and, after tanning, his pelt decorated many parkas at Kotzebue.

THE SEAL BOMBING PROGRAM troubled me more deeply as I filled in its details and effects. It seemed unlikely that fish thefts by seals could be much of a problem after the destruction of several thousand of these animals in a few brief years. When I broached this opinion to Harold, he confided his own increasing regret and guilt over engineering such a massively destructive program. He recounted instances of chaotic, callous, and inhumane behavior by the bombing crews that sickened him and were simply too revolting for me to record. We knew that squelching the program would be a locally delicate act, but it had to be done.

Some things worked in favor of scaling back or stopping all of the department's seal control activities. We could claim to have thinned out the seal population, even though that effect was quite localized and temporary. More important, a timely innovation, monofilament nylon gill nets, began replacing linen nets. The nylon nets were virtually invisible in water, meaning that fishermen who had been setting their linen nets primarily at night and in silty water so the fish wouldn't see them could now reduce crowding by dispersing into clear-water areas and set nets during daylight hours—a time when they could also see the seals and chase them off. In consequence, seal depredations declined significantly in most gill-net fisheries.

During this period we lost the services of both of the riflemen working in our Southeastern Alaska seal program. These hunters were not replaced, and the Copper River bombing operation was terminated as well. Clancy Henkins, an expert rifleman in the Taku River fishery, resigned to go into commercial fishing himself. And Clifton Kilkenny, who exercised rifle wizardry in the Stikine River area for many years, passed away.

I have the fondest memories of Clif Kilkenny, a grand old gentlemen who was grateful for the opportunity to be useful in his elderly years. On my first visit to Wrangell as his supervisor, he met me at the airplane float and insisted that I stay with him on his houseboat. I intended to take a room at the hotel, but he simply wouldn't hear of it. Clif's one-room home was so tidy that just opening my duffel bag seemed to create a mess. At dinner he plied me with smoked black cod, potatoes, and homemade bread and pastries. After a long evening of chatting, he showed me my bed. There was only one bunk so I asked where he would sleep. Oh, on the floor, he replied. That was too much hospitality for me. I won that argument only after convincing him that I would sleep either on the floor or in the hotel. It was the floor.

A veteran of World War I, Clif retired as a Marine Corps master sergeant. His sincere lament was that because of age he was not allowed back into service during World War II. As an expert rifleman, he made a science of accurate shooting. For seal hunting, he had two model 70 Winchester rifles with heavy target barrels chambered for .220 swift cartridges. He hand-loaded the cartridges with precision far beyond that of factory ammunition. Each year one of the rifles was rebarreled, because he believed that some accuracy was lost after several hundred rounds. A twenty-power telescopic sight assured deadly accurate shooting.

I awoke to the delightful aroma of frying ham. Clif had prepared a monstrous VIP breakfast of ham, eggs, and hotcakes. He had already packed a lunch and a thermos of coffee. It was to be a wonderful day with a great old-timer. The river mouth was full of eulachon (the anadromous smelt popularly called hooligan) and the sky was alive with screaming gulls and now and then a swooping eagle. In the course of the day, we saw many seals and shot five using a total of five cartridges. We recovered the seals so that I could collect biological information and specimens as well as remove the scalps that otherwise someone might find and submit for bounty payment.

CHAPTER TWENTY-ONE

Roar of the Lions

ONE FLIGHT AROUND THE ISLAND and I was sold. Several hundred sea lions lay on the narrow rocky strands and cliff areas, with many distinct harem gatherings. It looked like an excellent site for beginning my studies of the life history of sea lions.

It was late summer 1956, and Harold Hansen and I were flying an aerial survey of Steller sea lions in Prince William Sound. The site I liked was one of the Wooded Islands off the southwest coast of Montague Island. Although the is-

255

land had no secure anchorage for a boat, a convenient base could be established on Montague Island a few miles to the north. I could hardly wait to get back to Cordova and prepare a little expedition.

Harold offered me the use of a twenty-foot skiff and a couple of outboard engines. Dale Bosworth, a University of Alaska wildlife management student, would accompany me. Walkers seeing us load the boat in the dock harbor at Cordova offered dire advisories upon learning of our destination, which was ninety miles away, mostly across the open Gulf of Alaska. To avoid debate with these solicitous folks, we nodded in apprehensive agreement. But in fact, some of my boyhood escapades on Lake St. Clair made me look on this voyage, with a spare outboard motor, as relatively low-risk.

Our small craft was so heavily laden with gear and gasoline cans that progress was slow. We missed the slack tide at the notorious Hinchinbrook Entrance, which was already running a moderate sea despite the light wind. If we went on, the worsening seas would surely thrash us before we completed the crossing. I chose to wait over in Constantine Harbor at the east end of Hinchinbrook Island until the next slack water. Here we enjoyed watching the abundant sea otters in their amusing antics. We saw more than one mother otter lying on her back, grooming a pup held on her belly. For the first time I observed the often-reported behavior of sea otters cracking clamshells by striking them against a rock placed on their chest. I also had time to calculate our fuel consumption, which was adequate for our venture only if our speed increased dramatically as we burned fuel and lightened the boat. We proceeded on that assumption with the next slack tide.

Along the beautifully rugged south coast of Montague Island, a long-period ground swell made for a pleasant ride, tempered somewhat by the shattering impact of these waves meeting the rocky shore. Bundles of lumber and debris led our attention to a vessel and barge lying broken at the base of rocky cliffs. No wonder the Cordova people called this the graveyard of the North Pacific. We arrived without incident at the Nellie Martin River in Patton Bay and established our camp, taking care to erect the tent some yards away from well-used brown bear trails.

The next morning we stayed keenly alert as we motored toward the other island, not knowing what we would face in going among hundreds of sea lions on a breeding rookery. About a mile from the rookery, I stopped the engine to change fuel tanks. The distant, somewhat ominous, growls, roars, and even smell of the animals came to us on the light breeze. When we approached the island and began to circle it, hundreds of sea lions surrounded us in a noisy, splashy melee, barking and roaring, with many making porpoise-like leaps out of the water. The uncertainty of the situation passed quickly; our reception seemed to be a display of curiosity, annoyance, and perhaps even playfulness.

After this tumultuous introduction, we selected a small cove on the northeast side, anchored the skiff, and ignoring the animals around us, went ashore in our little plywood dingy. A ravine-like chute gave us access to the top of the island and a marvelous view of all that transpired below. The island was unnamed. I dubbed it Lewis Island, in honor of both my father and my son.

We were quickly and deeply affected by the beauty and uniqueness of this small facet of Alaska. Wind-deformed Sitka spruce crowned the rather flat top of the island, with an occupied eagle's nest in the largest tree. Lush rye grass, flowering Indian rhubarb, and Indian rice dominated the vegetation. Puffins, guillemots, oystercatchers, ravens, gulls, sparrows, and even hummingbirds showed themselves.

Many slate-colored sea lion pups, some being nursed, lay among the rocks and on flat places adjacent to our boat anchorage. With a fish-landing net and a spring scale, we caught and weighed the pups we could catch. Pupping had ended, but breeding bulls still defended their territories and harems. I was fascinated to see several larger animals, apparently yearlings, still nursing. This observation raised questions about reproductive biology that I wanted to examine. As the light waned in the evening, small creatures appeared, flying in tight circles around our heads. I first thought they were bats but soon realized they were Mother Carey's chickens (tiny storm petrels).

DALE AND I HAD AGREED to rotate the cooking and dishwashing duties, but Dale now suggested he do all of the cooking, and the dishwashing too. His comment came after I fried some sea lion liver and boiled a pot of rice. It wasn't clear whether my menu fell short of his gourmand expectations or simply failed to sound the depth of his stomach. Whatever, I let him stew for some minutes before agreeing to this most sensible arrangement.

Our liver entree came from a female we had taken that held special interest because she was nursing one of the large yearlings. I wanted to determine whether she was again pregnant, as well as noting her stomach contents, body weight, and measurements. We ferried the carcass to a site near our camp for convenience in doing the work. This decision led to a truly close encounter with a large brown bear.

After completing the autopsy, we moved the skiff up the river to our camp. Dale walked to the tent while I fussed with things in the boat. Some movement caught my eye: a bear swimming in the river and about to land some ten or twelve yards downstream. I wondered which direction it would take, and whether I should pick up my rifle from the boat or unlimber the Leica camera that hung around my neck. I decided on the Leica. The bear emerged, shook, turned, and began walking toward me. I felt chills or something equivalent; fate would take its course. The beach was narrow, perhaps only twenty feet between the skiff and the trees. The bear split the difference as I snapped pictures. Through the viewfinder, I noticed the animal's lips suddenly protrude like a person kissing but trying to avoid contact. At the same time I heard a soft, snortlike sound but nothing else to show an awareness of my presence. After several more steps, it turned and walked into the woods.

I experienced a somewhat similar incident in another setting with a different bear. While fishing for steelheads on the Setuk River, standing in water well out from the bank, I saw a brown bear walking up the middle of the river toward me and already quite close. The situation was startling, like having an airplane engine quit, and it required a quick decision: hold my position or move away quickly. I feared that fleeing could trigger an attack and so chose to remain fixed as a statue. The bear continued coming and walked on by within fifteen feet, looking straight ahead. The only sign it gave of being aware of me was a series of clicking sounds. But we were probably equally apprehensive; when it was only a few yards beyond me, the bear made splashing lunges for the opposite shore.

Then I heard a voice behind me, and looked around to see my hunting companion, Stan Swanson, some distance away holding his rifle. From the nearby cabin, Stan had seen my predicament and took a position to help should the bear attack. Stan's presence was reassuring after the fact, but it diminished my sense of spunkiness in facing a brown bear while armed only with a slender wand of split bamboo.

ONE DAY FROM THE SEA LION ROOKERY we sighted a vessel far off to the south, moving very slowly, and intermittently hidden by a ground swell. We figured it was a halibut schooner working its gear. I had quit smoking when we arrived on Montague Island and thrown my remaining packs of cigarettes into the Nellie Martin River. The pangs of nicotine withdrawal kept me fidgeting, and now they encouraged me in a social visit to the fishing boat.

We approached on the vessel's port side while the fishermen worked the roller and handled fish on the starboard side. As Dale secured our painter, I climbed over the gunwale farther aft to approach the crew. The skipper was standing halfway out of the wheelhouse doorway, speaking to his men. On turning back, he saw me. He jerked like a released spring, wide eyes fixated, mouth agape. Then he stammered: "Who are you?"

Before I could answer, he rolled his eyes skyward with an awestruck facial expression. I realized that the fellow was truly suffering shock, and perhaps with cause. He had been at sea for many days with his small crew, and he was now miles off shore, with no other boats in sight; also no airplanes, balloons, or parachutes—and then to have a figure out of nowhere appear on deck. Were he a religious man, I know what he would be thinking.

I told him my name and asked if he had any spare cigarettes. The skipper shouted at his men: "Cigarettes! Get cigarettes!"

The situation began to settle down as Dale appeared and we pointed out our skiff tied alongside. Captain Ken Jung of the halibut schooner *Northland* out of Juneau then introduced himself and crew. The encounter had an impact on Captain Jung, for on returning to port he went straight to the newspaper. By his account, he was astounded to encounter a fellow bumming cigarettes from a small skiff during foul weather in the middle of the Gulf of Alaska.

On a day when a fierce storm stymied our attempt to return to Lewis Island, we explored the woods and west shore of Patton Bay. Low tide exposed sheared-off tree trunks and root systems studding the beach out at least two hundred yards from the present tree line, proclaiming this to be a seismically active place. Sea otters and harbor seals were in sight just off shore, and two black-tailed deer wandered in and out of the forest edge in front. Inland, large Sitka spruce grew so densely that only moss seemed to thrive on the forest floor, which was deeply etched by meandering brown bear trails. In the evening, surf smelt began spawning on the beach near our camp. We caught enough with our hands for a fine dinner. At that time, this corner of Alaska fit anyone's dreams of a pristine wilderness. We had no reason then to imagine how private ownership, logging roads, and earthquakes would disfigure this scene in the future.

After many round trips between our camp and the rookery, a dwindling gas supply forced our return to Cordova. With a low overcast, a light drizzle, and light winds, we set a course directly from Patton Bay to Strawberry Entrance, sixty miles across the Gulf. We passed Seal Rocks south of Hinchinbrook Entrance and noted many harbor seals, a few sea otters, and several nonbreeding sea lions. Farther along, south of Hinchinbrook Island, a puzzling spectacle appeared to the north. Beneath the clouds and through the dreary mist, a vivid emerald apparition projected from the island with a brilliance and purity that challenged the reality that it was simply sunlight reflecting off vegetation. Perhaps a thin place in the overcast and atmospheric moisture somehow split the sun's spectrum and reflected back only the emerald color. Whatever it was, for me this giant jewel testified that Alaska has its own emerald isle.

I PROPOSED TO DIRECTOR ANDERSON that the Fisheries Department commit a little more money and expand studies of the sea lion, hoping he would allow me to combine the research with graduate school. He smiled approvingly and said that it should help both me and the department, but that I would have to carry on with my administrative duties and assure continuity of the work already under way. This was fine with me.

I was accepted in 1956 into the zoology Ph.D. program at the University of British Columbia, at Vancouver. In a loaded pickup truck, Bertha, Lewis, and I drove the Alaska Highway from Fairbanks, arriving in Vancouver in time for the fall semester.

During the following spring semester, affairs of high interest to me were taking place in Juneau. The Territorial Legislature created a Department of Fish and Game that included the existing Department of Fisheries. As a territory, we had no authority to manage resources; federal agencies would hold on to that power until statehood. But the lawmakers sensed statehood was near and wanted a fish and game management capability in place. Anderson came to Vancouver to bring me the good news and discuss how to frame a larger organization. He expected me to head up the game side of the department. The prospects were titillating, and I easily ignored the major effect on my career: of likely becoming a bureaucrat rather than a scientist.

By the end of the 1957-58 school year, I had completed the Ph.D. course work and passed the oral exam, still looking forward to pursuing sea lion research for my doctoral dissertation. Bertha, Lewis, and I moved to Juneau, our new home, in the spring of 1958. Anticipation of statehood was feverishly high, causing most people to now seriously wonder how they would be affected. Those of us long striving and preparing for statehood enjoyed a cautious euphoria.

CHAPTER TWENTY-TWO

The 49th Star

THE DREAM OF STATEHOOD for Alaska had been moving toward reality for years. Delegates had convened in Fairbanks in the fall of 1955 for a Constitutional Convention. Most Alaskans were delighted, as was I, though federal employees generally frowned. Many of my friends in the U.S. Fish and Wildlife Service imagined all manner of bad things happening should animal-management authority be turned over to a new state lacking established organizations and experienced personnel.

265

A University of Alaska wildlife group—mostly faculty, students, and former students including me—lobbied the delegates for a constitutional article that would keep politicians from meddling in fish and game management. The idea was to place fish and game regulatory control in a bipartisan, independent commission. Some convention delegates thought the constitutional creation of a commission would fragment government and excessively insulate resource issues from the people. They voted to leave the matter to the legislature, and the people of Alaska ratified the constitution on April 24, 1956.

In retrospect, I think some of us were naive in believing that management of fish and game could be shielded from politics. There would always be political battles in the competition among commercial, subsistence, and recreational users, and conflicts over timber cutting, mineral extraction, and water use.

I was in Dillingham on June 30, 1958, when word reached us over the radio that Congress had that day passed the Alaska Statehood Act. With my colleague Cal Lensink, I went to Anchorage but was too late to join in the pandemonium and celebration that erupted there. Then we learned that oil had been discovered on the Kenai Peninsula. There seemed no way of telling what the discovery might mean; it was wait and see. More immediate uncertainty struck with the news that Clarence Rhode, of the U.S. Fish and Wildlife Service, my first employer as a student biologist, was missing on a flight to the arctic coast. Twenty-one years would pass before the wreckage of Rhode's plane was discovered by two backpackers near the Ivishak River in the Brooks Range.

Cal and I flew on to Cordova and journeyed from there in a skiff to Lewis Island to continue studies of the sea lion rookery. There we heard over our tiny transistor radio on

July 7 that President Eisenhower had signed the Alaska State-hood Act. What a sense of exultation. I had lived more than half my life under territorial status, hoping and planning for statehood. It was time to sample our Everclear and cider.

The evening before departing for Cordova we again felt a need to celebrate something, maybe just our well-being, but then we remembered we had used our only remaining Everclear to preserve biological specimens. We agreed that, without diminishing our devotion to science, it would be OK to open a couple of specimen jars and salvage a little alcohol, with the sacrifice of only two deceased shrews and a pair of ovaries from a sea otter found dead on the beach.

On January 3, 1959, Alaska statehood was officially pro-claimed. The American flag now had forty-nine stars. But the feds withheld jurisdiction over fish and game until the state had laws and agencies to manage them. Governor William Egan now looked to us few souls in the Territory's fish and game agency to draft a proposed law that would define the authority and duties of the State Department of Fish and Game. I had a pretty free hand writing the sections dealing with game, even to the extent of prescribing license fees. The same duties fell to Ed Marvich for sport fisheries and to Walt Kirkness for commercial fisheries.

We included in our draft a provision for a Board of Fish and Game that would have regulatory authority but no ad-ministrative powers. Extraordinary power would be granted the department head (the commissioner) to control fishing and hunting, as needed, in specified areas by field order and announcement. This authority could be delegated to field managers, to create an efficient, real-time regulatory system. The governor submitted our draft to the legislature, and it became law quickly with little change, probably because few lobbyists were around to complicate proceedings.

In a flash of acumen during this first state legislative session, I saw a chance to do something I had vainly urged on others. Under the Statehood Act, Alaska was granted the right to select more than 100 million acres of "vacant, unappropriated and unreserved" federal lands. Among the selections, how about including the Walrus Islands? C. L. Anderson, now the commissioner of fish and game, approved my broaching the subject with the commissioner of natural resources, who instructed the director of lands to move on it. A relatively small acreage was involved, it was easy to describe, had good justification, and, I could speculate, would show fairness in the selection process, which would soon involve very large tracts of relatively featureless lands with petroleum potential.

To the surprise of many, title to the Walrus Islands was the very first land conveyed to the new state. But one problem surfaced: the new State Land Act provided that no area larger than 640 acres, which amounted to a fraction of the Walrus Islands, could be reserved for single-purpose use except by approval of the legislature. This obstacle was overcome by legislators who had nurtured the department in territorial days and by old friends Harold Hansen and Jay Hammond, who won seats in the first state election. They passed another law, creating the Walrus Islands State Game Sanctuary. This action was deeply gratifying, though ominous threats to other areas were incubating.

SHORTLY AFTER THE FIRST LEGISLATURE adjourned, Dr. Edward Teller, the famed nuclear physicist, was in Juneau to brief the governor and seek his endorsement for Project Chariot, an Atomic Energy Commission (AEC) plan to use nuclear energy to blast a harbor at Ogotoruk Creek near Point

Hope in northwestern Alaska. The governor was recovering from gall bladder surgery and wasn't available. The Alaska secretary of state, Hugh J. Wade, asked for assistance from Commissioner Anderson, who in turn asked me to meet with Teller, a guest now at the governor's mansion. Representing the governor fell to me only because no other biologist was immediately available who had much knowledge of the Arctic or the Inupiat Eskimos.

Scientists from the AEC had been touring Alaska, drumming up support for the project. The Chambers of Commerce, the president of the University of Alaska, unions, and editors and publishers of Alaska's largest newspapers embraced the plan. The legislature even passed a resolution of support. The only objections came from a few faculty members at the University of Alaska, who pointed to the absence of studies to evaluate public health and ecological risks. Governor Egan had yet to express a position.

I listened carefully to Teller, fascinated both by his explanation of Project Chariot and by his extraordinarily bushy eyebrows, which seemed to fortify his message. He said the blast would create a harbor that would help develop Alaska, with assurance of no detectable risks to the people or the environment. To reassure doubters, he had authorized biological and ecological research that was even then under way. Sensing he was about to end his monologue, I asked for information the governor should have on the question of public safety.

I wanted to know how such a massive nuclear excavation could avoid injecting substantial amounts of radioactive debris into the atmosphere. Teller replied, in essence, that little if any radioactive release would occur, but if it did, it would be safely diluted in the atmosphere. In public statements, he had claimed that radiation risks associated with

Chariot were less than those from his wristwatch. I didn't ask about the possibility of radioactive isotopes entering food chains, because he had just assured me that such questions were being researched.

The pronouncements of Teller and his associates that Alaska was being favored with a project that would aid development of its tremendous natural resources had won over many people. But I was confident that, as applied to Ogotoruk Creek, Teller's assessment was so much malarkey. Though a giant in nuclear physics, he had probably never met an Eskimo, and was even less familiar with arctic ecology and economies. I asked him how and when Project Chariot would generate economic gains, and he winced that such a question should be posed. Perhaps because the allure of economic benefit was the sole basis for garnering support in Alaska, he retorted in high irritation that if the Soviet Union should surpass the United States in the development and use of nuclear energy, it would be one of the worst setbacks in his life.

I seemed to be in a minority in wanting to pin Teller down on the realities of Project Chariot. A lot of people appeared to be mesmerized as they shared Teller's grand visions of geographical engineering, of literally reshaping the world for man's benefit and pleasure. In due course, however, Project Chariot was abandoned. The reason given by AEC spoksmen was that technical events elsewhere had overtaken the need for Chariot. Environmentally concerned people, especially the Inupiat, believed their vigorous opposition won the day.

The federal government got its way on another plan for nuclear explosions in Alaska when the AEC used Amchitka Island for underground tests. Amchitka Island is part of the Aleutian Islands Reserve created by federal executive order in 1913 as a wildlife refuge, but the order permitted use of the reserve for military purposes. The distance of Amchitka Island from human populations and the Cold War tensions of the time helped the AEC justify the program. Project Longshot was fired off in October 1965 followed by Project Milrow in October 1969, both modestly scaled experiments. Then in November 1971 came Project Cannikan, a 5-megaton bomb that collapsed cliffs, drained lakes, and killed, among other things, seven hundred to a thousand sea otters. Given the national-security concerns of the time, these effects were generally considered acceptable.

CHAPTER TWENTY-THREE

I Become a Bureaucrat

IT WAS A HECTIC RUN-UP to January 1, 1960, when the state of Alaska officially took over authority for fish and game. We had only a few months to hire good people, set up our offices, and draft the full scope of fish and game regulations. My new role as a bureaucrat, casting me with people and institutions rather than with wildlife in the open air, was sobering. I was never more conscious of my new situation than when I saw the department's new employees dashing off to the field to carry out the kind of animal studies I used to thrive on. I was shackled to a desk while Sam Harbo began his wildlife research in the Bering Strait region, working out of Nome. As Bob Weeden started his fieldwork on ptarmigan and grouse, I spent my time at meetings. Although I had a valuable role to play in Juneau, I was in a sense on the sidelines as Ronald Skoog headed out to follow the caribou and Robert Rausch got close to moose and wolves.

Our first state hunting and trapping regulations surprised much of the public accustomed to the inflexible style of the federal managers, with few if any changes from year to year. For example, the hunting of hooters (cock blue grouse) in the spring became legal for the first time, making honest hunters out of innumerable sourdough grouse poachers. Hunting seasons for deer were extended and bag limits were increased in response to high abundance. Beaver trapping rules were liberalized.

Perhaps the most startling change fractured dogma by providing for the taking of cow moose in parts of the Matanuska Valley and the Kenai Peninsula. From the earliest game protection laws in Alaska, there was no more serious violation than shooting a cow moose. Forbes Baker, my old commanding officer in the Territorial Guard and a longtime member of the federal Alaska Game Commission, proclaimed hunting seasons for cow moose unthinkable. Yet in some places, there were too many moose with too little food; the result was winter starvation and poor reproductive success. Proper management required the removal of some cows, which outnumbered bulls at least ten to one.

My long-standing concern about killing walruses for ivory in the Bering Strait region found some relief when the Board of Fish and Game placed a cautionary restraint on the harvest of cows: five per hunter annually, but with no limit on bulls. This wasn't a realistic regulation since walrus hunting was largely a communal activity, not an individual one, but the rule was mainly intended to foster the concept of conservation. Later we realized the walrus had reached the peak of a long period of population growth; their numbers were now dropping, simply because there wasn't enough food for them all. If we had recognized this cycle earlier, it might have been possible to slow the rate of population increase and postpone the eventual downturn by approving more killing of walruses, not less. But this would have entailed an appalling level of slaughter, and who could advocate such action or predict the consequences? This experience revealed the uncertainties in trying to manage wildlife populations that have their own long-term ecological rhythms, probably spanning the careers of four or five generations of game managers.

On another front, the board extended the ban on use of poisons to include government agencies. This new rule caused the federal wolf control program to go away. The regional director of the federal Bureau of Sport Fisheries and Wildlife was less than happy about the new restriction on his agency. So Pete Nelson decided to show the flag, in what to me seemed mischievous intent, by sending federal agents to Barrow to ticket Eskimos for shooting eider ducks out of season. No one before had ever questioned the traditional harvest of these birds, which simply aren't at Barrow during the official open hunting season.

After John Nusungingya, an Inupiat duck poacher (and state legislator), was apprehended, hunters rebelled. A total of 138 Eskimos brought ducks to the federal agents and offered themselves for arrest. The cases were dismissed, and the incident served as a major catalyst for the Natives' effort to gain legal recognition of their various rights.

The board began requiring airborne wolf hunters to have a permit issuable at the discretion of the department – and it took a further step to promote a more temperate perception of wolves by classifying them as game as well as fur animals. I think these measures began to soften the legislature's support for bounty payments on wolves.

The bounty system aimed at other "offenders" as well: seals, wolverines, coyotes, eagles, and earlier, even trout. All were issued the death penalty because they were seen as interfering in some way with human activities such as salmon fishing. Based on a recommendation in the 1920s by a federal salmon expert, the powerful salmon industry itself initiated payment of bounties on trout and persuaded the Territory to share the cost. The target species was nominally Dolly Varden, though in some areas, fishery biologists found an overwhelming dominance of rainbow trout and juvenile coho salmon tails being presented for bounty. Trout bounty payments ended during World War II. Until 1959 the Territory paid a bounty of fifty cents on bald eagles, even though research showed their predation on salmon was of no significance.

With increasing criticism, the entire bounty system slowly faded, with legislative appropriations falling short of claims. The legislature finally shed itself of the program by delegating authority to the Board of Fish and Game to designate which of the state's twenty-six designated game management units qualified for bounties. In a 1970 board meeting, member Jim Rearden moved that no unit qualify. The motion passed, effectively ending the bounty system.

I STOPPED THE AERIAL HUNTING of polar bears for the 1965 season, and then the fun began. Aerial hunting of the bears had increased steadily from the 1950s. From only a few bears to begin with, the trophy count reached a hundred a year, then two hundred and climbing. Fearing a genuine conservation problem in the making, I issued an emergency regulation stopping aerial hunting for the season. The guides were outraged. The legislature was in session, and Senator Bob Blodgett from Teller, where a few guides located their operations and patronized his trading post, flew into a frenzy. His ravings may have intimidated some legislators into siding with him.

Walt Kirkness, who had succeeded C. L. Anderson as commissioner of fish and game, and I were called before the Senate for an accounting. We had several good and reasonable friends there, though their voices were drowned out by the raucous shouting of Blodgett and his trading partners. The dressing-down was laced with personal vindictiveness. We refused to back down.

The result was Senate Resolution 12, censuring Walt and me, which passed by voice vote. Worse was to come. Unknown to us, Senate Resolution 13 was being circulated. This document noted the "high handed, arrogant actions of the Department served by a rubber-stamp Fish and Game Board." It threatened that "a reactionary legislature would rise up against the Department and remove its vicious, dictatorial powers and slash the game budget to a skeletal force." It went on to accuse the Department of Fish and Game of "a despotic attempt to force a no bounty system on the people of the state." I was certainly guilty of the last accusation, though I'd have to dispute "despotic." Resolution 13 also passed by voice vote, though the high decibel "yeas" possibly drowned out a larger vote of "nays."

Fortunately I had assigned Jack Lentfer, a brilliant, tough-as-rawhide biologist, to collate available data on the polar bears and design a research project. He developed a plan that promised to yield a better understanding of the life history, the range of movement, and the abundance of polar bears. Coincidentally, all countries around the polar basin began fretting about the well-being of polar bears.

Our efforts to control the killing of polar bears didn't go unnoticed. U.S. Senator Bob Bartlett of Alaska and Secretary of the Interior Stewart Udall called an international conference to consider actions for conservation of the bear. The Department of Fish and Game made arrangements for the First International Scientific Meeting on the Polar Bear, in September 1966 at Fairbanks. The attendance was extraordinary, with Canada, Russia, Norway, and Denmark (for Greenland) sending delegates. Jack Lentfer and I attended as delegates and were pleased to find that Alaska, largely due to Jack's efforts, was well advanced in research relative to what others were doing.

A high point of the meeting for me was to chat with Bob Bartlett. When I mentioned that I had once spent time in his father's cabin on the Little Delta River while waiting for an airplane pickup, he eagerly asked for more details about the place. As a boy he had spent many happy months there. Until Bob's death, a few years later, we corresponded regularly on such matters as Native reservations and the pleasures and risks of using tobacco. He never voluntarily quit cigarettes; I did.

BROWN BEARS WERE ON THE AGENDA, too, including a tricky situation that can be traced back to a Russian undertaking in 1795. In that year Russians brought a small number of tough Siberian cattle to Alaska's Kodiak Island. The original animals multiplied to about 250 head by 1833, but may have numbered no more than 60 by the early 1880s. These animals were kept for milk and meat production; they were closely tended and not reported to be much troubled by bears. Some of the descendants of the original cattle are said to have survived in pure form until other types were introduced in the 1920s.

The first efforts at open-range cattle raising on Kodiak Island began in the mid-1920s, but intensified during the 1930s with the coming of several experienced stockmen displaced from the Lower 48 states by the Great Depression. They saw wonderful possibilities for open-range cattle production based on the profusion of foliage during the summer. The realities of hard winters and wet spring weather would later disillusion them as the cattle starved, or came through so weakened that calf survival suffered. Brown bears scavenged carcasses and began killing cattle. Losing cattle after they had survived the winter infuriated the stockmen. Bears were shot at every opportunity.

A few ranchers hung on for some years before selling out to others who entertained visions of becoming cattle barons. Very little meat was marketed through the years. For the next few decades many people cycled through hardship and failure trying to make a living from cattle on Kodiak Island. Because each rancher had so few animals, any loss to bears was considered catastrophic. Ranchers appealed in vain to the U.S. Department of Agriculture for a bounty of fifty to one hundred dollars on bears. It was said that such a bounty would have made a dead bear worth more than a live cow.

This situation prevailed up to the time of statehood and was to cause our department some trouble and embarrassment. Federal law in Alaska had long permitted the killing of wildlife in defense of life and property, and game agents assisted ranchers in removing problem bears. State law contained this same provision, so our department continued the practice of helping ranchers with bear control.

For a few years, everyone seemed content with this program. But in 1963 the man in charge of the department's Division of Protection at Kodiak became overburdened with other duties and assigned the bear control task to David Henley, a pilot on his staff. Henley dabbled in cattle ranching himself before taking the state job, and remained president of the Kodiak Stock Growers Association for a while. As a former Air Corps fighter pilot, Henley knew something about aircraft and guns. The new assignment led him to mount an M1 rifle atop a Piper airplane owned by one of the cattle ranchers.

Either alone or with Gilbert Jarvela, a bush pilot and a member of the legislature, Henley began killing bears at a record rate with the Piper fighter plane. Officers in the Division of Protection kept mum about the bear shootings, which continued for some time before they came to the attention of Commissioner Kirkness and me. We immediately put a stop to Henley's hunting; there was no justification for shooting so many bears because now and then one was accused of molesting cattle.

A biologist named Jim Heming learned of the aerial shootings and tipped off the editor of *Outdoor Life* magazine, who in turn contacted Jim Rearden. Rearden called Commissioner Kirkness and asked about doing a story on the program for *Outdoor Life*. Walt said, "Fine, go ahead. Tell it as you see it—no restrictions."

That's just what Rearden did. The cover of the August 1964 issue of *Outdoor Life* featured a painting of a Piper aircraft with a mounted rifle, attacking a bear. As the story unfolded, I was ever more surprised and embarrassed; it did justify questions about how the department had dealt with the issue of bears and cattle. Rearden concluded that the root problem came from the federal creation of a wildlife refuge followed by the leasing of federal land next door for cattle raising.

Al Erickson of the Division of Game went to Kodiak to learn more about the bear killings and got trapped in a meeting with ranchers and their sympathizers, including a couple of legislators. Al was a notoriously plucky, dynamic guy, rarely if ever intimidated by man or beast. Because he was the only speaker willing to say that bears, too, had value, he drew the group's wrath. He was maligned by this intolerant bunch that was seeking a scapegoat for erosion of their cattle-ranching aspirations, which were already problematic, bears or no bears. A powerful state senator and esteemed pioneer lady, Irene Ryan, harshly impugned him at the meeting for seeming to be as concerned about the welfare of bears as for the welfare of cattlemen. Her complaints rattled around in high places, thereafter causing Erickson and all the department's professionals to be a little gun-shy when politicians were working their constituents.

CHAPTER TWENTY-FOUR

On Thin Ice

IN 1967 I REALIZED a startling fact: I had been in charge of game management for Alaska, both territory and state, for ten years. My initial excitement at fashioning something new and better was fading as we implemented the reforms of previous years. It was hard to find satisfaction in the ever-lengthier meetings of the Board of Fish and Game, with their ritualized haggling over hunting seasons, bag limits, and such. A career change was in the wind. The new governor made my decision for me.

Walter J. Hickel, a Republican, defeated Governor Bill Egan, a Democrat, in the 1966 gubernatorial election. Wally and I shared a little personal history in that we both reached Alaska in early 1940 aboard the SS *Yukon*, traveling steerage class. That's about all we had in common; from there our interests and careers took very different paths. Of course, as governor he wanted to put his own stamp on his administration. Hickel sent an assistant named Carl McMurray to our headquarters in Juneau to tell Walt Kirkness, Ed Marvich, and me that we were dismissed

Walt and Ed accepted federal jobs in Washington, D. C., but I couldn't abide the thought of leaving Alaska. When I heard the Alaska Flag Song, it stirred me almost like the national anthem. Bertha liked Juneau and enjoyed her work with a state agency, but my job prospects there were nil. While mailing out job inquiries and applications, I became pretty dejected, feeling shut out of my beloved career field. I sort of went to the dogs, literally.

For many years, training retrievers for hunting and field trials was my favorite hobby. Now, with time on my hands, I traveled around the state and even to the West Coast of the Lower 48 to compete in retriever field trials with our Labrador, Taku Tiger, and our Chesapeake, Bobby. Whatever temporary solace these sojourns offered, they exacerbated another problem. Bertha and I were drifting apart after twenty-one years of marriage. Lacking the spark of earlier times, we could no longer take difficult challenges in stride, and we divorced. Lewis would stay with his mother. Bertha also wanted to keep Tiger, a wonderful companion in house or field.

I credit my good friend Clarence Pautzke Sr. with reviving my career. A former deputy commissioner of fish and game in Alaska, he was now commissioner of the U.S. Fish and Wildlife Service. One day I got a call from Thomas

Baskett, head of the agency's wildlife research branch. He offered me a research position focusing on polar bears; the job would be based in Anchorage. I accepted, and with my dog, Bobby, loaded the station wagon and left Juneau with mixed feelings of hope and sadness.

Upon arriving in Anchorage, I received a phone call from my father in Detroit. He was in a hospital, and I think he just wanted to say a last good-bye. By the time I arrived in Detroit, he had died. The year was not a good one for me — displaced from my chosen career, divorced from my wife, and now the loss of my father.

I RELISHED THE PROSPECT of working in the Arctic again. I would be collaborating with Jack Lentfer, who was still leading the polar bear research project for the state Department of Fish and Game. Jack would work out of Barrow, and I would operate from Cape Lisburne on the Chukchi Sea.

There was a lot we didn't know about polar bears, so there were many questions. How many polar bears are present on the ice pack off Alaska? Do individual bears roam the entire arctic basin or are they part of regional populations? Where do pregnant bears make their dens? How often and at what age do they breed?

The plan was to capture live bears and record their sex, size, and reproductive condition. Jack had come up with a technique for catching bears by shooting them with an anesthetic-loaded dart from a helicopter. We would place plastic tags in the ears, take a premolar tooth for age determination, and tattoo an identifying number inside the lip. To be sure we wouldn't mistakenly recapture one of the bears, we painted a conspicuous, indelible number on the side of each animal. The hunting guides despised us: the paint nullified the trophy value of the bear.

We located polar bears the same way guides and hunters did. Two aircraft flew together over the ice pack. Bears were usually found by following their tracks, although they were often seen simply by flying along open-water leads. When guides sighted a bear, they would land nearby with their hunter while the second aircraft hazed the bear toward them. We were sometimes disappointed to find a "red bear" — a carcass stripped of its hide and its head — after following a track for miles. Someone had his trophy.

My pilots that first year were Mort Clement with his Cessna 185, a fellow who had experience as a polar bear guide, and helicopter pilot Joe Soloy, the first person to fly helicopters in support of an Antarctic whaling fleet. With the additional help of field assistant Sterling Eide, we flew every day that weather allowed in temperatures ranging from 30 degrees above zero Fahrenheit to 30 degrees below, from late February to the first of April. On our first morning over the ice, Sterling pointed out a line of evenly spaced holes across a thinly frozen lead. A polar bear had crossed, swimming underwater and, about every twenty yards, breaking holes through the ice to breathe.

During the first field season we caught, processed, and released forty-eight polar bears. Over the next four years I worked with a succession of fine pilots and assistants. Flying over the ice pack and handling polar bears became routine — mostly. We carried a .30-06 caliber rifle just in case. Whenever we approached a bear that we had hit from the air with an anesthetic dart but wasn't yet completely out, we kept the rifle ready while I approached to add more drug by hand syringe.

I only needed the rifle once. We had fired the darts at a sow bear and her two cubs. The cubs were more than two years old, and big — about the size of adult black bears. As usual, the cubs ended up lying very close to their mother.

When I walked up to the animals, I saw that one cub seemed alert, turning its head to look at me. While preparing a hand syringe, I looked for the location of the dart that had been fired into the cub. There was no dart. This bear then stood on all fours and faced me. With my equipment bag in hand, I slowly moved back a few steps, and the bear came forward. I moved faster and it moved faster. I turned and started to run. After giving me a head start of several yards, the bear came after me. Just as I thought it was about to grab me, I swerved to my right and opened a gap. At that moment I heard a rifle shot, and the bear stopped.

Cub Martin, my helicopter pilot, had fired the rifle, not to hit the bear but rather to distract it. I turned and ran directly toward the helicopter. The bear came after me again at a full run. I accidentally dropped my instrument bag, and the animal hesitated briefly as it came to the bag.

When I reached Cub, I took the rifle and told him to get into the helicopter. As he ran around the front of the aircraft, I opened the side door and jumped in. The bear lunged up into the doorway. With the rifle across my lap, I pushed the muzzle at its throat and pulled the trigger. It was the sorry end to this experience and left me with a lousy feeling. I was there to help the bears, however indirectly, and now I had killed one.

After the 1966 international meeting at the University of Alaska dealing with polar bears, similar meetings to coordinate research took place elsewhere annually until 1972. Jack Lentfer and I attended them all. Savva Uspensky of the USSR was the arctic patriarch among us. He had devoted much of his career to studies of the animals of eastern Siberia, along the way discovering that Wrangel Island, off the northeast coast of Siberia, was a main center of polar bear maternal denning. Other areas of denning by pregnant bears were located around the polar basin, but we came to conclude that most of the bears in the Chukchi Sea probably originated on Wrangel Island. We were also beginning to get some rather encouraging information about the well-being of polars bears in various arctic regions. In 1972 the U.S. Congress enacted the Marine Mammal Protection Act, giving polar bears in areas of U.S. jurisdiction total protection from hunting, except for subsistence taking by Alaska Natives.

ONE YEAR I ASKED USPENSKY if I might get permission to visit Wrangel Island. He didn't seem optimistic, but he said he would look into it with Soviet authorities. Then Uspensky asked me about the possibility of obtaining musk ox from Alaska's Nunivak Island for transplant to Wrangel Island, and I gave him about the same reply. We both came up empty-handed: the time wasn't right.

I finally got to see Wrangel Island from the air, anyway. At Cape Lisburne we were within flying range of Wrangel — that is, if we carried as much fuel as possible and had the right weather. Almost as a lark I mentioned the idea of such a flight to my pilots, Charlie Allen and Cub Martin. They were game for it, even when I mentioned the possibility of being intercepted and maybe held by the Soviets. I justified the flight on grounds that I was just doing my job, and on this day we would be looking for polar bears across the central part of the Chukchi Sea.

On March 29, 1972, under a high-pressure system with little wind, a clear sky, and the temperature at minus 30 degrees Fahrenheit, we loaded extra fuel in five-gallon cans aboard both aircraft, mostly jet fuel for the helicopter, and in loose formation steered a heading of 305 degrees for Wrangel Island. I was riding with Cub in his helicopter; Charlie was flying his Cessna 185. On the way I counted every polar bear track that we crossed. We landed several times to transfer fuel from the cans into the aircraft tanks. For the last hundred miles to Wrangel Island, we flew very low, hoping to avoid showing up on Russian radar screens. This got a little spooky when we crossed many miles of open water just east of Wrangell Island.

We flew westerly along the south shore of the island until we spotted several buildings and an antenna tower. We quickly turned back and flew to Herald Island, which we circled. I suspect this little-known, remote island is also used for denning by pregnant polar bears. I counted 121 bear tracks on the four-hour outbound flight to Wrangel Island, with tracks common even in the central Chukchi Sea.

Our return-flight course to Alaska had an accidental dogleg. Cub Martin and I in the helicopter trusted Charlie Allen to do the navigating because our magnetic compass was erratic. Still, we thought that Charlie's heading was several degrees too far north. When questioned about it, he sounded miffed. We continued flying without sighting the coast.

Finally, Charlie called the FAA radar station at Point Lay to ask for our position. What a surprise. We were ninety miles to the west, on course for Wainwright. Charlie quickly figured out the problem. Empty metal fuel cans in the cabin had slid forward under the instrument panel, causing deviation in his compass. Point Lay gave us a steer for Cape Lisburne. With the air temperature still at minus 30 degrees, and the light—as well as our fuel supply—fading, we had to decide whether to go directly to the beach or head straight home. Going home entailed more risk, but promised more rewards.

Eventually we landed back at Cape Lisburne by starlight, with a mere nine pounds of fuel left in the helicopter. Despite a little tension due to the navigation error toward the end, it had been a gratifying trip. We had flown eight hours and forty minutes in lovely weather over the absolutely clean, beautiful, and seemingly endless ice pack. For fear of embarrassing Uspensky, I never told him about our unauthorized flight to Wrangel Island.

THE DISCOVERY OF OIL near Prudhoe Bay jolted my attention away from polar bears for a while back in 1968. The immensity of this discovery on the arctic coast wasn't yet known, so it stirred little notice in the environmental community. I wanted to get to Prudhoe Bay and see firsthand the effects on the land.

Along with Averill Thayer, manager of the Arctic National Wildlife Refuge, I spent several days talking with oilmen and examining disturbed tundra from the air and on the ground. Seismic operations involving surface detonations had left ugly craters scattered widely over the region. We also noted severe scarring of the tundra from moving heavy drilling equipment. Once the insulating vegetative surface of the tundra is broken, the underlying permafrost thaws, multiplying the damage. Liquid waste from drilling was stored in open, overflowing ponds. The oil operators were showing no concern for the environment.

After a follow-up visit to Prudhoe Bay, I wrote a report to my Washington supervisor. It was the first heads-up on the situation that the Fish and Wildlife Service had received directly, and it excited considerable interest. The report was published and found its way to a number of congressional offices. I suspect that it hastened the decision to get moving on a full-fledged environmental impact statement. In 1969 I received a commendation for the report from the new U.S. secretary of the interior, Wally Hickel—the same Wally Hickel who had dismissed me from my job as direc-

tor of the state Division of Game when he became governor of Alaska.

YOU MIGHT SAY I also have Wally Hickel to thank for bringing me back into state employment. After Hickel quit the
governorship to head the Department of the Interior, he was
succeeded by Keith Miller, who then lost in the 1969 general
election to Bill Egan, the first governor of the state. Egan
had been governor during most of my time as head of the
state Division of Game, and now I got word that he wanted
me to return to my old job. I pondered the offer briefly. Returning to Juneau in that capacity would have been a short-
term political move, neither financially nor professionally
rewarding. I declined, but said I would consider appointment as the overall boss — Commissioner of Fish and Game,
head of both the game and fish divisions.

I received no response to this proposal, so I thought no
more about state employment. But then in July 1972, I received a phone call at home. A familiar voice said, "Jim, this
is Bill. How are you? I've been meaning to call you. I'd like
you to come down and be my Commissioner of Fish and
Game. Would you consider that?" Without hesitation I said
I would be very happy to accept the appointment.

In Juneau the familiar old leaky-roofed Subport Building still served as headquarters, and many friends welcomed
me back. Soon thereafter, on a state business trip to Anchorage, I was met at the airport by a lovely lady friend of mine
who was in a joyous mood. She had fallen in love with a fine
gentleman, a successful businessman widowed a few years
earlier, who was everything she desired in a mate. They were
soon to be married. Instantly, I felt a hollow place inside, but
also gladness in seeing her have what she so rightfully de-

served. I also felt thankful, perhaps rationalizing that the time she had devoted to me had bridged an uncertain phase in her life leading to this wonderful new course. Before long, another woman altered the track of my own life.

To my surprise, Peter and Christa Bading, good friends in Anchorage, were divorced. Peter had served in the German Army during World War II. After the war he emigrated to Canada and on to Alaska where he became a naturalized U.S. citizen. He was a proud man, sometimes a little pompous, but also charismatic to those he liked and respected, usually government officials or successful professional or business people either German or American.

For some reason, his own business ventures seemed to flower and wilt, without noticeably dampening his enthusiasm. During a visit to Germany in 1965, he met and married Christa Helfrich, a somewhat younger, very attractive physician, and brought her home to Anchorage. The following year they had a daughter, Beatrice.

The Badings were gracious hosts, and their home seemed to be a hostel for a constant flow of guests, mostly Germans of some notable official, artistic, or business stature. During lulls, Peter and Christa occasionally invited me to dinner, followed by an evening of chess. I was unaware of problems between the couple beyond some indication that, as a former busy doctor in Germany, Christa chafed at her new, unending role of hostess that included a raft of charwoman duties.

Aside from tending her flower garden, her only chance for outdoor activity was training her Chesapeake retriever. But the marriage failed, with Christa then being a mother with a young daughter, no work opportunity in her profession, and the prospect of returning to Germany disillusioned. I saw her as a very pretty, energetic woman who shared many of my interests; ideas of romance came easily. I invited Christa to Juneau to have a look at this beautiful part of Alaska. She liked it. Suffice to say, some months later we were married, and I adopted Beatrice. Peter quickly remarried. We remained friends and chess adversaries until his death some years later.

The mountains and forests surrounding Juneau beckoned Christa; with our dogs she hurried to hike every trail, climb on the local mountains, search out and harvest the mushrooms and berries. These activities were reliving the delights of childhood. She had grown up in Bavaria, living in an old government castle assigned to her father, who managed the state forests, including the wildlife. The outdoor pursuits marvelously complemented Christa's more serious devotion to reviving her medical career.

She studied at our dining room table over a couple of years to gain facility in English medical and technical language, and then passed the federal examination to have her foreign medical training recognized in this country. When she accepted a residency at St. Lukes Hospital in Fargo, North Dakota, we sent Beatrice, now in the third grade, to live with her grandparents in Germany and attend an American school that served U.S. military children.

In the summer of 1976 we were all reunited in Juneau. Christa got her medical license in Alaska and began assisting other physicians part time, but then arranged a more formal association with another physician, Linda Larsen. About a year later, Dr. Larsen's unfortunate death shocked and bewildered Christa. After reviewing the new situation, she decided to buy Larsen's business assets and to open her own clinic. From that point, our personal and professional lives meshed well, although we seemed to have less and less time for the outdoor activities we loved so much.

CHAPTER TWENTY-FIVE

Tightrope Walking

FISH AND GAME can lead to fightin' words in Alaska. When it comes to the salmon and bears and wolves and other creatures of this great land, everyone has a strong opinion. So it's no surprise I ended up in the middle of a few controversies during my time as commissioner of fish and game: it comes with the job.

Take the summer of 1972, for example, when over thirty dead caribou were found closely clustered on Donnelly Dome south of Fort Greely. The *Fairbanks Daily News-Miner* reported speculation that the animals died as a result of secret military activities. Public concern grew out of the known presence of a small nuclear power plant at Fort Greely, as well as suspicions about experiments related to biological and chemical warfare. Governor Egan was alarmed and asked me to look into it.

I felt queasy about the situation. I remembered back to a period before 1967 when I had top-secret security clearance to act as liaison between the governor and military people at Fort Greely. Periodically a uniformed Army general accompanied by civiliain scientists would come to my office to brief me on experiments involving aerosols, pathogen simulants, dispersal projections, and other ominous aspects of biological and chemical warfare—along with their assurances that there was no danger to public safety. Neither the governor nor I knew whether such tests had continued beyond 1967—but if they had, was it possible now that something had gone wrong?

The mystery deepened when my department's biologists examined these caribou and autopsied some of them, finding nothing abnormal. Then one biologist noticed the hair between the animals' hooves appeared to be burned. They returned to Donnelly Dome to check the site of the deaths and discovered streaks and veins of charred soil and duff not obvious in the overlying vegetation. The caribou mystery was solved: the animals had been killed by lightning.

IF YOU WANT TO SEE a furor erupt, just try withdrawing what some Alaskans consider a God-given right. In late 1972 I concluded that aerial shooting of wolves should be stopped. I directed that no more permits be issued for shooting wolves from aircraft unless we knew that wolves were killing ex-

cessive numbers of big game. This action was the first significant legal restraint ever on killing Alaska's wolves.

I stopped this type of hunting for a number of reasons.
From 1960 until 1967 I had worked to bring changes in the
management of wolves, and now I felt a keen interest in
reviewing how our treatment of the animals fit the contem-
porary scene. Segments of the public had begun to question
the rightness of aerial hunting, prompted by abuses such as
poaching in Denali National Park. Aerial hunters sometimes
wounded wolves without being able to complete the kill,
leaving injured animals. And there was nothing sporting
about instances in which wolves were killed but the carcasses
were then just left on the ground. Unfortunately, Alaska's
free-for-the-asking permits for aerial shooting of wolves
seemed to bear out official recognition of the wolf as a harm-
ful, unwanted animal. In contrast, federal law already pro-
hibited aerial shooting on federal lands except as part of an
animal control program.

As soon as word got out that the state had also banned
the practice, aerial hunters screamed about this outrageous
protection of wolves. And of course people who favored the
ban got into the act. The uproar drew wide, even national,
attention in the media. In defense of wolves, petition-style
letters arrived signed by whole classrooms of children who
argued that the wicked nature of wolves was nothing but
nursery-rhyme fiction. Governor Egan's correspondence
secretary, Reva LaFavour, was near panic trying to cope with
the deluge of mail, and I helped her compose replies.

Even though we stood our ground, I soon learned that
denying permits for aerial shooting lacked any real effect. It
didn't change the behavior of hunters and it didn't reduce
the number of wolves killed. The hunters simply began landing on the ground and shooting the wolves they had spot-

ted from the air. Or they claimed that is what they did, if they were accused of aerial shooting. In other words, the hunters exploited a loophole in the rules.

The Board of Fish and Game quickly found the wolf to be a lively agenda topic, particularly on the question of whether wolf control was needed in some areas. Most board members were careful in their judgments, but one unabashed wolf hater, Ivan Thorall from Fairbanks and Chisana, tried to quell debate by citing the Bible's book of Genesis as a testament to man's dominance over all living things. No one at the table had an audible response to Ivan.

In 1975 an aerial survey of the western arctic caribou herd indicated an astounding collapse in numbers from 240,000 to 50,000 animals within the preceding five years. There were a lot of possible causes—too much hunting, predation by wolves and bears, bad weather, disease. But in any case, it looked like a situation where wolves were at least partly responsible for killing caribou that could have been used for food by people living in the herd's range. So we issued permits for aerial hunting of wolves in the range. Forty-eight wolves were taken by aerial hunters and three times that number by hunters and trappers on snow machines (snowmobiles).

These efforts were thought to have removed about 20 percent of the wolves present at the beginning. The caribou herd then appeared to stage an extraordinary recovery. Killing of the wolves generally got the credit, and at the time I was happy enough to entertain this notion. On reflection, however, it seems highly dubious that minor jiggling of predation levels—getting rid of 20 percent of the wolves—could trigger such a quick and extreme response. By the year 2001, the herd had grown to a half million animals and expanded its range southward through the Seward Peninsula and beyond. The humbling conclusion may simply be that a wild-life population can sometimes take its own course, confounding our best assessments and remedies.

We also issued permits for aerial shooting of wolves in 1975 in a large area south of Fairbanks because there were indications that wolves were killing too many moose. After that the number of moose increased modestly. Drastic thinning of wolf numbers in the Nelchina River basin brought little or no enduring change in the moose population. These results, not at all spectacular, probably typify the uncertain effects of wolf predation.

Without human interference, wolves and moose likely trend toward sparser numbers. Early explorers in Alaska and the Yukon reported a scarcity of moose as the common condition, evidently the consequence of a freely operating predator-prey system with no tinkering by man. The relatively great abundance of moose in more recent times suggests they somehow escaped the bonds of predation. I believe this began to happen soon after the arrival of non-Native hunters and trappers with their guns, steel traps and snares, and especially strychnine to kill the natural predators such as wolves. With a greater density of moose, and probably sheep and caribou as well, other agencies of population control accordingly came into play.

I have to say that in my years of trying to manage predation by wolves, about the only clear result is that it prompts a terrific amount of public debate.

IT SOMETIMES FELT like walking a tightrope as we tried to balance competing interests in the fish and other sea life of Alaska. The salmon failures in 1972 and 1973 were unprecedented. In all regions except the Yukon and Kuskokwim

Rivers, salmon failed to return in anything like expected numbers (the result of earlier harsh winters that killed many juvenile salmon). We set severe restrictions on fishermen to assure that fish could escape to spawning areas. Imagine the frustration of the fishermen who reported fish in never-before-seen abundance, the water surface allegedly silver with jumpers as far as the eye could see. It turned out this was nearly the case in the Noyes Island district, but the fish were sockeyes (red salmon) bound for Canada. Alaska fishermen had no legal right to these fish.

Another tricky issue involved the sale of roe taken from salmon that were caught for subsistence use (for the personal use of the people doing the fishing). The law said that fish caught for subsistence could not be sold. This included the roe, which wasn't traditionally used by subsistence fishermen but was in great demand as caviar by Japanese buyers. Natives appealed for permission to sell this otherwise wasted by-product. My sympathies were with them. I ignored the advice of Carl Rosier, the director of commercial fisheries, and persuaded myself that the Natives would benefit and not abuse the right to sell roe.

Then came the flack. Senator Bob Palmer alleged that the move was politically motivated, an attempt to curry favor with the Natives. I was further embarrassed when fishermen betrayed my trust by catching more salmon than they needed for subsistence, discarding the surplus fish after stripping the roe. I had to reverse my original decision, incurring the wrath of all sides.

This disagreement was nothing compared with the battles over the state's rules on catching king crabs. During the 1960s the Alaska king crab industry had developed into perhaps the most economically rewarding fishery in the world. These giant crabs, looking like spiders that measured three feet across outstretched legs, were coveted by seafood dealers and consumers. By 1972 the fishery faced trouble from excessive harvests and competition. Regulations were aimed at conservation and at sharing the fishing opportunities, but of course not everyone was satisfied.

In August 1973 a group of king crab vessel owners in Seattle complained in a letter to U.S. Senator Warren G. Magnuson of Washington state that some Alaska crab regulations are "aimed solely at excluding us from competing with their [Alaskan] small fleets, and also with our Japanese, Korean, and Russian counterparts." In turn, Governor Egan called the Seattle group "a classical example of non-residents who still feel they can come to Alaska, exploit our resources wantonly and get out without contributing anything...."

After more jostling back and forth, the situation turned serious. Shortly before the scheduled July 1, 1974, opening of the Bering Sea king crab fishery, owners of the Seattle fleet announced they would not recognize the regulations or the jurisdiction of the state beyond three miles off shore. They declared their own fishing season, with an opening date of June 24. We quickly learned that many king crab pots were indeed already set and fishing in the Bering Sea. I promptly sent telegrams to the Seattle group, making it clear that the season in the Bering Sea would be delayed until the illegal crab fishing stopped and all crab pots were removed. Alaska had unquestioned authority to regulate within three miles, and because the crabs had to be delivered in live condition to shore plants for processing we held a strong hand.

With their huge fleet now mostly at anchor in Dutch Harbor, the Seattle owners retreated to a more conciliatory position. Their spokesman, Ron Jensen, appeared in Juneau to discuss the stalemate with me, offering assurances that the fleet would comply with state regulations. I knew Ron as a sophisticated, honest person and an astute businessman whose word was as good as gold, but the situation was aggravated by the illegal pots in the Bering Sea. There could be no compromise on the need to move all pots to designated storage areas, with gates open, and then to inspect the holding tanks of the vessels.

We didn't have an easy time verifying removal of the crab pots. We were limited to using chartered aircraft and two vessels. The immensity of the area to be searched coupled with bad weather made the task agonizingly slow, and fishermen's tempers frayed. But when I was finally satisfied that no significant illegal fishing was possible, I opened the king crab season. For the time being, at least in this case, the authority of the State of Alaska was affirmed.

THE MUSK OX ON NUNIVAK ISLAND became quite an issue, prompting a showdown between state and federal authorities, with the Soviet Union also in on the tussle. An environmental agreement between the U.S. and the Soviets in 1972 led to a deal for relocating some musk ox from Nunivak, which is part of a federal wildlife refuge, to Wrangel Island and northeast Siberia. Originally roaming Siberia, musk ox had long ago been wiped out by humans for food. Alaskans would be happy to sample some of their own musk ox meat from Nunivak, so we asked the U.S. Fish and Wildlife Service to allow limited hunting. The agency said no.

I decided that if Americans couldn't enjoy the benefits of harvesting musk ox, we shouldn't give them away either. I notified the U.S. Fish and Wildlife Service of my opposition to the relocation. Despite this objection, the plan went ahead; the musk ox were caught on Nunivak and transported to Bethel on the Alaska mainland in preparation for the move to Russia. But Governor Jay Hammond agreed that the musk ox belonged to Alaska. State troopers halted the move, pending my issuance of a state export permit. The stalemate was broken when the Fish and Wildlife Service gave the go-ahead for limited musk ox hunting on Nunivak Island. The crated musk ox were then whisked away by a Soviet transport plane.

I didn't have a lot of time to enjoy the resolution of this crisis before a few people in Fairbanks, who had it in for me because I banned aerial shooting of wolves, saw the musk ox controversy as an opportunity to take me down. Independent journalist Joe La Rocca, whose writing appeared mainly in the *Fairbanks Daily News-Miner,* filed suit, alleging I had no authority to permit export of the musk ox and claiming it amounted to unlawfully giving away state property. I was subpoenaed to appear in Fairbanks district court, where I gave the judge a statutory citation authorizing my action. He promptly dismissed the case.

AS COMMISSIONER of fish and game, I inevitably was pulled into the dispute over subsistence hunting and fishing rights. It's an issue that's not yet settled, and I would simply describe my limited involvement with it as unrewarding.

The Alaska Native Claims Settlement Act of 1971 compensated Alaska's indigenous Natives for land rights mostly ignored by the federal government since the purchase of Alaska. The act conveyed 44 million acres of land and $942 million to Natives, but it gave no protection to aboriginal hunting and fishing rights. From the perspective of the Natives, Alaska's rapid population growth and advances in transportation and in hunting and fishing technology gave plenty of reason to ring the alarm bell.

In 1973, members of a delegation representing the Alaska Federation of Natives asked me to meet with them on the subject of subsistence. I had some vague anxiety about what was in store for me. These were Native leaders with an entourage of non-Natives bent on a cause: hunting and fishing by Natives must have priority over other uses such as sporting, commercial, or even personal use by urban dwellers.

The Board of Fish and Game had adopted a subsistence policy that took account of the bush population's dependence on fish and game, but did not allocate among Alaskans because the Alaska Constitution declares that fish and wildlife are reserved to all the people for common use. So the board's regulations, applicable to everyone, were especially considerate of rural residents. Now, Native leaders were dissatisfied. They wanted statutory guarantees for preservation of cultural and lifestyle traditions that were changing or being abandoned. Indeed, the aboriginal way of life had already vanished in its pure form.

When I finished reciting the board's past actions and its policy to the delegation, the response was immediate, boisterous, and disapproving, conspicuously led by non-Natives. There was no doubt that I had been set up. Activists within the Rural Alaska Community Action Program, professional counselors to the Natives, had staged this encounter to ventilate and intensify claims for an assured Native subsistence priority. They clearly were also testing their powers of intimidation. The community action people accused the department of racism and genocide, demanding that I, as commissioner, apologize.

Whatever hope I had that we could talk about specific complaints was dashed: these folks were on a political mission. While they were laying the hickory on me, I thought how interesting it would be to put these proxy-Natives, identifying so passionately with subsistence, on a diet of beluga meat and seal oil for a while, even allowing a little pilot bread and Labrador tea. However unpalatable to them, they would not dare grumble for fear of drawing a stark distinction between themselves and the Natives.

The subsistence issue found political resolution, or at least mutation, in federal law in 1980, when the Alaska National Interest and Lands Conservation Act defined subsistence uses to mean "customary and traditional uses by rural Alaskan residents of wild renewable resources...for personal or family consumption or barter." The act gave a priority to subsistence users over other users. The state failed to approve conforming legislation, so the federal government later took control of fish and wildlife jurisdiction on federal lands and waters in Alaska.

The process of allocating priority hunting and fishing opportunities to a class of people, identified as rural by place of domicile, continues to move forward. There is disagreement on whether the process should be a state or federal function. State involvement would first require Alaskans to vote on amending their Constitution, an action the legislature has so far refused to initiate. Rural folks seem comfortable with the status quo, trusting federal officials to tilt more favorably toward them. Ever greater tilt may be needed because the unprecedented rural birth rate means ever more rural people will have to share finite resources.

Meanwhile, Native leaders seem determined to see that a rural priority is principally viewed as a priority for Natives. A prominent Native leader, Byron Mallott, told the 2001 Alaska Federation of Natives convention: "Rural means Native, and if people don't understand that they are either incredibly stupid or naive."

MY FIVE-YEAR TERM as commissioner of fish and game was up in 1977, and I decided to retire from state government and find other work. Department employees staged an overwhelming retirement party. I got to hear a lot of folks, including Governor Hammond, offer words of praise that I knew were overstated, yet they made me realize I must have done a few things right.

I think little decisions were responsible for this showing of kindness and regard from the people I had worked with. I remembered how I occasionally called for a "sun break" when the sun came out after weeks of Juneau rain: it meant that employees could go home after lunch. And I welcomed dogs in the Fish and Game building—the only state building that permitted this kind of trespass. As fast as the Buildings and Grounds officials posted their No Dogs Allowed signs, I had them removed. Then there were the Christmas gatherings, and every birthday among staff members was good reason for coffee and cake. I managed to help a few employees overcome alcohol problems, and I dealt fairly with another who resisted help. During my years as commissioner, I found real pleasure in seeing the good spirit that grew among employees and hearing that Fish and Game was a great place to work.

By this time I had accepted a job offer from the National Marine Fisheries Service, and was given an intimidating title: Alaska region chief of management and enforcement. Marine mammals as well as commercial fisheries fell within my purview. I would be dealing with the momentous new federal law that extended U.S. fishery jurisdiction out two hundred miles from the coastline, in a fishery conservation zone. This law came into being after foreign fleets had virtually destroyed many fish stocks close to our shores. Canada and the USSR, with expansive adjacent waters of their own, quickly declared similar zones.

CHAPTER TWENTY-SIX

In the Zone

I HAD A LOT OF TERRITORY to cover in my new job, in more ways than one. To begin with, the huge geographical region posed a challenge in monitoring the activities of foreign fishing boats. Most left our zone when directed; some weren't inclined to go willingly.

Our special agents were assigned to Coast Guard cutters, and foreign vessels caught violating our rules were seized. Impounded foreign vessels became a common sight at Kodiak and Dutch Harbor. The Japanese minimized their risk of being caught fishing illegally by a system of tracking Coast Guard cutters, referred to in radio traffic as great white sharks. The Japanese fishing companies must have found the fishery so profitable that occasional vessel seizures were an acceptable cost of doing business. To the contrary, the skipper of a Soviet vessel was in big trouble back home if apprehended for illegal fishing.

The agency that was set up to deal with the waters off Alaska, the North Pacific Fisheries Management Council, developed plans for Alaska's huge groundfish resource, with the intention of reducing foreign fishing fleets and encouraging U.S. fishing efforts. But Americans had no groundfish catcher-processor ships and only a few vessels rigged for trawling. A further complication was an absence of domestic markets for many species including pollock, the dominant high-tonnage fish. For Americans to get started, it was necessary to enter into joint ventures with foreign companies who agreed to buy their catches at sea. Foreign fleets were permitted to take that part of the total allowable catch not harvested by U.S. fishermen.

By 1985, through a combination of enterprise and political savvy, U.S. entrepreneurs were taking full advantage of the opportunity given them by the expanded fishery zone. One hundred U.S. trawlers were delivering ever larger catches to foreign processors; American factory trawlers were also appearing on the scene. Five years later, U.S. flag vessels and shore processors (some with substantial foreign equity) had completely displaced foreign operations and were harvesting the total allowable catch of over 2 million metric tons.

The trawlers were striving for high catch rates, with little concern about incidental killing of sea lions. These abundant animals had a bad name among Alaskan fishermen for stealing black cod and halibut as longlines were being retrieved and for biting through buoys attached to crab pot lines. I winced at hearing fishermen laugh as they described how to catch sea lions by fast-dragging their trawl gear at the surface after raising it from the bottom. As many as fifty sea lions were said to be taken at once.

The killing of sea lions, by accident or on purpose, was greatest in areas adjacent to large rookeries or haul-out sites but also occurred far at sea. Fishing vessels attracted both killer whales and sea lions; observers reported sea lions attempting to climb the sides of ships in futile efforts to escape a violent end in the whales' jaws. Over a period of years, sea lion abundance declined in the entire region of trawl fishing. The sea lion population in western and central Alaska coastal regions declined sharply. Meaningful steps by the management council toward protecting the animals began only after lawsuits by environmental groups and the listing of Steller sea lions as threatened under the Endangered Species Act.

ALASKA'S ESKIMOS were hit in 1977 with a total ban on the taking of bowhead whales, imposed by the International Whaling Commission out of fear the whale population was declining. The implications to villages with a traditional dependence on bowheads were grave indeed. It was critical to the well-being of these people that they gain some relief from the prohibition. I was familiar with Eskimo bowhead whale hunting practices, having many times unsuccessfully stalked these whales with the hunters of Little Diomede Island and the village of Wales.

New to me was the modern manner of hunting bowheads at Barrow. With wealth from taxes levied on North

Slope oil companies, many people could now afford to buy aluminum boats, large outboard engines, and whatever whaling gear they fancied. A number of hunters began pursuing bowheads during their fall migration with small, fast boats, striking large numbers of whales but not retrieving them. During the 1976 fall season, estimates of struck but lost whales, though probably exaggerated, exceeded eighty. The whaling commission's scientific committee believed that more whales were being killed than were being born and growing to maturity, so they imposed the ban.

In late 1977 I went to Barrow as representative of National Marine Fisheries along with people from the National Oceanographic and Atmospheric Administration to meet with the Eskimos. We hoped to agree on an appeal to the whaling commission for a relaxation of the bowhead moratorium to satisfy the subsistence needs of the nine Eskimo whaling villages. We were successful, and the commission authorized a subsistence quota.

Now my office had to monitor the hunting. We hit a brief snag when a Barrow whaler who resented our agent's on-scene monitoring laid claim to one of our snow machines, alleging that the agent lost it in a poker game. The accusation was false, but it served the intended purpose of stirring up discontent.

With our encouragement and some financial support, the Eskimos organized their own Alaska Eskimo Whaling Commission to allocate the whale quota among the nine villages. In 1981 the authority of the Eskimo Whaling Commission was formally recognized. It was soon tested when whaler John Nusungingya refused to stop hunting after the Barrow spring whale quota had been reached. Eskimo Whaling Commission leaders persuaded Nusungingya to get off the ice, but only after what seemed to be a face-saving delay. The National Marine Mammal Laboratory involved the Eskimo commission in research that led to more confident, and much higher, estimates of bowhead numbers. These arrangements pleased the Eskimos, advancing their long-term strategy of gaining management control over all subsistence resources.

Until the ban imposed by the International Whaling Commission, the Eskimos showed no outward concern about the large number of whales that they had struck and lost. This seeming indifference toward the animals was shared by the Bering Strait Eskimos in their killing of walruses. From my time living with these Eskimos, I could understand how this attitude might not change quickly. For three thousand or more years, their hunting technology and practices had given them the means to thrive in one of the world's harshest environments. The limitations of their weapons seldom allowed them to kill more animals than they could actually use. Then came modern weapons and modern boats, which made hunting easier but didn't necessarily change the hunters' attitudes toward the animals.

Since statehood, Natives have increasingly participated in fish and game management. The bowhead whale experience led to somewhat similar cooperative arrangements in managing walrus and waterfowl. This active interest by Natives has surely advanced their understanding of conservation principles that weren't relevant back in their ancestors' day.

CHAPTER TWENTY-SEVEN

Bad Wolf, Good Wolf

EVER SINCE MY CHILDHOOD days when I gazed in wonder at the drawing of a lone wolf in a snowy, moonlit scene, my fascination with wolves has never dimmed. I've studied them, and I've hunted them; in my years with the state, I tried to manage them. Through it all I never lost my respect for this animal so central to any concept of Alaska. So I watched with growing concern as the state declared that big game would be managed for abundance, in order to guarantee enough caribou, moose, and wild sheep to satisfy sport and subsistence hunters—a strategy that cast wolves and bears in the roles of the bad guys. The issue prompted me to jump back into the fray briefly in the 1990s.

By that time the Department of Fish and Game had embraced the killing of wolves by pursuers who spotted them from the air, then landed to shoot them (it remained illegal to shoot from an aircraft). People favoring a more ecological cast to game management recommended less hunting of big-game animals rather than killing the animals' natural predator, the wolf. These dissidents were duly assailed as being anti-hunting, or worse.

With the election in 1990 of Wally Hickel as governor, once again, and the appointment of my old friend Carl Rosier as commissioner of fish and game, the manage-for-abundance concept began to move forward. In the fall of 1992, the department announced a wolf control program that incited political and public relations turmoil, including threats of tourist boycotts. This wolf flap grew out of what seemed to be an innocent move by the department and the Board of Game to appoint an Alaska wolf management planning team. The team produced a report born of much study and public participation that described a zoning system to guide decisions on wolf control.

What happened next was notably revealing—not so much about the effects of wolves on big-game animals as about a subtle strategy within the management system to achieve a previously determined result. Acting ostensibly in accord with the report, the department soon announced plans to kill several hundred wolves over five years in three immense areas of the Interior. It did not go unnoticed that the department had already placed radio collars on twenty-five wolves (called Judas wolves by some) in as many packs. The wolf packs would now be easy to find and kill.

With growing protest over the plan, Governor Hickel delayed its implementation and called for an Alaska wolf summit. He wanted to hear the opinions of experts and representatives of interest groups including national and international conservation and environmental organizations. Wayne Regelin, director of the state Division of Wildlife Conservation, invited me to attend the meeting scheduled for mid-January 1993 in Fairbanks. The invitation wiped out my reluctance to get involved again in the messy issue of wolf management.

At Fairbanks I found that wolf control advocates had called a rally for the locals at Alaskaland, a facsimile of a historic mining community. About five hundred people were there, listening to how outsiders and environmentalists were trying to undo their Alaskan way of life. That these outsiders had been invited by the governor didn't seem to lessen their threat. People at the rally were told that unless wolves were controlled by killing them, wolf packs would destroy the moose, caribou, and sheep.

On the first morning of the summit, pickets with signs and banners that vilified wolves filled the parking lot at the Carlson Center. A sign attached to a dog said "A Wolf Ate My Sister"; a counter-protester came up with a dog bearing a sign that said "My Sister Is a Wolf." The Alaska Independence Party, led by my cranky old friend of almost fifty years, Joe Vogler, was especially visible and vocal. In a crude gesture, I suppose to taunt those not keen on wolf control, unknown persons arriving early placed the bloody carcass of a wolf, freshly killed, at the entrance to the center. People had to walk over it or around it. Inside the center, both uniformed and plainclothes police stood around quietly. A reporter estimated attendance at fifteen hundred.

The summit was professionally managed, and everything proceeded pretty much as expected. Two panels gave presentations, the audience had a brief chance to comment, and the invited participants broke into groups that came up with a batch of recommendations. Game managers and hunters wanted to be sure there were as many big-game animals as possible, by eliminating a good number of wolves. Environmentalists, on the other hand, wanted to let nature take its course—or, in the jargon of game management, "to maintain multispecies interacting wildlife communities." My thinking is that the summit came off as a unique social experience exposing a lot more about human nature than about predator-prey relationships.

IN THE AFTERMATH of the wolf summit, the department and the Board of Game reduced the scope of the wolf control program, but (except for member R. T. Wallen) remained stubbornly determined to hold as much ground as possible. They went ahead with a plan to remove some wolves from popular moose hunting areas south and east of Fairbanks. The quickest and cleanest way to get this job done would have been to simply spot the wolves from helicopters and then immediately shoot them. But I suppose that the state was gun-shy after the revelation that it had previously marked some wolf packs with radio collars. The state decided to use snares and foot-hold traps instead, and professional trappers taught department personnel how to use them. Huge numbers of snares were put in place, hung in clusters around large baits—seemingly without concern that moose and caribou would also be entangled. While many wolves were caught during the winter of 1993-94, the snares also killed a dozen moose, a couple of caribou, and various fur animals.

The snaring program ended in a distressing incident that roused public protest both locally and nationally. One day in 1994, wildlife activist Gordon Haber spotted four wolves caught in snares. He said that only one wolf was dead, caught around the neck as intended; the other three were caught around the body or legs and were still alive. Haber said that when a department biologist arrived in a helicopter to kill the wolves, he used ineffective ammunition in his .22-caliber pistol. He shot the first wolf once in the forehead, once in the body, and twice behind the ear. The wolf flinched at each shot, then sat passively while the biologist returned to his helicopter for more powerful cartridges. Haber videotaped much of the incident and released it to television.

I felt sorry for Ken Taylor, one of the department's finest field biologists, who said, "I know this will be ugly. I think that everything that could go wrong went wrong." And Ken was right. The bungled snaring operation cost the department and Board of Game credibility and even inspired an initiative to ban the use of snares, which later failed at the polls. I strived for professionalism in the state's first wildlife programs, and I felt only dejection at this entire wolf fiasco. It was not the last insult to enlightened wolf management.

The Board of Game refused to reform land-and-shoot wolf hunting in the face of abundantly chronicled abuses. In dismay I joined with some retired members of the Board of Game, retired Fish and Game employees, and former governor Jay Hammond to seek change through a public ballot initiative. Our initiative called for a prohibition on the killing of wolves the same day a person has been airborne, thereby eliminating land-and-shoot hunting. It was easy to get enough signatures to put the initiative on the November 1996 ballot; it passed and became a law that could not be changed by the legislature for at least two years. And that's just what happened. A bill to rescind the prohibition cleared the legislature. For me and the others who put together the successful initiative, it was back to the drawing board. This time we managed to get the aerial hunting issue before the public in the fall 2000 election as a ballot referendum.

Opponents tried to exploit a puzzling, unprecedented incident that occurred about this time. A wolf bit and injured a six-year-old boy at a logging camp at Icy Bay northwest of Yakutat. The boy's father shot the wolf, and rabies tests were negative. The wolf had been seen from time to time around two logging camps and may even have been fed by humans. It had previously been handled by humans, since it was wearing a radio collar placed on it when it was a pup, so it could hardly be considered a typical wild wolf. This wounding incident was a rarity in a state that has recorded only two fatal wolf attacks on humans—in 1942 and 1943, both involving rabid animals. All other instances of wolves biting humans in Alaska occurred while tame or habituated wolves were being fed or while a person tried to break up a fight between dogs and a wolf. In comparison, the Alaska Trauma Registry during the years 1991 through 1997 recorded 190 hospital admissions for injuries caused by dogs, 39 injuries caused by cats, 23 by horses, 18 by bears, 6 by moose, 4 by cattle, and 1 by a rockfish. Invoking the Icy Bay wolf attack to vilify wolves was a transparently weak and desperate tactic. Our referendum easily passed, once again showing the public's opposition to land-and-shoot aerial wolf hunting.

It will take both objectivity and wisdom if state game officials are ever to achieve an acceptable balance of interests in how wolves are treated. New faces in the Department of Fish and Game and on the Board of Game since the 1990s are bringing a more sensitive appreciation of public interests. I expect that calls for the state to carry out wolf control operations will decline as legal hunting and trapping continue to be successful. A survey by the Alaska Trappers Association showed wolves to be the most sought-after of all furbearers. Hunters and trappers with their snow machines and all-terrain vehicles have been taking more than a thousand wolves annually.

If government wolf control becomes necessary in a particular area, shooting from a helicopter would be the most efficient and humane means. I would not return to public aerial hunting nor pander to emotionalism by resorting to sterilization, relocation of the wolves, or other inefficient means. An essential part of any control operation would be follow-up to see if the number of game animals increases and, most important, to determine if killing the wolves is really what caused any increase — or if other factors are at work. With better science supporting wolf management, some of the public skepticism and criticism will go away. But not all of it. Individuals will always covet their own feelings about wolves, be they rooted in hate, fear, economics, fascination, mystery, or sympathy.

CHAPTER TWENTY-EIGHT

Home

THE UNIVERSITY OF ALASKA FAIRBANKS awarded me an honorary Doctor of Science degree in 1989, and it came as a touching surprise. Strange fate. In my earlier life, such an award would have ranked with the least likely of eventualities. When I should have been in high school, I was riding freight trains as a hobo, or surviving as a trapper in Alaska's Interior. And when I lied about high school graduation to qualify for Army pilot training, I didn't seem like much of a candidate for academic recognition. Christa and I flew to Fairbanks for spring commencement ceremonies and enjoyed the congratulations and hospitality of old friends and colleagues.

Then in 1991 I decided to retire from the National Marine Fisheries Service. Ever since my work as a pilot and biologist with the Fish and Wildlife Service in 1951, I had enjoyed a ringside seat if not always a place in the performing arena in matters of wildlife conservation during times of great change.

Christa and I could now devote much of our time to a new wilderness adventure—enjoying the cabin we had bought at Farragut Bay, which indents the mainland ninety miles southeast of Juneau. Total population of the place when we bought the cabin in 1985 was four: Joe Cook, his wife Donna, and their two young sons. The bay is accessible only by boat or airplane, so I bought just the plane we needed: a Cessna 185 on amphibious floats. It not only got us to our cabin, but put us within a day's flying range of all of Alaska. Our time at Farragut Bay brought pure pleasure. In the spring and summer we hiked a lot. Christa also worked in her vegetable garden while I took on such chores as cutting firewood or relocating the outhouse. Late summer and fall were harvest times: I hunted waterfowl and both of us looked for mushrooms and picked berries.

We found it was a mistake to assume the cabin would be unoccupied during our annual absence from late October to the following April, when we lived at our home near Juneau. On our first arrival one spring, we discovered that white-footed mice had found a fine winter home, well provisioned and furnished with bedding materials. It took a day or two to clean up after them. But this was child's play compared with what we faced a couple of years later. We had left an upstairs screened window slightly open for ventilation on our final visit in the fall. What a mistake.

In the spring we were greeted at the cabin by a chirping marten in the upper window, now opened wider with the screen torn away. In the cabin we were stunned by the horrific mess and stench. Two marten departed through the window.

They and perhaps others of their kin had obviously lived the high life for six months. Moments later they came back and noisily challenged our intrusion. It seemed strange they could look so sparkling bright and clean in the midst of such filth. The main floor was covered with cooking oil, syrup, oatmeal, cornmeal, flour, rice, peas, broken jelly jars, lamps, and more, all leavened with feces. The shelves had been cleared as though they had served as a race track. As bad as this was, the upstairs sleeping area appeared to be their major toilet site. Nothing was spared: pillows, bedding, floor, and stored clothing were all fouled. Christa bravely said I should go to Juneau alone and bring back all that we needed to make the place livable and she would stay and start the cleanup. That worked out, though it took us a good week of scraping, scrubbing, and burning before we could feel comfortable.

On another arrival, Christa walked to the rear of the cabin and found a different kind of devastation. The steps had been torn apart and scattered around, the door frame mostly chewed away, but the locked door was still in place. A bear had worked hard to break in but finally gave up and apparently vented its frustration by knocking down the stacked woodpile and biting paint and fuel cans on the deck.

A later bear incident was much more personal, and exciting. A sow black bear with twin cubs had been spending much leisure time under a patch of large spruce trees about a hundred yards from the cabin, avoiding our immediate area while we respected their chosen ground. Soon after dark one night, noise on the deck told me that we had a visitor. The dogs barked excitedly; Christa held them away from the door while I shined the flashlight out to see a cub tugging ferociously on one of the dead geese that I had hung on strings from the rafters of the back deck, along with a number of ducks. The sow and the other cub stood quietly a few yards away. When the string broke, the cub with its loot and the rest of the family retired into the woods.

I was certain they would return, so I had to put the birds out of reach. I put them into a heavy canvas duffel bag, which I hoisted and tied to the rafters about seven feet above the deck. All was ominously quiet for a while except for the hooting of a great horned owl. Sometime later we were awakened by a couple of powerful thumps that actually shook the cabin and panicked the dogs into a barking fit. The flashlight revealed the sow bear departing with the bag of birds. Quickly putting on my shoes, I loaded my shotgun with two rifled slugs for protection and, directing the flashlight beam ahead, went after the thieves.

Not more than thirty yards from the cabin, three pairs of green eyes reflected the light beam, and I could distinguish the bird bag at the feet of the sow. This was where she would show her willingness to yield, or to do something else. After a few seconds, she and both cubs moved to my left about five yards, where madam stood on her hind legs with one front paw resting on a tree trunk and looked at me. I had won the battle of nerves and could have my birds back. Without paying further attention to the bears, I walked to the bird bag, grabbed the attached strap, and went back to the cabin.

SEEING AND HEARING WOLVES at Farragut Bay gradually became common. I surprised Christa, and myself too, when I called a lone wolf to within a hundred yards of the cabin, where it lay in the grass for a while before beginning to hunt mice in the manner of a fox or coyote.

Early one morning we were fascinated with watching the hunting tactics of this wolf pack, consisting of six animals. Far across the marsh, beyond a flock of grazing Canada geese, we saw the pack disappear into a slough. About twenty minutes later, a single wolf showed itself on the near side of the geese, only about two hundred yards from our cabin. It wandered around rather aimlessly in plain view but did not move toward the geese. Very slowly, the grazing birds drifted toward where we had last seen the other wolves. Perhaps one of the wolves became impatient and allowed a sentinel goose to see it because, with a sudden outburst of honking, the flock took wing. After botching the ambush, the whole pack of wolves promptly appeared and gave the grazing area a good inspection.

Christa believes she interrupted a planned attack on one of our dogs. As she was picking bog cranberries near our cabin, she looked up to see a wolf walking by. A few moments later, the wolf dropped to its belly and began moving on its elbows. It was apparently stalking our little Chesapeake, Tootsie, who lay only about thirty yards away. Christa hollered and waved, putting the wolf to flight. Feeling the danger past, just for fun she hailed the animal with her version of a wolf howl. Several wolves appeared at the edge of a nearby crab apple thicket. After looking at Christa for a few seconds, they drifted back out of sight.

Christa's playful wolf howl brought her more than she bargained for one April day in 2001. She was walking with our dogs Jessie and Skipper in a boggy area covered with occasional small spruce trees, some dead, a few crab apples, and cranberry bushes, a place traversed by moose and bear trails. "At some point I began my wolf howl," Christa said in a later note to our daughter Beatrice. "I don't know why I did it, it probably just felt suitable for this eerie region."

She was answered by the howling and yipping of many wolves, and then the sight of the animals between the tiny trees and shrubs, rushing back and forth. "Jessie was stunned and moved between my legs," Christa wrote. "Skipper was frightened to a mere shaking something, running and falling toward me and burying himself between my legs.... Daddy had convinced me that wolves would not attack people, but what about people with dogs between their legs?" Then Christa worked her way across the boggy area and away from the animals, with Jessie at her heels and Skipper still shaking between her legs. "As we walked home on the higher ground, twice I felt the urge again to howl. Each time it was followed by the appearance of a single large and beautiful wolf across the slough, watching us for a little bit, then walking off."

That same day we had been surprised by the appearance of several wolves, early in the morning, in the yard by our cabin. We stood enthralled, watching from the window as they explored outside. These wolves in mid-April had not yet begun to shed, and they appeared to be in excellent condition with one, perhaps pregnant, being heavier in the belly than the others. The animals focused intently on one another. When one or two moved, the others stood still and watched until satisfied that a new discovery or peril was not about to unfold. When I related this rare and beautiful sighting to friends at our trap-shooting club, one of them responded "Wow! Didn't you have a gun?"

FARRAGUT BAY IS CULTURALLY CHANGING. Our wilderness retreat has become relatively congested, with a half dozen new buildings ranging from nice cabins to rather large homes scattered across the delta. The wildlife now share their home with two Norwegian fjord horses using eighteen fenced acres of vegetated wetlands. In one spot where we usually see black bears eating the new grass in the spring, we found only a single bear, and it lacked its skin and head; someone had taken a trophy. Crab fishing in the bay has intensified since several Vietnamese families moved to Petersburg, and I have to pay close attention when landing and taking off in the plane to avoid crab-pot lines and buoys. The Forest Service management plan calls for logging the north side of the bay. Newcomers enjoy the beauty and bounty of the place, but the cumulative footprint of man is becoming pretty obvious to Christa and me.

Natural geologic processes are working even greater changes. Broad sloughs that a few years ago meandered through the grass flats and filled with water on every high tide are now mere ditches because of sedimentation and land uplift. Where the land rises above tidal influence, woody vegetation is displacing grasses, which in turn are rapidly pioneering the emerging new land to seaward. One effect of all this is that floatplane access to our cabin is becoming ever more restricted. Some years ago, I could taxi the airplane to the cabin on any high tide; now I have this easy access only with the highest cycle of tides, a few days a month.

We were at least partly persuaded by these developments to purchase *Wonderon*, a three-cabin diesel trawler. This capable vessel stirred pleasing reveries of earlier watercraft, beginning with the leaky wooden contraption that I nailed together and, with my sister Hazel's help, hauled to the Fox Creek canal on a wagon. Christa and I, always with two Chesapeakes, found much joy in visiting out-of-the-way places in Southeastern Alaska aboard *Wonderon*. Our comfortable cruises often brought to mind starkly contrasting voyages in the past—crossing the Gulf of Alaska in an outboard-powered skiff, or sharing a crowded umiak with the walrus hunters of Little Diomede.

Our airplane also carries us across beautiful, far-flung expanses of backcountry Alaska. On a recent trip through northern and western regions, this time with my son Lewis, we saw herds of caribou, many moose, and a few grizzly bears. At a remote mountain lake in late June, just a few days after it cleared of winter ice, we thrilled at seeing lake trout swimming under the floats of the airplane as we beached it. And these fish eagerly fell for a leech tied on a No. 10 hook fished with a fly rod.

At home, sixteen miles northwest of Juneau, we often watch humpback whales, harbor seals, sea lions, and land otters from our parlor windows. A large pod of killer whales comes by every couple of months. Bald eagles launch themselves from a spruce tree in our yard to snatch surfacing fish or rob an otter of its catch. And from the nearby Herbert Glacier trail, I can hear wolves howling—fulfillment of a child's wonderment and of a young man's straying from the east side of Detroit.

SUBJECT INDEX

NAME INDEX

ABOUT THE AUTHOR

JAMES W. BROOKS left his boyhood home in Michigan and made his way to Alaska as a seventeen-year-old in 1940. Here he found a new world that offered occupations suited to an adventurous young man: fisherman, railroad worker, Caterpillar operator, trapper, musher, wartime flyer, walrus researcher, bush pilot, whale biologist. He led the Territory of Alaska's wildlife management program into the era of statehood and later served as commissioner of the state Department of Fish and Game. Brooks has published numerous scientific and popular articles on Alaska's living resources. He received an honorary Doctor of Science degree from his alma mater, the University of Alaska, in 1989. With his Cessna 185 amphibian airplane, Brooks and his wife, Christa, continue to visit friends and range widely over the state.

Recommendations for readers
interested in learning more about Alaska through memoirs
and biographies of notable Alaskans:

ACCIDENTAL ADVENTURER
Memoir of the First Woman to
Climb Mt. McKinley
Barbara Washburn, $16.95

ARCTIC BUSH PILOT
From Navy Combat to Flying
Alaska's Northern Wilderness
James "Andy" Anderson
& Jim Rearden, $16.95

RAISING OURSELVES
A Gwitch'in Coming of Age Story
from the Yukon River
Velma Wallis, $14.95

ART & ESKIMO POWER
The Life and Times of Alaskan
Howard Rock
Lael Morgan, $16.95

SPIRIT OF THE WIND
The Story of Alaska's George Attla,
Legendary Sled Dog Sprint Champ
Lew Freedman, $14.95

FLYING COLD
The Adventures of Russel
Merrill, Pioneer Alaska Aviator
Robert Merrill MacLean
& Sean Rossiter, $19.95

TALES OF ALASKA'S BUSH
RAT GOVERNOR
The Extraordinary Autobiography of
Jay Hammond, Wilderness Guide and
Reluctant Politican, $17.95

JIM REARDEN'S ALASKA
Fifty years of Frontier
Adventure
Jim Rearden, $17.95

CHIPS OFF THE CHOPPING
BLOCK
More Tales from Alaska's Bush Rat
Governor
Jay Hammond, $17.95

ON THE EDGE OF NOWHERE
Jim Huntington & Lawrence
Elliott, $14.95

TUNDRA TEACHER
John Foley, $14.95

These titles can be found or special-ordered at your local bookstore.
A wide assortment of Alaska books also can be ordered at the publisher's
website, www.EpicenterPress.com, or by calling 1-800-950-6663.